EVERYDAY...
MATTERS

A Daily Devotional

Rod & Joni Parsley

EVERYDAY...
MATTERS

A Daily Devotional

Rod & Joni Parsley

RESUL**T**S
PUBLISHING

EVERYDAY...MATTERS: A Daily Devotional

Copyright © 2017 by Rod & Joni Parsley
All Rights Reserved.
Printed in the United States of America
ISBN: 1-935794-26-4

Published by Results Publishing
World Harvest Church
PO Box 100
Columbus, OH 43216-0100, USA
www.RodParsley.com

Unless otherwise noted, all Scriptures are taken from the Modern English Version of the Bible. Copyright © 2014 by Military Bible Association. Used by permission. All rights reserved.

Scripture quotations marked MSG are from The Message. Copyright © 1993, 1994, 1995, 1996, 2000. 2001, 2002 by Eugene H. Peterson. Used by permission. All rights reserved.

Scripture quotations marked NIV are from the HOLY BIBLE, NEW INTERNATIONAL VERSION. Copyright © 1973, 1978, 1984 International Bible Society. Used by permission of Zondervan Bible Publishers.

Scripture quotations marked KJV are from the King James Version of the Bible.

The Bible Reading Plan is formulated from the One Year Bible Online, copyright © 1996-2015. One Year® is a registered trademark used by permission, Tyndale House Publishers, Inc.

Contents

Contents

Introduction

Everyday...Matters is designed to help you find God in your routine, normal, sometimes stressful daily life and to help you make every day matter. It is God's desire that you walk in victory and make each day count for Him!

There are two very special features in this year's devotional that I am excited to share with you. My extraordinary wife, Joni, will be showcased in a weekly feature entitled, "A Day with Joni." You'll laugh, cry and be touched in a special way. Joni is the greatest Christian I know, and I believe you will be blessed by her writings. The second feature is the inclusion of the One Year® Bible that I believe will help you experience the eternal truths and promises of God's Word in fuller measure.

Joni and I have been married for 30 years and have shared the triumphs and trials of marriage and ministry together. We know what it's like to stand in faith, to trust God despite your circumstances, and to stand firm on the Word of God through the large and small trials of life. And over the past year we have been tested.

God is a wonder! He has mightily healed me of cancer on my vocal cord, and I am walking in His power with a seven times greater anointing than I had before the enemy tried to take my voice. I know what it's like to walk through trials, and I can tell you that the Lord Jesus Christ has already won the victory and is walking every step of the way with you. He will not leave you alone. Hang on to our Heavenly Father with all that's in you and praise Him in the good times, bad times and times in between.

Make every day matter this year as you open your heart to God's extraordinary plan, purpose and blessings for your life.

JANUARY

A Firm Foundation

Whoever hears these sayings of Mine and does them, I will liken him to a wise man who built his house on a rock. And the rain descended, the floods came, and the winds blew and beat on that house. And it did not fall, for it was founded a rock.

— Matthew 7:24-25

January 1
Focus on God

So here's what I want you to do, God helping you: Take your everyday, ordinary life—your sleeping, eating, going-to-work, and walking-around life—and place it before God as an offering. Embracing what God does for you is the best thing you can do for him. Don't become so well-adjusted to your culture that you fit into it without even thinking. Instead, fix your attention on God. You'll be changed from the inside out. Readily recognize what he wants from you, and quickly respond to it. Unlike the culture around you, always dragging you down to its level of immaturity, God brings the best out of you, develops well-formed maturity in you.

— Romans 12:1-2 (MSG)

The best thing you can do for God at the beginning of this new year is to fully embrace His plan and purpose. God is sovereign, and He knows what is best.

When my children were little, they did not have to ask me, "Father, what is your will for me, today?" They knew, if it was a school day, they were to eat their breakfast, wash their dishes, then get their bookbags and head off to school.

The will of God is not something you spend your life seeking. You wake up in His will and live in it daily. God gave you His will in the pages of His Word. All you have to do is read the Word of God and follow His instruction. Where the will of God is known, perfect faith abounds!

Today's Bible Reading Plan: Genesis 1:1-2:25;
Matthew 1:1-2:12; Psalm 1:1-1:6; Proverbs 1:1-1:6

Jesus, I trust You; I embrace Your perfect plan for me!

January 2

For I Know My Plans For You

For I know the plans that I have for you, says the LORD, plans for peace and not for evil, to give you a future and a hope.

— *Jeremiah 29:11*

God's plan is good and not evil. He has established an incredible kingdom and wants you to enjoy its fruit. Once you dine with the Master, He dispatches you to spread the Good News of His marvelous love and His plan for eternal life.

You are God's light, reflecting His beauty to a dark and chaotic world. Whether you're in the grocery store, or in your office, or walking through the park, no matter where you go, you are God's bright shining light (Isaiah 9:2).

There is no greater love you can show your family, friends, coworkers, neighbors, or even complete strangers, than to reflect the love and glory of God in every situation. When things look darkest, that's when you can shine brightest, because the love and power of God surrounds you and emanates from you. Allow the Holy Spirit access to have His way and use you in your everyday life.

Today's Bible Reading Plan: Genesis 3:1-4:26; Matthew 2:13-3:6; Psalm 2:1-2:12; Proverbs 1:7-1:9

King of the universe, have Your way in me, today. Let Your purpose and plan be fulfilled in my life!

January 3

For God So Loved...

For God so loved the world that He gave His
only begotten Son, that whoever believes in Him
should not perish but have eternal life.
— John 3:16

This truly is Good News! You have been given a marvelous gift.

You have an extraordinary eternity to look forward to, and you can also experience the Lord's salvation in your everyday life. Jesus rescues us, saves us daily, many times during the day, from the hazards of life.

For instance, the Holy Spirit can prompt you to leave the house five minutes earlier to run errands, so that you miss that car accident the enemy had planned for you.

Another example, the Holy Spirit can impress you to go left instead of right, where you will encounter someone who is in need of comfort, at which time He will give you words of comfort to speak.

Every day, you can have a beautiful encounter of the God kind, as you enjoy His presence in your everyday, walking-around life.

Today's Bible Reading Plan: Genesis 5:1-7-24; Matthew 3:7-4:11; Psalm 3:1-8; Proverbs 1:10-19

Precious Holy Spirit, guide me through my day
so that I will be used for God's honor and glory.

January 4

Peace Like a River

For thus says the LORD: *I will extend peace to her*
like a river and the glory of the nations like a flowing stream.

— *Isaiah 66:12a*

Peace is not only the lack of conflict, it is shalom: nothing broken, nothing missing and nothing lacking.

During His earthly ministry, Jesus walked in total victory. He responded promptly each time He heard His Father speak; therefore, He lived a powerful and victorious life bathed in God's shalom.

Just think how incredible it would be to live a life filled with God's presence surrounding you and filling you to overflowing each day. This abundant life is possible when you follow God's direction and let Him carry you along His living waters of peace, cleansing you, making you whole and complete.

Jesus is our Prince of Peace, and He is our Passover Lamb. He willingly laid down His life, so that we can experience salvation, healing, deliverance, prosperity, security and victory every day of our lives!

Today's Bible Reading Plan: Genesis 8:1-10:32; Matthew 4:12-25; Psalm 4:1-8; Proverbs 1:20-23

Jesus, my Prince of Peace, thank You for shalom today,
with nothing broken, nothing missing, and nothing lacking.

January 5

God Is Good All the Time

Every good gift and every perfect gift is from above and comes down from the Father of lights, with whom is no change or shadow of turning.

— *James 1:17*

As we go about our daily lives, we must always remember to thank God for the many things He does for us. Turn to God and rely on Him for today's needs, but also remember to thank Him for what He has already done and what He is yet to do.

My beautiful wife, Joni, was washing dishes one day, and tears of joy were streaming down her face into the dishwater as she thought about the goodness and mercy of the Lord. We need to be sensitive to God's presence even in the seemingly mundane chores of our day; for He is there, abiding and caring for us.

Pray to be filled with a spirit of thanksgiving and gratitude. After all, we can't breathe in if God doesn't breathe out. Our very lives are totally dependent on His goodness and blessings. Pray that the Holy Spirit will make you acutely aware of His presence every moment of every day.

Today's Bible Reading Plan: Genesis 11:1-13:4; Matthew 5:1-26; Psalm 5:1-12; Proverbs 1:24-28

My Lord and King, make me deeply aware of Your divine presence in and around me today.

7

January 6

Shout Now!

It will not be necessary for you to fight in this conflict.
Take your positions, stand, and observe the deliverance
of the LORD for you... Do not fear or be filled with terror.
Tomorrow, go out ... and the LORD will be with you.

— *2 Chronicles 20:17*

Each day is filled with wonder and sometimes fear, but you can walk in a perpetual state of victory.

Whether you need the Lord's intervention in your finances, on your job, in your health, or with your relationships – no matter what you face – God is there just waiting for you to exercise your faith in Him.

Move forward in the battle; God is forever faithful and will never mislead you. Don't retreat by giving in to the enemy. My pastor, the late Dr. Lester Sumrall, liked to joke that he didn't even like to use the reverse gear on his car.

There is no one greater you can turn to than Jehovah Joshua Messiah, the Lord Jesus Christ. No matter what you face today, trust Him to lead you mightily into victory. And remember, don't wait until the battle is over. Shout now!

Today's Bible Reading Plan: Genesis 13:5-15:21; Matthew 5:27-48; Psalm 6:1-10; Proverbs 1:29-33

> *Jehovah Joshua Messiah, thank You for every*
> *battle You have fought and won on my behalf.*

8

January 7 ~ A Day with Joni

Trust and...

Trust in the LORD, and do good;
dwell in the land, and practice faithfulness.

— *Psalm 37:3*

It is truly an everyday reminder: *Trust in the Lord.* Whatever this day may bring, you can be confident, for your God is in control.

In all the challenges and choices you'll face today, realize the psalmist's admonition doesn't stop there. It reads: Trust in the Lord *and do good.*

Allow this verse to call you to self-examination. Ask, "Am I doing what I can to *do good?* Who can I bless? What can I change?"

When these two things become consistently one across your thoughts and actions—you're trusting Him AND doing good—then you are practicing faithfulness.

Today's Bible Reading Plan: Genesis 16:1-8:15; Matthew 6:1-24; Psalm 7:1-17; Proverbs 2:1-5

Heavenly Father, O for the grace this day – and every day – to trust You and do good. Will You open my eyes to see opportunities to love, encourage, and bless others whose paths I cross today? I'm trusting You with my life today. In Jesus' name!

January 8

Rivers of Living Water

On the last and greatest day of the feast, Jesus stood and cried out, "If anyone is thirsty, let him come to Me and drink. He who believes in Me, as the Scripture has said, out of his heart shall flow rivers of living water." By this He spoke of the Spirit, whom those who believe in Him would receive.

— John 7:37-39a

Jesus promises you not just a river, but <u>rivers</u> of living water, plural. What an amazing promise! When you drink from the well of God's abundant love, rivers of living water will flow out of your heart, because the Spirit of God lives in you!

In an ever-increasing world of chaos and confusion, the power and presence of God will maneuver you safely through the land mines laid by your adversary. You have a passing through anointing!

As you bask in the presence of God, you will be renewed each day, and your heart and mind will be miraculously transformed.

I pray for rivers of living water to flow from you today, emanating from the very throne room of God, surrounding you and saturating you in His powerful anointing that breaks every yoke of bondage.

Today's Bible Reading Plan: Genesis 18:16-19:38; Matthew 6:25-7:14; Psalm 8:1-9; Proverbs 2:6-15

Holy Spirit, renew my heart and mind today. Let Your rivers of living water overflow to all those around me.

January 9

Angels Unemployed

Because you have made the LORD, who is my refuge,
even the Most High, your dwelling,
there shall be no evil befall you,
neither shall any plague come near your tent;
for He shall give His angels charge over you
to guard you in all your ways.

— Psalm 91:9-11

God assures you that because you have made Him your refuge and dwelling place, He will assign angels to protect you. There are myriads and legions of angels ready to hearken to the voice of the Word of God, but you have to employ them by speaking His Word.

Before you and your loved ones begin the day, don't forget to dispatch the angels that have been assigned to you. Assign those angels the task of guarding you and those you love throughout the day's activities.

Once employed, God's angels are all around you, surrounding you, going ahead of you, providing protection behind you, upholding you on your right, standing guard on your left, weapons drawn.

Today's Bible Reading Plan: Genesis 20:1-22:24; Matthew 7:15-29; Psalm 9:1-12; Proverbs 2:16-22

Almighty God, today I dispatch the angels
You have assigned me, so that no evil nor sickness
will befall me or my loved ones.

11

January 10

The Book Is Right

All Scripture is inspired by God and is profitable for teaching,
for reproof, for correction, and for instruction in righteousness,
that the man of God may be complete, thoroughly equipped for
every good work.

— 2 Timothy 3:16-17

The Book is right, and they are wrong. The Bible does not change with age. We must always hear truth as truth, not our version of truth. Truth is not relative, where the Bible means one thing to me and something else to you.

The good news is that you can search the Scriptures to find the truth, and God's Word will not change according to the latest fads or trends of the day. When the Word is your standard of conduct and your code of ethics, the enemy of your soul cannot convince you to accept a wrong precept, which then draws you into misconception and error.

The Holy Spirit pricks your conscience when the enemy tries to deceive you. Your conscience, guided by the Holy Spirit, is your rudder through life and will convict you of error and convince you of the truth.

Today's Bible Reading Plan: Genesis 23:1-24:51; Matthew 8:1-17; Psalm 9:13-20; Proverbs 3:1-6

Holy Spirit, thank You for
revealing the truth of God's Word.

January 11

Alive & Active

For the word of God is alive, and active, and sharper than any two-edged sword, piercing even to the division of soul and spirit, of joints and marrow, and able to judge the thoughts and intents of the heart.

— Hebrews 4:12

Beware of any teaching that tries to entice you away from God's Word. For example, one false teaching, called Gnosticism, says your spirit is good, and your flesh is evil; therefore, it doesn't matter what you do in your flesh, because your spirit will be acceptable to God.

The problem with that teaching is it makes excuses for sinful behavior. The truth is, when you're immersed in the Holy Spirit, you have a passion for the things of God. You hate what God hates and love what God loves. You don't try to justify the sinful desires of your flesh.

Submitting to the instruction of God's Word in your everyday life will have an impact on the culture around you. Make His Word alive and active in you!

Today's Bible Reading Plan: Genesis 24:52-26:16; Matthew 8:18-34; Psalm 10:1-15; Proverbs 3:7-8

Lord, help me to reflect Your Word to the culture around me, so they can experience the power and the glory of Your kingdom.

13

January 12

Your Word Is Truth

Sanctify them by Your truth. Your word is truth.

— John 17:17

God is a good, good Father, and He has given us His written Word (the Bible) and His living Word (Jesus) to sanctify us and set us apart.

Even though we are in the world, we are not of the world, just as Jesus was not of the world (John 17:14). We indeed are sanctified by the truth of God's Word.

You will, at times, experience persecution for your faith. Just as the world hated Christ, they will hate you because you follow Christ. Don't be afraid to live what you believe. You have not been taken out of the world, but John 17:15 lets you know Jesus prayed for you, that you will be kept from the evil one.

Today's Bible Reading Plan: Genesis 26:17-27:46; Matthew 9:1-17; Psalm 10:16-18; Proverbs 3:9-10

Father, as You sent Jesus into the world, so send me, for I know I am not alone; You are with me now and always.

January 13

The Truth Will <u>Make</u> You Free

And ye shall know the truth, and the truth shall make you free.

— *John 8:32 (KJV)*

I firmly believe it is the truth that you know that makes you free. Truth won't even ask if you want to be free, but it will genuinely <u>make</u> you free! When you know the powerful truth that Jesus saves, you will live in the joy of His salvation. When you know the truth of God's faithfulness, you will be filled with faith.

If you do not know the truth of God's Word, the storms of life can batter you and leave you fraught with worry and anxiety. Don't wait until a crisis to draw near to God and learn the truth. Give the Holy Spirit full access to your everyday, practical life.

It is in the mundane daily activities that you can hone your spiritual skills and learn to be sensitive to God's voice. Then, as you learn in your daily life that God is faithful, you will be up for the task when a crisis occurs.

I pray that you will take time to learn the truth of God's Word and then apply it to your life every day.

Today's Bible Reading Plan: Genesis 28:1-29:35; Matthew 9:18-38; Psalm 11:1-7; Proverbs 3:11-12

I will look to God for truth and wisdom, for when I know the Truth, He will make me marvelously free!

January 14 ~ A Day with Joni

How? to Wow!

God is love.

— 1 John 4:8b

Poor examples in the pulpits to the pews, broken hearts and broken homes, pain and suffering – it's no wonder many wrestle with the message that our *God is love.*

I did, for many years. It was the extravagance of His love that finally moved me from *"How could God love me?"* to *"Wow! God loves me!"*

The dictionary defines extravagant as, "exceeding the limits of reason and necessity and unusually high in price." What a fitting description of God's love. He so loves you and me that while we were yet sinners, He sent His Son to die for our sins. How's that for beyond reason and unusually high price?

Carry a fresh reminder of this truth into your day: He loves you! Live today as a beloved child of God!

Today's Bible Reading Plan: Genesis 30:1-31:16; Matthew 10:1-23; Psalm 12:1-8; Proverbs 3:13-15

Father – and what a blessing it is to call You Father – I am so overwhelmed by Your love. There are so many times when I feel unworthy. Thank You for the reminders; You will never leave me nor forsake me. May Your love shine through me, today and always. Amen.

16

January 15

Yesterday, Today & Forever

Jesus Christ is the same yesterday, and today, and forever.

— Hebrews 13:8

It is comforting to know that God never changes. What we know about God today will be true about Him tomorrow. We know that God is love; and if He is love today, He will be love tomorrow. We know that God is faithful; and if He is faithful today, He will be faithful tomorrow.

Whatever you know to be true about God today will be true about God forever. He is not wishy-washy like men and women. He does not love you today and hate you tomorrow. He will not show you compassion today and treat you with contempt tomorrow.

How do you know the character of God? Read His Word. His Word describes Him perfectly. That's who He was yesterday. That's who He is today. And that's who He will be forever. He will now and forever be your salvation and your Savior, your healing and your Healer, your deliverance and your Deliverer, your protection and your Protector, your provision and your Provider, your victory and your Victorious King!

Today's Bible Reading Plan: Genesis 31:17-32:12; Matthew 10:24-11:6; Psalm 13:1-6; Proverbs 3:16-18

God, You are everything to me, and You will never change!

January 16

God Is Not a Man

God is not a man, that He should lie,
nor a son of man, that He should repent

— *Numbers 23:19a*

This is good Gospel news! It is impossible for God to lie, because everything God says is true. Whatever He says becomes truth. So, don't believe what the enemy says about you. Believe what God says about you.

If God says He is your Shepherd (Psalm 23), then it's true and nothing can move Him away from you. If God says He will deliver you (Psalm 91:3), then it is true and nothing can hold back your deliverance. If God says you are healed (Isaiah 53:5, 1 Peter 2:24), believe the truth of His Word!

There is absolutely nothing and no one that can make God lie! He is your refuge and your fortress, and you can trust Him at all times (Psalm 91:2). Men will disappoint you, but God is not a man. Men will try to destroy you, but God is not a man. Men will steal from you, but God is not a man. Men will lie to you, but God is not a man. Hallelujah!

Today's Bible Reading Plan: Genesis 32:13-34:31; Matthew 11:7-30; Psalm 14:1-7; Proverbs 3:19-20

Jehovah Joshua Messiah,
I proclaim You to be God Almighty, El Shaddai!

January 17

Born Again to the Bone

Jesus answered him, "Truly, truly I say to you, unless a man is born again, he cannot see the kingdom of God."

— *John 3:3*

The born again experience is truly unique to the believer in Christ. You are not just a good person who is trying to do better. You must have a deep longing for God to transform you. You cannot have your life and His, too. It's all Him or nothing.

True repentance requires you to change the way you think and act. What you used to love, you don't love anymore. Where you used to go, you don't have the desire to go anymore. Instead, you have a passion for God and a tremendous love for Him.

According to 2 Corinthians 5:17, if anyone is in Christ, they are a new creature, a new creation that has never existed before. Old things pass away and all things become new. When you accept Christ, be sure to go all the way and become born again to the bone. Let Jesus wash you and strip you of your old thoughts and your old way of doing things. Allow the Holy Spirit to lead you into God's abundant life!

Today's Bible Reading Plan: Genesis 35:1-36:43; Matthew 12:1-21; Psalm 15:1-5; Proverbs 3:21-26

Strip me of the old man and make me a new creation today!

January 18

Life Is But a Vapor

Come now, you who say, "Today or tomorrow we will go into this city, spend a year there, buy and sell, and make a profit," whereas you do not know what will happen tomorrow. What is your life? It is just a vapor that appears for a little while and then vanishes away.

— James 4:13-14

"The river of life is so broad and so wide, its depths so deep, and its current so slow that it appears to pause. This is the deceitfulness of life. We do not notice that we have moved toward the rapids of age and the falls of death until we ask, 'Where did it all go and how hitherto have I come?'"

I wrote this in my journal as I battled cancer on my vocal cord. I couldn't talk, so I'd jot things down. The point is that your life can radically change in an instant.

No matter what you face, today, know this one thing: Jesus paid it all, and He extends grace, mercy, forgiveness and freedom to you. The blood of Jesus paid for your salvation, healing, deliverance, prosperity, security and victory!

Today's Bible Reading Plan: Genesis 37:1-38:30; Matthew 12:22-45; Psalm 16:1-11; Proverbs 3:27-32

Lord, help me to make each day count for You.

January 19

Abundant Life!

The thief does not come, except to steal and kill and destroy.
I came that they may have life,
and that they may have it more abundantly.

— John 10:10

The world tells you if you could only be happy, life would be beautiful. After all, according to the world, the height of achievement is to be happy.

The problem is God says you can't be truly happy until you are holy; the good news is you can receive the forgiveness of God, through the sacrifice of His Son, and thereby be made holy.

You are then blameless, not because of anything you've done, but because of what God has done for you.

Jesus is the Good Shepherd. Hear His voice as you undertake the assignments of the day. There is no lack in Him in any area. By the power of His Spirit, He will lead you through this day in victory!

All you have to do is accept the forgiveness He offers and receive the abundant life He wants you to enjoy in your practical daily life.

Today's Bible Reading Plan: Genesis 39:1-41:16;
Matthew 12:46-13:23; Psalm 17:1-15; Proverbs 3:33-35

Lord, demonstrate Your abundant life
in me and through me today.

January 20

The Righteousness of God

God made Him who knew no sin to be sin for us,
that we might become the righteousness of God in Him.

— *2 Corinthians 5:21*

There are things that the enemy will try to use to bring you guilt and shame and condemnation. The adversary reminds you of negative situations from your past. He accuses you of unrighteous deeds, making you believe you will never be good enough.

When those thoughts overwhelm you, causing your countenance to be twisted and your shoulders to be rounded, look to Jesus. He will lift you out of the pit of despair. Look to His righteousness. Your Savior will quickly rescue you from Satan's accusations and deliver you into the presence of God, where you are loved.

You are not who the world says you are. You are not who your friends say you are. You are not who your enemies say you are. You are who God says you are. When you are in Christ, no matter what accusation the enemy hurls at you, remember what God says about you: you are the righteousness of God in Christ!

Today's Bible Reading Plan: Genesis 41:17-42:17; Matthew 13:24-46; Psalm 18:1-15; Proverbs 4:1-6

I am who God says I am:
the righteousness of God in Christ!

January 21 ~ A Day with Joni

Seasons of Change

To everything there is a season,
a time for every purpose under heaven…

— *Ecclesiastes 3:1*

Who likes change? Sure, every once in a while, changing something minor up can be fun. But if we're honest, we're creatures of habit and don't like our habitats disturbed.

I love Robert Frost's poem *Nothing Gold Can Stay* because he uses the changing colors of the leaves to represent the continuing and inevitable seasons of life.

Change equals challenge. But here's what I've learned: With every gain there's a loss, and with every loss there's a gain. Life is in motion. *To everything there is a season.* And my friend, God's got this. Regardless of what changes, your God does not. His unchanging hand will lead you gracefully from one season to the next and have you to discover His peace and purpose along the way.

Today's Bible Reading Plan: Genesis 42:18-43:34; Matthew 13:47-14:12; Psalm 18:16-36; Proverbs 4:7-10

Almighty God, You are of unchanging nature, character and purpose. Will You help me today to rest in You – my rock of safety and surety – even as all around me is in motion? You are my anchor. You are my strong tower. I look to You. Amen.

January 22

Raise the Standard

So shall they fear the name of the LORD from the west
and His glory from the rising of the sun;
when the enemy shall come in like a flood,
the Spirit of the LORD shall lift up a standard against him.

— *Isaiah 59:19*

God lovingly gave us His instructions for living, His commandments. His instructions weren't given to punish us; they were given to protect us.

There are consequences in the natural realm for murder and theft. In the spiritual realm, there are consequences when we don't place God first in our lives, or when we don't give honor to His name, or when we worship false gods.

God's original intent is that we love Him and love each other. When we read God's Word and obey it, we carry out those commandments practically in our day-to-day relationships.

Today's Bible Reading Plan: Genesis 44:1-45:28; Matthew 14:13-36; Psalm 18:37-50; Proverbs 4:11-13

Holy Spirit, help me to raise the standard of God in my home, on my job, and in my neighborhood.

January 23

Leave & Cleave

Jesus answered them, "Due to the hardness of your heart he wrote you this precept. But from the beginning of the creation, God 'made them male and female.'
For this cause shall a man leave his father and mother, and cleave to his wife, and the two shall be one flesh.' So then they are no longer two, but one flesh. What therefore God has joined together, let not man put asunder."

— *Mark 10:5-9*

When Joni and I were married, my pastor, the late Dr. Lester Sumrall, during the ceremony, described the following three ways to get married: the shortest lived marriages are those who marry due to physical attraction; those who marry due to a connection of the soul and mind last a little longer; the marriages that truly last are those who marry in the spirit, which is a combination of all three – body, soul and spirit.

The Word of God says men are to leave and cleave: leave their fathers and mothers and cleave to their wives. *Cleave* literally means to be joined together in a fashion that requires surgical separation. Marrying the third way, in the spirit – spirit, soul and body – creates a covenant that will not be broken.

Today's Bible Reading Plan: Genesis 46:1-47:31; Matthew 15:1-28; Psalm 19:1-14; Proverbs 4:14-19

Holy Spirit, touch marriages today – spirit, soul and body.

25

January 24

The D Word

*Then the rib which the LORD God had taken from man, He
made into a woman, and He brought her to the man. Then
Adam said, "This is now bone of my bones and flesh of my
flesh; she will be called Woman, for she was taken out of Man."
Therefore a man will leave his father and his mother and be
joined to his wife, and they will become one flesh.*

— Genesis 2:22-24

Throughout Scripture, God gave many instructions about marriage. He places a very high priority on how we form our families and how we behave after our families are formed. It doesn't end at the altar. That is just the beginning.

God created marriage and family for your pleasure. It's not hard to live right when you have a beautiful family, a loving family, a family rooted and grounded in God's love and love for one another, as God desires.

Joni and I said on our wedding night that the D word, divorce, would never be mentioned among us or in our home, and we have kept that promise to one another. God's love and our love for one another is what joined us, and it is what keeps us together.

Today's Bible Reading Plan: Genesis 48:1-49:33; Matthew 15:29-16:12; Psalm 20:1-9; Proverbs 4:20-27

Lord, renew our covenant today!

January 25

A Prayer for Your Family

"Therefore pray in this manner: Our Father who is in heaven, hallowed be Your name. Your kingdom come; Your will be done on earth, as it is in heaven. Give us this day our daily bread. And forgive us our debts, as we forgive our debtors. And lead us not into temptation, but deliver us from evil. For Yours is the kingdom and the power and the glory forever. Amen.

— Matthew 6:9-13

My dad was not a spiritually boisterous man at all; but the few times our family was in a crisis, he would kneel down in the living room and say, "Come on, Mom. Come on, kids. Let's pray."

I can hear him just as clearly today as I can hear my own voice. He started every prayer by saying, "God, here is our family…"

Families are so very important to God. Whether you're single and a family of one, a family of two, husband and wife, or have a family with children, I pray that God will provide your family with righteousness, and peace and joy in the Holy Spirit (Romans 14:17).

Today's Bible Reading Plan: Genesis 50:1-26; Exodus 1:1-2-10; Matthew 16:13-17:9; Psalm 21:1-13; Proverbs 5:1-6

Thank You, Lord, for Your Holy Spirit, who leads, guides, and directs us.

January 26

The Kingdom of Heaven

Jesus spoke to them again by parables, saying, "The kingdom of heaven is like a certain king who arranged a marriage for his son, and sent out his servants to call those who were invited to the wedding, but they would not come ... For many are called, but few are chosen."

— Matthew 22:1-2,14

The Master calls, "Come and dine. Come celebrate and rejoice at the marriage supper!" The messengers are dispatched with the Good News!

Alas, not all who hear the call will respond. Some will mock the messengers and then go on their merry way. Some will ask to be excused because they have to tend their garden; others will not come because they have a business to run. Still others will treat the Master's messengers cruelly and kill them.

In the end, it is only the Master's faithful bride who immediately responds to His call. She is ready, eager to come to the celebration of the marriage supper. She has waited so very, very long, and now she enters the banquet with joy in spotless white!

Today's Bible Reading Plan: Exodus 2:11-3:22; Matthew 17:10-27; Psalm 22:1-18; Proverbs 5:7-14

Holy Spirit, open doors of opportunity for me to extend the Master's invitation to come and dine at the wedding banquet!

January 27

The Kingdom of God

When He was asked by the Pharisees when the kingdom of God would come, He answered them, "The kingdom of God does not come with observation. Nor will they say, 'Here it is!' or 'There it is!' For remember, the kingdom of God is within you."

— *Luke 17:20-21*

For believers in Christ, we will experience the kingdom of heaven as described in yesterday's reading; however, the kingdom of God is already within us. We experience daily His salvation, healing, deliverance, prosperity, protection, peace and victory.

You don't have to wait until the sweet by and by to encounter God's kingdom. When you received Jesus as Savior and Lord, you entered His kingdom. As Jesus instructed in Matthew 7:7, *Ask and it will be given to you; seek and you will find; knock and it will be opened to you.*

By the power of the Holy Spirit, everything you need to enjoy the kingdom will be given to you. *But seek first the kingdom of God and His righteousness, and all these things shall be given to you* (Matthew 6:33).

Today's Bible Reading Plan: Exodus 4:1-5:21; Matthew 18:1-20; Psalm 22:19-31; Proverbs 5:15-21

*Jehovah Joshua Messiah, reveal
the kingdom of God within me today.*

January 28 ~ A Day with Joni

Think First

For My thoughts are not your thoughts,
nor are your ways My ways, says the LORD.

— Isaiah 55:8

Take time to think it through … with Him.

If you're at all like me, there are some times when you really contemplate things, but every now and then you just react and spew out an opinion in haste. Lord help us! I've often said if a thought could just go from the brain through a checkpoint before it hits the tongue, it would be great for all concerned. Taking a moment to ponder a difficult situation with the Lord can act like that checkpoint.

Very often, in taking a moment to think, we realize the truth in Isaiah 55:8 – His thoughts and His ways are not ours. From there, we can pray for a glimpse from His perspective, and come to trust Him even if we don't understand. And beloved, here's the best realization: It is a very good thing that His thoughts and His ways are not ours!

Today's Bible Reading Plan: Exodus 5:22-7:25; Matthew 18:21-19:12; Psalm 23:1-6; Proverbs 5:22-23

Gracious Lord, I praise You, for You made me and know me inside and out. Will You search my every thought and inclination, and show me where my heart needs to be more aligned with Yours? Help me to think – and to speak and to walk – more closely with You.

January 29

Forgiveness

"And when you stand praying, forgive if you have anything against anyone, so that your Father who is in heaven may also forgive you your sins. But if you do not forgive, neither will your Father who is in heaven forgive your sins."

— *Mark 11:25-26*

Jesus gives a stern warning that if we do not forgive, we will not be forgiven. That is a very daunting prospect.

What most don't seem to realize is that forgiveness is just as much about the one issuing forgiveness as it is about the one receiving forgiveness. It is unimaginable to think I would not forgive someone, when Jesus willingly experienced undeserved, horrible humiliation and an excruciating death in order to extend God's forgiveness to me.

Forgiveness is a verb, and it is an ongoing act. I cannot forgive you today, but refuse to forgive you tomorrow. If I am to walk as Jesus walked, I must completely forgive all past, present and future wrongs done to me. The Lord forgave me yesterday, forgives me today, and will forgive me tomorrow. Hallelujah!

Today's Bible Reading Plan: Exodus 8:1-9:35; Matthew 19:13-30; Psalm 24:1-10; Proverbs 6:1-5

*Holy Spirit, give me a heart
always eager to love and forgive.*

January 30

God Is Greater!

You are of God, little children, and have overcome them,
because He who is in you is greater than he who is in the world.

— 1 John 4:4

The adversary has no power over you. The Lord Jesus delegated power and authority to you *to trample on serpents and scorpions, and over all the power of the enemy. And nothing shall by any means hurt you* (Luke 10:19).

You are superior to the forces of darkness that are arrayed against you. The marching hordes of the alien armies of the antichrist have no power whatsoever over you.

Not long ago, due to cancer on my vocal cord, I could only experience a World Harvest Church service through streaming video on iHarv.tv. With tears streaming down my face, I couldn't even bring myself to utter a whisper.

God was faithful, and I am healed! Now I can shout again! You and I are on the victory side today. God's Word in Luke 10:20 declares that we can rejoice because our names are written in heaven!

Today's Bible Reading Plan: Exodus 10:1-12:13; Matthew 20:1-28; Psalm 25:1-15; Proverbs 6:6-11

Jehovah Ropheka, thank You for
Your healing power demonstrated in my life today.

32

January 31

Follow Jesus

Then Jesus said to His disciples, "If anyone will come after Me, let him deny himself, and take up his cross, and follow Me."

— Matthew 16:24

Self-sacrifice is entry level Christianity. You cannot have your life and His, too. Romans 1:16 declares, *For I am not ashamed of the gospel of Christ. For it is the power of God for salvation…*

The cross is the foundation of our faith in God. The cleansing stream of the cross is sweet, but the fountain from which every blessing flows came at the awful price of Christ's suffering and sacrifice.

Sadly, we've raised an entire generation who have no earthly idea why they even need the atonement of Jesus, much less what it is. To some, coming to the altar is a necessary religious ritual, but it has no real meaning.

We must get back to the firm foundation of the Gospel of Christ. Following Jesus means your life will change; and when your life changes and reflects His image, you will shake this planet!

Today's Bible Reading Plan: Exodus 12:14-13:16; Matthew 20:29-21:22; Psalm 25:16-22; Proverbs 6:12-15

Jehovah Joshua Messiah,
I give my life wholly and completely to You today!

FEBRUARY

Influence the Culture

For God is not the author of confusion,
but of peace,
as in all churches of the saints.

— *1 Corinthians 14:33*

February 1

Think On These Things

Finally, brothers, whatever things are true, whatever things are honest, whatever things are just, whatever things are pure, whatever things are lovely, whatever things are of good report, if there is any virtue, and if there is any praise, think on these things. Do those things which you have both learned and received, and heard and seen in me, and the God of peace will be with you.

— *Philippians 4:8-9*

Even though our culture is in chaos, we can be assured that, *The peace of God, which surpasses all understanding, will protect your hearts and minds through Christ Jesus* (Philippians 4:7).

As we think on those things that are true, honest, just, pure, lovely and good, our minds will focus on Jesus. Our expectation, even in these dark times, must be that the goodness of God will prevail for those who follow Christ.

The atmosphere of expectancy truly is the breeding ground of your miracle. Start each day expecting the best from Almighty God, surveying the day for a divine encounter.

Today's Bible Reading Plan: Exodus 13:17-15:18; Matthew 21:23-46; Psalm 26:1-12; Proverbs 6:16-19

I wait with expectancy for Your divine touch, today.

February 2

Speak the Word

By faith we understand that the universe was framed by the word of God, so that things that are seen were not made out of things which are visible.

— Hebrews 11:3

The Word of God is powerful enough to create the universe; therefore, we can change our world by declaring and decreeing what thus saith the Lord. Once we speak His Word, we must then act on it, because James 2:17 says, *So faith by itself, if it has no works, is dead.*

Even though the culture would rather I be silent, I cannot. My conscience, love of country, and most of all, obedience to the Spirit of God compels me to continue broadcasting an urgent warning to our nation.

I pray that you will join the remnant who have been stirred up and are proclaiming truth wherever they go. When believers stand in faith and live the life Christ has called us to live, our culture will be profoundly impacted as we shine His light in the darkness.

Today's Bible Reading Plan: Exodus 15:19-17:17; Matthew 22:-1:33; Psalm 27:1-6; Proverbs 6:20-26

*Lord, have Your way in my life, today,
so that all those I encounter may see Your glory!*

February 3

A City on a Hill

You are the light of the world.
A city that is set on a hill cannot be hidden.

— *Matthew 5:14*

I have labored in Christian ministry for decades. I have preached the truth to millions, and I will continue to speak, because I know it is not too late for this generation. Even now with worldwide crises shaking this planet, we can still chart a course in America to become the shining city on a hill of which our forefathers dreamed.

This dream, however, is being attacked from without and dismantled from within. We need to renew our commitment and reclaim our lost heritage. There is much to be gained by a return to the discarded values of the past. It is time to remake our nation into the just, compassionate, noble society she was meant to be.

Rise up, today, and share the Good News of our King. Commit to make a difference in your home, in your neighborhood and on your job. It's not too late.

Today's Bible Reading Plan: Exodus 17:8-19:15; Matthew 22:34-23:12; Psalm 27:7-14; Proverbs 6:27-35

Jehovah Joshua Messiah, use me today
to show Your marvelous kingdom in action.

February 4 ~ A Day with Joni

People Problems

If you fulfill the royal law according to the Scripture,
"You shall love your neighbor as yourself," you are doing well.

— James 2:8

One of life's greatest challenges is that life is full of people.

Each of our stories has a cast of characters playing all sorts of roles; heroes, villains, a supporting cast and extras. And that's by God's design. Every role is important to His bigger narrative and our place in it.

God is the Author and Finisher of His redemptive story. Other than our own salvation, most of the Gospel message concerns our loving and serving others.

James gives us a measuring standard. Today's a great day to look in the mirror and ask, how am I doing at loving my neighbor?

Today's Bible Reading Plan: Exodus 19:16-21:21; Matthew 23:13-39; Psalm 28:1-9; Proverbs 7:1-5

My Father, I confess I often fall short of the royal law. Will You deepen my love for my neighbor, my awareness of their needs, and my appreciation for the role they're playing in my life and in Your redemptive story? Thank You that I can love – because You first loved me. In Jesus' name.

February 5

Make God Welcome

He who dwells in the shelter of the Most High
shall abide under the shadow of the Almighty.

— *Psalm 91:1*

The spirit of the world says our society ought to be secular: no prayer in our schools, no God in our pledges, no faith in our politics. God has been driven from the marketplace of ideas.

The same First Amendment of the Constitution that bars government from restricting belief has been used to drive Christianity from the national public square.

What can we do to bring God back to the forefront and make Him a priority in our nation again? To change a nation, each person must change individually and make a commitment to live out their faith everywhere they go.

Whether in the grocery store between the frozen peas and carrots or working in the local bank, we are to be a light in the darkness. We must be determined to exhibit the true character of God and thereby win the lost to Christ.

Today's Bible Reading Plan: Exodus 21:22-23:13; Matthew 24:1-28; Psalm 29:1-11; Proverbs 7:6-23

> *Holy Spirit, You are welcome here.*
> *Help me shine bright in a dark world.*

February 6

Strangers, Orphans & Widows

He executes the judgment of the orphan and the widow
and loves the foreigner, giving him food and clothing.

— Deuteronomy 10:18

The Message Bible says God makes sure orphans and widows are treated fairly and that He takes loving care of foreigners by seeing they get food and clothing.

As the world spins out of control, poverty suffocates millions. I was born to parents who grew up in Martin County, Kentucky, a county so poor that President Lyndon Johnson chose to announce his "war on poverty" there. My family will never forget what it means to be poor.

Grinding poverty sucks hope from the human soul. Haunting lack unchallenged by faith gives rise to fear and bitterness. With the abundance God has blessed us with, no one should suffer lack in our nation.

A serious commitment by this generation to the less fortunate could mean the end of poverty in our time. I pray that God will strip us of selfishness and fill us with compassion, so that we can truly make a difference in the lives of the poor.

Today's Bible Reading Plan: Exodus 23:14-25:40; Matthew 24:29-51; Psalm 30:1-12; Proverbs 7:24-27

Lord, use me to impact the culture.

February 7

One in Christ

You are all sons of God by faith in Christ Jesus. For as many of you as have been baptized into Christ have put on Christ. There is neither Jew nor Greek, there is neither slave nor free, and there is neither male nor female, for you are all one in Christ Jesus.

— Galatians 3:26-28

Although there is a rushing tide of racial strife and division in America, I believe the body of Christ, with God's grace and help, can turn it around. We who lay claim to biblical truth must first attack the segregation on Sunday mornings in our congregations. It is the most racially segregated time in our nation.

We, as believers in Christ, must set an example of love for one another, regardless of race. Just as aggressively as the enemy is trying to cause division, believers must uncompromisingly love one another, reaching across racial lines. Whether white, black, red, yellow, striped, or polka-dotted, we must set an example of God's love. I pray that the only color we see is the red blood of our Savior that was shed for us all.

Today's Bible Reading Plan: Exodus 26:1-27:21; Matthew 25:1-30; Psalm 31:1-8; Proverbs 8:1-11

Holy Spirit, help us to unite, regardless of race.

February 8

Owe No One
But to Love Them

Owe no one anything, except to love one another,
for he who loves another has fulfilled the law.

— *Romans 13:8*

God has poured out His blessings in unprecedented abundance. Yet, all have not enjoyed the benefits of prosperity. Income distribution has rarely been more lopsided. Something has gone terribly wrong.

The materialism and greed of our age has produced a culture of debt. We are drowning in an unrestrained lust for more toys. The more we have, the more we want. It is robbing us of peace, community and spiritual growth.

1 Timothy 6:6-9 gives us clear instruction. *Godliness with contentment is great gain ... If we have food and clothing, we shall be content with these things ... those who desire to be rich fall into temptation and a snare ... which drown men in ruin and destruction.*

Instead of worshiping at the throne of materialism, we must worship God Almighty! We should truly owe no one anything but love; in doing so, we fulfill the law of God.

Today's Bible Reading Plan: Exodus 28:1-43; Matthew 25:31-26:13; Psalm 31:9-18; Proverbs 8:12-13

Lord, deliver us from materialism and greed.

February 9

Our True Reward

Then I looked. And there was a great multitude which no one could count, from all nations and tribes and peoples and tongues, standing before the throne and before the Lamb, clothed with white robes, with palm branches in their hands.

— *Revelation 7:9*

Our true reward is to finally stand before our King! Temporary, instant gratification in this life cannot even remotely compare to the eternal reward that awaits us.

Our Lord is a Rewarder of those who diligently seek and draw close to Him. The word *diligent* means more than just a casual glance and it means more than just a curious gaze. It means steadfast and focused interest, with a willingness to push everything else aside. It is to seek after something that means more to you than material possessions, food or even sleep.

Keep pressing forward to the true prize. As you seek the Lord in unwavering and steadfast faith, He will reward you for your faithfulness, and His reward will be the one that remains forever!

Today's Bible Reading Plan: Exodus 29:1-30:10; Matthew 26:14-46; Psalm 31:19-24; Proverbs 8:14-26

I have settled it in my heart to follow Jesus and receive the reward of my Lord now and forever.

February 10

Walk in the Light

But if we walk in the light as He is in the light,
we have fellowship one with another, and the blood of
Jesus Christ His Son cleanses us from all sin.

— 1 John 1:7

Jesus is your light, and when you walk with Him, His light shines in you. When we display the Light of Jesus, then many times just our presence causes people to adjust their behavior.

You may have had someone make a point of apologizing to you when they have used coarse language in your presence. You may have never shared the Gospel with them directly at all, but because you have been a light in their presence, others know there is something different about you. That is the impact you can have in your home, in your neighborhood, on your job and everywhere you go.

We are called to be influential in an obvious way, like a lighted candle in a dark room. Even when you walk in the blackest night of trouble, trial and tribulation, there is a light because Jesus dwells within you. Let your light shine brightly!

Today's Bible Reading Plan: Exodus 30:11-31:18; Matthew 26:47-68; Psalm 32:1-11; Proverbs 8:27-32

Holy Spirit, make my life so shine with the Light of Jesus
that I become a beacon of hope to everyone I encounter.

February 11 ~ A Day with Joni

What a Friend We Have in Jesus

But I have called you friends…
— John 15:15b

Friends are so important. I thank the Lord for every friend I have in this life – they are such a blessing. But I have to tell you, there is no friend in this world as abiding as Jesus Christ! Have you discovered this most faithful of friends? You're never alone – in Jesus, you have a constant companion, every second of every day. He is with us in our darkest hour, and can unfold it into a beautiful sunrise just because we looked to Him in our time of need. Just like the old hymn says:

What a friend we have in Jesus, all our sins and griefs to bear! What a privilege to carry everything to God in prayer!

He sees every tear and knows every hurt. The question is, do you look to Him as your friend and companion? What is before you this day? God doesn't intend for you to face it alone, without His help, and apart from His presence. Lean into Jesus!

Today's Bible Reading Plan: Exodus 32:1-33:23; Matthew 26:69-27:14; Psalm 33:1-11; Proverbs 8:33-36

Heavenly Father, thank You for the blessing of friendship in this life. Thank You most of all that Jesus is a friend who sticks closer than a brother! Please remind me to lean into my relationship with Jesus when I am feeling alone – that I'd sense Your arms around me, I pray.

February 12

Don't Forget

In the same manner He took the cup after He had supper,
saying, "This cup is the new covenant in My blood. Do this, as
often as you drink it, in remembrance of Me."

— 1 Corinthians 11:25

We must never forget what Jesus has done for us. I take communion every single day, because I want to remember and commemorate every day what the Lord has done for me. For me, that makes every day matter in a very significant way.

Holy communion stands as a monument to every adversary, to every sickness, to every force of the enemy. It is a reminder that you are covered by the blood of the Lamb every moment of every day. What Jesus did was unfathomable, and it was rooted in love.

The love between Father and Son was extended to all mankind through one selfless act. As you go about your day meditate upon this unconditional, everlasting love. It is a love so great that Jesus Christ suffered the deathblows of Calvary so you could bask in the fullness of God's presence.

Today's Bible Reading Plan: Exodus 34:1-35:9; Matthew 27:15-31; Psalm 33:12-22; Proverbs 9:1-6

Jesus, thank You for Your perfect love
that has given me access to my heavenly Father.

February 13

A Light to the Nations

He says, "It is a light thing that you should be My servant to raise up the tribes of Jacob and to restore the preserved ones of Israel; I will also make you a light to the nations so that My salvation may reach to the ends of the earth."

— Isaiah 49:6

You are called to be a light to the nations. Jesus declared, *You are the light of the world. A city that is set on a hill cannot be hidden* (Matthew 5:14).

The purpose of shining brightly is so that we will show forth the salvation of the Lord. Light that is hidden is of no use to anyone, not even the person responsible for it. *Neither do men light a candle and put it under a basket, but on a candlestick. And it gives light to all who are in the house* (Matthew 5:15).

Far better that we obey Jesus' command to *Let your light so shine before men that they may see your good works and glorify your Father who is in heaven* (Matthew 5:16).

When you walk with Jesus, you walk in the Light!

Today's Bible Reading Plan: Exodus 35:10-36:38; Matthew 27:32-66; Psalm 34:1-10; Proverbs 9:7-8

Jesus, shine Your light in me and through me so that I will glorify God everywhere I go.

February 14

There Is No Other

For thus says the LORD, who created the heavens, who is God, who formed the earth and made it, who has established it, who did not create it in vain, who formed it to be inhabited: I am the LORD, and there is no other.

— *Isaiah 45:18*

We must worship God alone. Even though today's culture is distracted by things such as entertainment and materialism, believers in Christ must remain focused on Jehovah Joshua Messiah, the Lord Jesus Christ, and seek to develop an intimacy with Him.

God, who created the heavens and the earth, is our Savior, and there is no other. In Isaiah 43:11, God declares, *I, even I, am the LORD, and besides Me there is no savior.*

Let's worship the one true God! Let's glorify Him instead of glorifying people and things. Let's change the way we think and act. That is true repentance.

Today's Bible Reading Plan: Exodus 37:1-38:31; Matthew 28:1-20; Psalm 34:11-22; Proverbs 9:9-10

Lord God Almighty, I worship You and You alone!

February 15

The Heavens Declare His Glory

The heavens declare the glory of God,
and the firmament shows His handiwork.

— Psalm 19:1

I love being outside, taking in the wondrous beauty of God's creation. Whether it's watching a glorious sunrise or sunset, sitting quietly by a stream, taking a stroll through the woods, or walking through the untouched expanse of new-fallen snow, being outside helps me focus on the magnificence of Almighty God.

The stresses of everyday life can sometimes temporarily distract us from understanding who God really is. We should stop telling God how big our problem is, and instead tell our problem how big our God is.

God is bigger than our problems, bigger than our fears, bigger than any burden we will ever bear. No matter what we go through, it will never equal the burden Jesus bore for all mankind on the cross. Because of His sacrifice, we can relish each day in His creation and experience His marvelous glory.

Today's Bible Reading Plan: Exodus 39:1-40:38; Mark 1:1-28; Psalm 35:1-16; Proverbs 9:11-12

Lord, You are now and forever truly amazing!

February 16

The Maker of Us All

*"But now ask the beasts, and let them teach you; and the birds
of the air, and let them tell you; or speak to the earth, let it teach
you; and let the fish of the sea declare to you. Who among all
these does not know that the hand of the LORD has done this,
in whose hand is the soul of every living thing
and the breath of all mankind?"*

— Job 12:7-10

If we want to affect our nation and the world for
God, we must step away from our agenda and
embrace God's agenda. We must sometimes step back
from our plan and see the entirety of His plan.

Job 12:7-10 explains that even the animals know
that the Lord God has created everything! When I
consider the works of His hands, it makes the things I
worry about pale in comparison.

Wars are fought over boundary lines; yet, God
established it all. Congregations are ripped apart
because of doctrinal differences; yet, God is still the
Maker of us all. Instead of focusing on our differences,
we must step back and see the wonder and glory of
God, which outshines us all.

Today's Bible Reading Plan: Leviticus 1:1-3:17;
Mark 1:29-2:12; Psalm 35:17-28; Proverbs 9:13-18

*Holy Spirit, help me to put things in perspective
and see everything through Your eyes.*

February 17

They Are Without Excuse

The invisible things about Him—His eternal power and deity—have been clearly seen since the creation of the world and are understood by the things that are made, so that they are without excuse.

— *Romans 1:20*

There is no greater evidence of God's existence than His creation. Whether it be trees, animals or people, we are proof of God's creation, and we bear His mark. Romans 1:20 says that we should understand by what has been made that there is a God. Even though He may be invisible, what He has made is very evident.

The fact that there is a watch proves the existence of a watchmaker. You can gather car parts and toss them in a garage, but they won't land in perfect order and make a properly functioning automobile.

The evidence of the Creator is His incredible creation. We stand as His testimony, whether people accept it or not. Those who refuse to believe in the existence of God have *traded the glory of God who holds the whole world in His hands for cheap figurines you can buy at any roadside stand* (Romans 1:23 MSG).

Today's Bible Reading Plan: Leviticus 4:1-5:19; Mark 2:13-3:6; Psalm 36:1-12; Proverbs 10:1-2

You are great, O God, and I exalt You above all things and people.

February 18 ~ A Day with Joni

Growing Up

Therefore be perfect, even as your Father
who is in heaven is perfect.

— Matthew 5:48

When we are young, we cannot wait to grow up. When we're finally grown up, all we want to do is recapture our youth. We say, "Youth is wasted on the young." But I wonder, is wisdom wasted with age?

No matter how old you are, growing comes with growing pains. There will be nights when we walk the floors, asking all the wrong questions, getting none of the right answers. Growth includes taking many long, hard looks in the mirror. Who am I? Who am I becoming?

Growth is about gaining perspective. Christian growth is about gaining God's perspective. Let His Word be your mirror. Grow in Him, so that as you look in the mirror you see His reflection more than your own.

Today's Bible Reading Plan: Leviticus 6:1-7:27; Mark 3:7-30; Psalm 37:1-11; Proverbs 10:3-4

Heavenly Father, search me and know me. Reveal to me things I need to see differently, hold more dearly, or let go. Grow me up in You so the people in my life, those You've surrounded me with, see more of You and less of me. In Jesus' name, Amen.

February 19

Worship with All of Creation

Then I heard every creature which is in heaven and on the earth
and under the earth and in the sea, and all that are in them,
saying: "To Him who sits on the throne and to the Lamb be
blessing and honor and glory and power, forever and ever!"

— *Revelation 5:13*

Stand with all of creation and worship. All of creation gives God glory! Let us magnify and exalt His name together!

God inhabits the praises of His people. As Psalm 22:3 proclaims, *But You are holy, O You who inhabits the praises of Israel.* As followers of Christ, we have been grafted into Israel and can partake of the richness of the olive tree. (Romans 11:17) We are no longer *strangers to the covenants of promise* (Ephesians 2:12).

Just imagine the day when all of creation gives God glory and honor. What a thunderous roar of praise that will be! Until that glorious day, give God your best praise. Praise Him with all that is in you. Let all of creation know you praise God Most High, Jehovah Joshua Messiah!

Today's Bible Reading Plan: Leviticus 7:28-9:6; Mark 3:31-4:25; Psalm 37:12-29; Proverbs 10:5

I will forever praise the Lord God Almighty!

February 20

Praise the Lord!

Let everything that has breath praise the LORD.
Praise the LORD!

— Psalm 150:6

I don't think we can ever give God too much praise. We especially need to praise Him when we are going through hard times. Hebrews 13:15 declares, *Through Him, then, let us continually offer to God the sacrifice of praise, which is the fruit of our lips, giving thanks to His name.*

This verse says to <u>continually</u> offer to God the sacrifice of praise. This is a powerful way to impact our culture. Giving the Lord praise affects the spiritual realm in ways we could never do in the natural.

Giving a sacrificial offering means you may not necessarily feel like giving that offering at the time. Everything may not be going wonderfully in your life. Try offering the sacrifice of praise to God continually. You just might have a Psalm 30:11-12 experience.

For You have turned my mourning into dancing; You have put off my sackcloth and girded me with gladness, so that my glory may sing praise to You and not be silent. O LORD my God, I will give thanks to You forever.

Today's Bible Reading Plan: Leviticus 9:7-10:20; Mark 4:26-5:20; Psalm 37:30-40; Proverbs 10:6-7

Lord God, fine tune my spirit so that praise and worship will flow from me to you continually.

February 21

Let Us Exalt
His Name Together

Oh, magnify the LORD with me,
and let us exalt His name together.

— Psalm 34:3

When the saints of God gather to praise the Lord, it creates an atmosphere of expectancy that is the breeding ground for miracles. Countless times our church family has come together in praise and witnessed God pour out miracle, after miracle, after miracle.

Praise and worship is the time to draw near to God and invite Him to draw near to you. Praise is not limited to a designated time and place in a church service.

Times of praise and worship are divine encounters you have with God Almighty, where an exchange takes place: you give Him the glory and honor for which He alone is worthy, and He touches your life in a miraculous way.

Today's Bible Reading Plan: Leviticus 11:1-12:8; Mark 5:21-43; Psalm 38:1-22; Proverbs 10:8-9

Lord, to You alone be all glory, honor, praise and worship.

February 22

Praise God!

Praise the LORD. Praise, O you servants of the LORD,
praise the name of the LORD.
Blessed be the name of the LORD
from this time forth and for evermore.
From the rising of the sun to its going down,
the LORD's name is to be praised.

— Psalm 113:1-2

What a paradigm shift there would be in our nation and homes if we would praise the name of the Lord from sunrise to sunset. Can you imagine what it would be like to walk through the grocery store and hear praises coming from the loudspeakers instead of disco music from the '70s?

Imagine hearing praises ring through your neighborhood instead of rock music. What an awesome experience it would be to hear choruses of praise spontaneously break out at your favorite restaurant. Maybe it's just a dream, but this is what would happen if Psalm 113:1-2 were to become a reality. The very first verse says it begins with the saints of God. Oh, how I long for that day!

Today's Bible Reading Plan: Leviticus 13:1-59; Mark 6:1-29; Psalm 39:1-13; Proverbs 10:10

There is none greater than You, Jehovah Joshua Messiah!
I will praise You and give You the honor due Your name.

February 23

Give God the Highest Praise

Praise the LORD! Sing unto the LORD a new song,
and His praise in the assembly of the godly ones.

— *Psalm 149:1*

Psalm 149:1 stresses the importance of godly ones assembling together to give God praise. This is not talking about just singing a few songs. It's referring to the praise of the saints when they gather to worship as a congregation.

Individual times of praise and worship are good and should not be ignored, but there is something powerful about corporate gatherings to praise God.

Do not underestimate the power of praise and worship, individually or corporately. We serve a God who loves our praise. Genuine praise produces a close relationship with God, a cherished relationship He desires deeply.

Rejoice in the Lord and sing His praise. Thank Him for His promises and blessings. Praise Him for His matchless love and unfailing strength. Keep His praises ever on your lips and in your heart.

Today's Bible Reading Plan: Leviticus 14:1-57;
Mark 6:30-56; Psalm 40:1-10; Proverbs 10:11-12

All good things come from God above.

February 24

Hallelujah!

*Hallelujah! O my soul, praise GOD! All my life long
I'll praise GOD, singing songs to my God as long as I live.*

— *Psalm 146:1-2 (MSG)*

Sing hallelujah when you rise in the morning. Shout hallelujah when you go to work and as you return home. Breathe out hallelujah in the evening in gratitude for the completion of another day. Say hallelujah before you go to sleep in expectancy of a restful night and a new sunrise when you awaken.

Hallelujah combines two Hebrew words, hallel, which means praise, and Yah. Hallelujah = Praise Yah. Yah is short for Yahweh, the Hebrew name of God, which is where we get the transliterated English name Jehovah. When I declare the name Jehovah Joshua Messiah or Lord Jesus Christ in English, it is Yahweh Yeshua Mashiach in Hebrew.

Sing hallelujah today as you enjoy His goodness. Give Him a hallelujah He's never heard before!

Today's Bible Reading Plan: Leviticus 15:1-16:28; Mark 7:1-23; Psalm 40:11-17; Proverbs 10:13-14

> *Jehovah Joshua Messiah,
> I praise Your holy name!*

February 25 ~ A Day with Joni

Winter Weather

But if we hope for what we do not see,
we wait for it with patience.

— *Romans 8:25*

Ohio winters are long. The days are short, the nights are cold, and the skies are a lovely shade of gray. To every person who lives in a warm climate and whines when you have to wear a jacket, I ask you to forgive me, but I want to smack you with my snow shovel.

By February, you see, we have had it! Cabin fever. People are grouchy, bored, depressed – ready to swing snow shovels! Winter is harsh, but it's necessary. We can't always see it, but life is unfolding beneath the frost. Spring is coming – new life is quite literally springing forth. In the words of the Disney classic, The Lion King, it's the circle of life.

The same is true of seasons in our lives. God is at work in life's currents, even when we can't see it unfolding. If your hope is in Him, wait confidently. Winter gives way to spring.

Today's Bible Reading Plan: Leviticus 16:29-18:30; Mark 7:24-8:10; Psalm 41:1-13; Proverbs 10:15-16

Dear Lord, I pray for eyes to see, ears to hear, and a heart to wait patiently on You in every season of life. But I especially pray for Your presence in my soul's winter seasons. Will You comfort me? Encourage me? Deliver me – to the beautiful spring You have in store. Jesus, thank You for Your perfect sacrifice.

February 26

The Ultimate King

GOD is higher than anything and anyone, outshining everything you can see in the skies. Who can compare with GOD, our God, so majestically enthroned, Surveying his magnificent heavens and earth? He picks up the poor from out of the dirt, rescues the wretched who've been thrown out with the trash, Seats them among the honored guests, a place of honor among the brightest and best. He gives childless couples a family, gives them joy as the parents of children. Hallelujah!

— *Psalm 113:4-9 (MSG)*

This is the One I am privileged to serve. The buck stops here. There is no higher authority. He is majestic on His throne and rules a vast domain.

He rules in righteousness, and He does something extraordinary. Rather than oppress and misuse those who are less fortunate, He rescues the poor and wretched. Then He does something that is even more incredible. He seats them among His honored guests, a place of honor among the best. He doesn't stop there. Those who have no children are blessed by Him to be parents of children.

This is my King, the One I am privileged to serve.

Today's Bible Reading Plan: Leviticus 19:1-20:21; Mark 8:11-38; Psalm 42:1-11; Proverbs 10:17

Thank You, King Jesus, for choosing me to be part of your glorious kingdom!

February 27

A Born Leader

For unto us a child is born, unto us a son is given, and the government shall be upon his shoulder. And his name shall be called Wonderful Counselor, Mighty God, Eternal Father, Prince of Peace.

— Isaiah 9:6

When representatives are elected to public office in our nation, we cannot be sure what we will get. Some of our country's elected officials are involved in theft, fraud, misconduct and a host of other sins.

But we are told in Isaiah 9:6 that the government is not on the shoulders of corrupt men and women. By faith, we declare the government is on the shoulders of the Lord Jesus Christ. He is our righteous King and no other. Regardless of how things look today in our government, the government we look to has a Leader who is called Wonderful Counselor, Mighty God, Eternal Father, Prince of Peace.

We pray for the elected officials in our nation's government, but we know that no matter what they promise, they will always fall short. We patiently wait for the King of kings and Lord of lords to establish His kingdom forever.

Today's Bible Reading Plan: Leviticus 20:22-22:16 Mark 9:1-29; Psalm 43:1-5; Proverbs 10:18

Even so, come quickly, Lord Jesus.

February 28

Be Drenched in Shalom

Peace I leave with you. My peace I give to you.
Not as the world gives do I give to you.
Let not your heart be troubled, neither let it be afraid.

— John 14:27

As I mentioned earlier in the devotional, the Hebrew word for peace is shalom and means not only lack of conflict, but also wholeness and completeness, with nothing broken, nothing missing, and nothing lacking. It also means safety, prosperity and health.

The Hebrew definitions of shalom and salvation are very similar. The word for salvation in Hebrew is yeshua, which is also the Hebrew name for Jesus. Yeshua is defined as salvation, healing, deliverance, help, aid, victory, prosperity, security and well-being.

Of course, it's no coincidence that the definition of our Savior's name contains components of both words: *salvation* and *peace*. Jesus is the Prince of Peace. Be drenched now in His shalom. Hallelujah!

Today's Bible Reading Plan: Leviticus 22:17-23:44 Mark 9:30-10:12; Psalm 44:1-8; Proverbs 10:19

Lord Jesus Christ, Yahweh Yeshua Messiah,
thank You for Your peace, Your prosperity, Your safety,
Your shalom.

MARCH

Contend for the Faith

Beloved, while I diligently tried to write to you of the salvation we have in common, I found it necessary to write and appeal to you to contend for the faith which was once delivered to the saints. For there are some men who secretly crept in, who were marked long ago for this condemnation. They are ungodly men, who pervert the grace of our God into immorality and deny the only Lord God and our Lord Jesus Christ.

— Jude 3-4

March 1

No Weapon

No weapon that is formed against you shall prosper, and every tongue that shall rise against you in judgment, you shall condemn. This is the heritage of the servants of the LORD, and their vindication is from Me, says the LORD.

— Isaiah 54:17

No matter what seemingly insurmountable obstacle is in front of you, when you declare the Word of God over your situation, that mountain has to move! When the enemy has a plan to take you out, God always has a plan to keep you in.

No weapon that is formed against you will ever prosper, because you belong to Almighty God! Build on the foundation laid by the Lord Jesus Christ Himself. Have faith that every battle you fight was already won by our King at Calvary.

Jesus was not a victim at Calvary. He was an advancing warrior! God has never lost a battle, and He is not about to start now. He has already gone before you into the battle, and He has won the victory!

Today's Bible Reading Plan: Leviticus 24:1-25:46 Mark 10:13-31; Psalm 44:9-26; Proverbs 10:20-21

I claim victory in today's battle because of the battle that was won by Jesus at Calvary!

March 2

A Spiritual Battle

For our fight is not against flesh and blood,
but against principalities, against powers, against the rulers of
the darkness of this world, and against spiritual forces
of evil in the heavenly places.

— Ephesians 6:12

Even though there are wars in the natural realm that are raging all over the world today, those are not the battles believers in Christ should focus on. Our focus is the spiritual battle that is intensifying every day.

A harsh and cold-hearted approach is not the posture we should take toward unbelievers. The last thing I want to be is another screaming voice moving people to extremes and provoking them to folly. My desire is that people move, first, to compassion, then to wisdom and then to duty.

We must first recognize the many millions of people who are lost and dying without Christ. We must see them through God's eyes and wage our battle in the spiritual realm for their souls. The true battle has been won by Christ at Calvary. Declare the victory today for your family, friends, neighbors and coworkers.

Today's Bible Reading Plan: Leviticus 25:47-27:13
Mark 10:32-52; Psalm 45:1-17; Proverbs 10:22

Holy Spirit, prepare the hearts of those
I love and care about as fertile ground to receive the Gospel.

March 3

The Promise

The Lord is not slow concerning His promise, as some count slowness. But He is patient with us, because He does not want any to perish, but all to come to repentance.

— 2 Peter 3:9

My wife, Joni, is an extraordinary lady. She is the mother of my children, and she is the greatest Christian that I know. She exemplifies the life and heart of Jesus Christ. When we were married, I promised to love her, stick by her and never abandon her.

I take my promise to Joni very seriously and would give my life to protect her and my family. How much more does God love us and want to bless us by keeping His promise?

Even though it may seem like the promises of God are slow in coming sometimes, He is <u>always</u> faithful. His greatest promise is salvation. God is not mad at us. He is patiently waiting for the lost to come to Him in repentance. He does not want anyone to perish and suffer an eternity in hell.

Today's Bible Reading Plan:
Leviticus 27:14-Numbers 1:1-54; Mark 9:30-10:12; Psalm 44:1-8; Proverbs 10:19

Lord God, thank You for Your patience, Your mercy and Your unconditional, everlasting love.

March 4 ~ A Day with Joni

Tears to Triumph

Jesus wept.
— *John 11:35*

There it is recorded in the Bible for all to see. People talked about it. Why did Jesus weep? I tell you, it doesn't matter why. What matters to me is that Jesus wept. God broke down and cried. He proved himself the faithful high priest, understanding, sympathizing and suffering with His people. To Mary it seemed that God was running late. Can you relate to that feeling? I can. And to see Jesus arrive, with tears in His eyes – it's tremendously meaningful to me.

But then Jesus wiped His eyes and said, "Roll away the stone." Here we have a God who weeps with us in our pain, and then rolls away the stone of suffering.

Here is both Friend and Deliverer, Brother and Master, Sympathy and Salvation. He cried out of His humanity, then He spoke out of His divinity, and the dead rose to life. Where is God when you hurt? He weeps with you; He walks with you; and He works in you. Don't doubt Him, not even for a minute. He can still roll away the stone.

Today's Bible Reading Plan: Numbers 2:1-3:51
Mark 11:27-12:17; Psalm 47:1-9; Proverbs 10:24-25

It is so comforting, Lord, to know You care. When I hurt, Your heart goes out to me. Will You bring healing balm to my hurts? Hope to my hopelessness? I do believe. In moments where I wrestle with unbelief, thank You for reminders of Your presence. In Jesus' name.

March 5

Submit to God

Therefore submit yourselves to God.
Resist the devil, and he will flee from you.

— James 4:7

The formula to winning every battle is twofold. First, obey your Commander in Chief, the Lord Jesus Christ. Is He ruling in every area of your life? Have you submitted to His lordship and sovereignty? Personal transformation has its beginnings in the lordship of Jesus.

As you submit to His sovereignty, His resurrection power will be released to you and through you in a mighty way. Jesus provided all you need at the cross to live victoriously. Submit to His process, and through the work of the Holy Spirit He will equip you to walk in power. As you call upon the Lord, submit to His instructions to you and obediently submit to His authority.

When you obey the first step of the formula by submitting to God, the second step is relatively easy. Once you submit to Jesus and experience life in His light, living a life in darkness will be repulsive to you.

Today's Bible Reading Plan: Numbers 4:1-5:31
Mark 12:18-37; Psalm 48:1-14; Proverbs 10:26

I submit to the loving hands of my Savior
to make me whole — spirit, soul, and body.

March 6

An On-Time Word

For as the rain comes down, and the snow from heaven, and do not return there but water the earth and make it bring forth and bud that it may give seed to the sower and bread to the eater, so shall My word be that goes forth from My mouth; it shall not return to Me void, but it shall accomplish that which I please, and it shall prosper in the thing for which I sent it.

— Isaiah 55:10-11

The Word of God is always right on time. It is never early, and it is never late, but it manifests in His perfect timing. His Word will <u>always</u> accomplish what He pleases and will prosper in its purpose.

God has more for you than you could ever dream, and He has already seen you in your future. Apply His Word to your life. When things don't seem to be going your way, just remember that His Word will not fail you. Accept <u>all</u> of God's will for you, not just those portions that appeal to you.

Sometimes God's answer is, "Wait." Waiting does not mean no. It simply means wait. *But those who wait upon the LORD shall renew their strength; they shall mount up with wings as eagles, they shall run and not be weary, and they shall walk and not faint* (Isaiah 40:31).

Today's Bible Reading Plan: Numbers 6:1-7:89
Mark 12:38-13:13; Psalm 49:1-20; Proverbs 10:27-28

Lord, teach me to wait patiently on your perfect timing.

March 7

The Battle Belongs to God

And he said, "Pay attention all Judah, and those dwelling in Jerusalem, and King Jehoshaphat: Thus says the LORD to you, Do not fear, nor be dismayed because of this great army, for the battle is not yours, but God's."

— *2 Chronicles 20:15*

In this epic battle that never was, God required Israel to do nothing more than show up for the battle and then praise Him. In obedience, Israel showed up on the battlefield and began praising Yahweh.

In response to Israel's praise, the Lord set ambushes against their enemy, and the enemy became confused and defeated each other. The enemy was utterly annihilated, and Israel didn't even have to fight the physical battle, because God had already won the battle in the spirit and made it manifest in the natural!

The battle is not yours. It belongs to God. We draw our strength from battle. The battle actually forces us to trust God completely. So, do not shrink from the battle. Just show up on the battlefield and start praising God! He will cause your enemies to become confused and defeat one another.

Today's Bible Reading Plan: Numbers 8:1-9:23
Mark 13:14-37; Psalm 50:1-23; Proverbs 10:29-30

I believe God's Word and I declare His promises of victory, healing, wholeness, peace and deliverance in my life today!

March 8

Do the Right Thing

*Therefore, to him who knows to do good
and does not do it, it is sin.*

— James 4:17

If you do not do what you know to be right, that is sin, but choosing to do the right thing can sometimes cause conflict. As we learned in yesterday's reading, we must not shrink away from the battle. From your greatest conflicts come your greatest victories.

God is faithful to His Word. You do not have to perform religious works to demonstrate faith. Faith simply implies you will have corresponding action to activate your faith. When a word from God is given, reason is never required. Faith and faith alone must answer that door. The instructions you choose to obey determine the future you create!

Go into action by speaking the Word. What you believe, you will begin to speak. When your heart is filled with faith, then words of faith flow effortlessly from your mouth, and what comes out of your mouth will become your reality. Your words spoken today will frame your world tomorrow. What truth are you declaring now?

Today's Bible Reading Plan: Numbers 10:1-11:23
Mark 14:1-21; Psalm 51:1-19; Proverbs 10:31-32

I declare victory in every area of my life!

March 9

Live Free

*As free people, do not use your liberty as a covering for evil,
but live as servants of God.*

— 1 Peter 2:16

Enjoy the freedom that Christ gives, but don't use that freedom as an excuse to sin. Don't use your liberty in Christ to excuse adultery, or lying, or stealing. Don't make the excuse, "God knows I love Him," and then follow it up with behavior that dishonors God.

When you truly follow Christ and are filled with His Spirit, it is impossible for those around you not to know it. You don't say one thing and then behave contrary to the words you speak, "in the name of Jesus."

We need to apply biblical truth to our lives everywhere: home, school, work, neighborhood, marketplace and public square. There should be no area of our lives where there is an exemption and exclusion of the presence of God.

Today's Bible Reading Plan: Numbers 11:24-13:33 Mark 14:22-52; Psalm 52:1-9; Proverbs 11:1-3

Almighty God, thank you for Your presence.

March 10

Whose Report Do You Believe?

Who has believed our report?
And to whom has the arm of the LORD been revealed?

— *Isaiah 53:1*

Isaiah prophetically posed the question, "Who has believed our report?" He was, of course, speaking of the coming Messiah. He was asking who would believe in Jesus and in His promises? When confronted with this question, we have a choice to make. When we are given an evil report, we can discard our faith and give up or direct our faith and be lifted up.

The report is that Jesus bore our sicknesses and carried our pains (Isaiah 53:4). The report is by Jesus' stripes we are healed (Isaiah 53:5). The report says that He desires above all else that we would prosper and be in health even as our soul prospers (3 John 2).

God so values your right of freedom that He gives you the opportunity to choose for Him or against Him. When we choose to believe His Word, then He promises blessing and abundance not only for us but also for our children (Deuteronomy 30:19). When you get a bad report, whose report will you trust? Believe the report of the Lord!

Today's Bible Reading Plan: Numbers 14:1-15:16 Mark 14:53-72; Psalm 53:1-6; Proverbs 11:4

My faith rises within me to believe Your report, Lord!

March 11 ~ A Day with Joni

Face to Face

For I long to see you, that I may impart to you
some spiritual gift, so that you may be strengthened.
— Romans 1:11

I recently read a study of how social media and the internet are impacting society. We're becoming even more self-absorbed. It happens as people spend time within a system that is singular. We don't surf the internet in groups, we surf alone. As we surf, the sharks circle the advertising waters and smell the blood – our wallets and our vulnerabilities. We type and click hoping for fulfillment or satisfaction.

Something on a website or in an app is doing what people used to do – substituting for connection. Life is becoming increasingly more impersonal. I love Paul's letters. He begins them and ends them with personal greetings. In several he says, "I long to see you face-to-face." I believe we can easily lose sight of this blessing if we're not careful.

I'm no technology prude. I use a laptop, an iPad, an iPhone and I text and tweet with the best of them. But I refuse to let devices replace people and things that matter by stealing my time and my attention. The gospel calls us to follow the example of Jesus, who lived His life on earth for others and not for Himself.

Today's Bible Reading Plan: Numbers 15:17-16:40
Mark 15:1-47; Psalm 54:1-7; Proverbs 11:5-6

Lord, thank You for advances in technology. But help me to be aware – too much of even a good thing, becomes a bad thing, if it keeps me from the best thing. I was created in Your image, to be a relational being. You put me here for others, and others here for me. May I be fully present in these relationships today!

March 12

The Stronger Man

When a strong man, fully armed, guards his own palace, his goods are peacefully kept. But when a stronger man than he attacks and overpowers him, he seizes all the armor in which the man trusted and divides his spoils.

— Luke 11:21-22

Satan is the strong man, and he is guarding his palace and keeping his realm tightly under his control. The goods in his palace are stolen merchandise. They have been stolen from God's elect. In his palace are stolen health, security, peace of mind and freedom. He is fiercely guarding our stolen finances, relationships, opportunities and blessings.

Our Lord and Savior entered the strong man's house and plundered him. Jesus liberated the captives who had become bound. He spoiled principalities and powers and made a show of them openly. He manifested a mastery over demons, depravity and disease. When this Man spoke, even death had to listen. There is no one stronger than our Savior and King. By the power of the Holy Spirit, reclaim what the enemy has stolen from you. Satan has no authority, because Christ lives in you!

Today's Bible Reading Plan: Numbers 16:41-18:32
Mark 16:1-20; Psalm 55:1-23; Proverbs 11:7

I serve, Jesus — the Stronger Man — who lives in me!

March 13

The Weapons of Our Warfare

For though we walk in the flesh, we do not war according to the flesh. For the weapons of our warfare are not carnal, but mighty through God to the pulling down of strongholds, casting down imaginations and every high thing that exalts itself against the knowledge of God, bringing every thought into captivity to the obedience of Christ.

— 2 Corinthians 10:3-5

We read yesterday that the only way to invade the strong man's palace is to know the Stronger Man, Jesus Christ. With the Stronger Man living in us, we too can bind the strong man. How?

The weapons of our warfare are not carnal but are mighty through God to the pulling down of strongholds (2 Corinthians 10:4). We have the weapons of prayer, praise and God's Word with which to combat the enemy!

You can subdue Satan and deal him a deadening blow in your life when you use the spiritual weapons in your arsenal. Bind him, in Jesus' name, and take back everything he has stolen from you!

Today's Bible Reading Plan: Numbers 19:1-20:29 Luke 1:1-25; Psalm 56:1-13; Proverbs 11:8

Thank you, Jesus, for routing the enemy and setting me free!

March 14

Satan Is Not All That and a Bag of Chips

Be sober and watchful, because your adversary the devil walks around as a roaring lion, seeking whom he may devour. Resist him firmly in the faith, knowing that the same afflictions are experienced by your brotherhood throughout the world.

— *1 Peter 5:8-9*

The devil walks around <u>like</u> a lion, but he isn't one. He is <u>seeking</u> whom he may devour, but if you're a born-again, blood-bought, fire-baptized, Holy Ghost filled believer in Christ, he can't find you.

Jesus was a Lamb in His suffering and death, but He became a Lion when He victoriously pried open the devouring mouth of the grave. At Heaven's designated point in time, the Lion of the Tribe of Judah vanquished hell's roaring lion in one fell blow.

Allow the roar of the Lion within you to reverberate in the world around you. Be full of faith, not fear. For *the righteous are bold as a lion* (Proverbs 28:1).

Today's Bible Reading Plan: Numbers 21:1-22:20 Luke 1:26-56; Psalm 57:1-11; Proverbs 11:9-11

I am bold as a lion;
the Lion of the Tribe of Judah lives in me!

March 15

Put on the Whole Armor

Put on the whole armor of God that you may be able to stand against the schemes of the devil. For our fight is not against flesh and blood, but against principalities, against powers, against the rulers of the darkness of this world, and against spiritual forces of evil in the heavenly places.

— Ephesians 6:11-12

For most of us, we will never face hand-to-hand combat or experience the atrocities of war. But for the Israelites, it was a regular fact of life.

They depended upon the Lord of Battles to assemble a mighty unseen army to protect them and bring victory over their enemies. They trusted in Almighty God to save them. But whenever they trusted in the arm of the flesh, they faced certain defeat.

It is easy to forget that our warfare is not with flesh and blood but with principalities and powers. The battles we fight are spiritual battles. As such, they can only be won in the spiritual arena. That is why we must trust in the Lord for our success.

Today's Bible Reading Plan: Numbers 22:21-23:30
Luke 1:57-80; Psalm 58:1-11; Proverbs 11:12-13

*Father, I thank You that You are the Lord of Hosts,
and You are with me. You are my
refuge and my strong tower.*

March 16

Stand

Therefore take up the whole armor of God that you may be able to resist in the evil day, and having done all, to stand.

— Ephesians 6:13

There is a place you can get to in God where the evil one touches you not. Why? Because you are sheltered safe in the arms of God. (Psalm 91) In addition, He lives in you! In Christ, you have been given power over all the power of the adversary (Luke 10:19). You are Christ's ambassador, and you are speaking on His behalf (2 Corinthians 5:19-20). You stand in His authority, declare His works and He performs them.

As you walk in His Spirit, you can get to the point where what you say is what God said. You will begin to operate in the fullness of the authority given to you by Almighty God. You can exercise your power over all the power of the devil and make him put back everything he has stolen from you.

When you command Satan, it is not you commanding at all, but you speak in the very presence of God (2 Corinthians 2:17)! Greater is Christ who lives on the inside of you than he that is in the world. Alone you are no match for the devil, but you are not alone! Stand strong!

Today's Bible Reading Plan: Numbers 24:1-25:18 Luke 2:1-35; Psalm 59:1-17; Proverbs 11:14

Jesus, I stand in You, in Your presence.

March 17

The Ultimate Battle Gear

*Stand therefore, having your waist girded with truth, having put
on the breastplate of righteousness, having your feet fitted with
the readiness of the gospel of peace, and above all, taking the
shield of faith, with which you will be able to extinguish all the
fiery arrows of the evil one. Take the helmet of salvation and the
sword of the Spirit, which is the word of God.*

— Ephesians 6:14-17

This ultimate battle gear is not just a good defense; it
is the ultimate offense. Nothing can defeat you when
you are arrayed in this armor. Jesus is your salvation.
Jesus is the Truth. He is your righteousness. He is the
Good News of everlasting life. And Jesus is your
Shield. You are protected by the Anointed One and
surrounded by His anointing.

Not only is Jesus your Shield of faith, you have been
given His Word as a mighty sword of His Spirit
(Ephesians 6:16). You can deflect the fiery darts of the
wicked one when you stand and declare its powerful
promises. Shielded by the anointing, you can slip
through the clutches of sin, sickness, death and every
enemy force arrayed against you.

Today's Bible Reading Plan: Numbers 26:1-51
Luke 2:36-52; Psalm 60:1-12; Proverbs 11:15

> *Jesus, because You live in me,
> I am always in full battle array.*

March 18 ~ A Day with Joni

On Whom to Lean

Trust in the LORD *with all your heart,*
and lean not on your own understanding;
— Proverbs 3:5

We've all had days when things are going along just fine, and then ... something happens. It's called bad news. It can shake us to our core, leaving us confused, bewildered, startled, and unable to breathe. We are left feeling helpless as if we've been blindsided. We panic and cry out, "What am I going to do?"

If I'm being honest, that's my typical response. When I ask that question, I am leaving someone out. I'm "leaning on my own understanding," which means I'm leaning on the wrong person – me! When I lean on my own understanding, I try to figure out the who, what, when, why, and how of my bad news, I remember past failures, get confused and start worrying. But when I think on Him, I think about who He is and has been in my life. I think of how he has delivered me out of the lion's den many times. If we trust God with all our hearts, then we won't need to lean on anyone or anything else. You have the Lord. Lean on Him. Trust! Believe!

Today's Bible Reading Plan: Numbers 26:52-28:15 Luke 3:1-22; Psalm 61:1-8; Proverbs 11:16-17

Gracious Father, I need You all the time, but especially when bad news breaks into the everyday. I confess, those are times I tend to lean on my own understanding, as if I can figure it out and navigate it on my own. Rescue me! Remind me – it's too big for me, but not for You!

81

March 19

Pray for Preachers

Pray for me, that the power to speak may be given to me, that I may open my mouth boldly to make known the mystery of the gospel, for which I am an ambassador in chains, that I may speak boldly as I ought to speak.

— Ephesians 6:19-20

I love the Church, and I love preaching to the Church. But I also love speaking to our nation and the world. I cannot be silent when I see so many injustices. God has called me to speak out and spread the glorious Gospel of Jesus Christ to a hurting world.

Whether you speak to large crowds or small home groups, we who preach the Gospel need the prayers of all the saints. We are speaking to a world that only wishes we would shut up. I feel compelled to speak for those who cannot speak, who have been silenced by the enemy. I have a passion to speak the truth of God to those who know only the answers of this secular age.

Even if you only speak to one person at a time, you are still preaching the Gospel of Christ. Don't give up and don't grow weary. You are giving a lifeline to someone who is drowning.

Today's Bible Reading Plan: Numbers 28:16-29:40 Luke 3:23-38; Psalm 62:1-12; Proverbs 11:18-19

Holy Spirit, help me to be ready at all times to speak life.

March 20

Pray for the Fivefold Ministry

He gave some to be apostles, prophets, evangelists, pastors, and teachers, for the equipping of the saints, for the work of service, and for the building up of the body of Christ.

— Ephesians 4:11-12

The fivefold ministry, who are apostles, prophets, evangelists, pastors and teachers, are provided by God to equip the body of Christ. The Bible says that through this equipping, we all come into the unity of the faith and of the knowledge of the Son of God.

God is building us into a complete man, making us mature. The Message Bible describes this complete body as *moving rhythmically and easily with each other, efficient and graceful in response to God's Son, fully mature adults, fully developed within and without, fully alive like Christ* (Ephesians 4:13).

As God builds us, we will no longer be immature and subject to the trickery and craftiness of men and deceitful scheming. No, we will speak the truth in love and grow up in all things into Jesus, our Head, being joined together and connected, as every part effectively does its work and grows, building itself up in love.

Today's Bible Reading Plan: Numbers 30:1-31:54
Luke 4:1-30; Psalm 63:1-11; Proverbs 11:20-21

Lord God, thank You for equipping the body of Christ so that we can give You glory and shine Your Light to the world.

March 21

More Than a Conqueror

No, in all these things we are more than conquerors through Him who loved us.

— Romans 8:37

Because God has called you according to His purpose, and because He loves you, and you love Him, He works all things together for good. (Romans 8:28). How can you lose? Even when you make what seems to be a wrong choice, God works it for good when your heart is fixed on Him.

When you are called by God for His specific purpose, there is nothing that can stop His purpose from being fulfilled in your life. He knows far in advance what you will or will not do, and He has already worked it into His plan.

After all, your salvation is not dependent on your works. It is through faith you are saved, not works, lest you become boastful. *For by grace you have been saved through faith, and this is not of yourselves. It is the gift of God, not of works, so that no one should boast* (Ephesians 2:8-9).

Because of what Jesus did at Calvary, you have been put in right standing with God Almighty to do mighty exploits for Him.

Today's Bible Reading Plan: Numbers 32:1-33:39
Luke 4:31-5:11; Psalm 64:1-10; Proverbs 11:22

Father, I am so grateful that I can be in in right standing with You because of the obedience of Jesus at the Cross.

March 22

God Is On Your Side

What then shall we say to these things?
If God is for us, who can be against us?

— *Romans 8:31*

Nothing can ever separate you from the Father's love. Even though we all have sinned and fallen short of His glory (Romans 3:23), we have been made righteous, put in right standing with God through the sacrifice of His Son.

God has justified us. There is no more guilt, shame or condemnation. Jesus paid the ultimate price for our freedom, and we can now sing hallelujah and rejoice and dance in His presence!

No matter what battle we face, *we are more than conquerors through Him who loved us* (Romans 8:37). Nothing can ever make God stop loving us.

For I am persuaded that neither death nor life, neither angels nor principalities nor powers, neither things present nor things to come, neither height nor depth, nor any other created thing, shall be able to separate us from the love of God, which is in Christ Jesus our Lord (Romans 8:38-39).

Today's Bible Reading Plan: Numbers 33:40-35:34 Luke 5:12-28; Psalm 65:1-13; Proverbs 11:23

Father, thank You for Your love that will never cease.

March 23

Victory in Jesus!

*But thanks be to God, who gives us the victory
through our Lord Jesus Christ!*

— 1 Corinthians 15:57

The skies grew black at noonday. Women shrieked in horror, as the earth shook in horrible spasms. It seemed the Savior of the world was dying. Demons clapped their fettered hands in glee. It looked as though hell had won the battle of the ages.

At the darkest hour in human history, it looked as though God would forever be branded a liar and accused of not keeping His promise.

But hell did not win. Jesus, our King, let out a mighty cry of victory on the cross and declared and decreed, "It is finished!"

Don't write your report on Friday, because Resurrection Day is coming! Too often, we give up right at the point of breakthrough. It always appears darkest just before dawn, and Satan will always hit you the hardest before your greatest victory.

Don't give up! When you persevere, trusting in the Lord, you will prevail! We have victory in Jesus. He is Lord!

Today's Bible Reading Plan:
Numbers 36:1-13-Deuteronomy 1:1-46; Luke 5:29-6:11
Psalm 66:1-20; Proverbs 11:24-26

Jesus, thank You for total victory!

March 24

Faith that Overcomes

A thousand may fall at your side
and ten thousand at your right hand,
but it shall not come near you.

— *Psalm 91:7*

A precious single mother was struggling. She had held her family together, but they were living in a house so old that the foundations wouldn't even support a modern kitchen. They had no kitchen appliances, no kitchen sink, and this dear woman was saddled with a $10,000 debt.

Through it all, she did not lose her faith and belief in Almighty God. Although things seemed to be crashing in around her, she did not give up on God. Satan was unable to crush her faith. She held strong, knowing that it was the Lord Jesus who was the author and finisher of her faith (Hebrews 12:2).

The fruit of her faith? She recently received a $46,000 miracle! She paid off her debts and moved her family into a new home with a real kitchen. What would be her testimony to you today? No matter how dark it seems, do not grow weary, for in due season you will reap if you don't give up (Galatians 6:9).

Today's Bible Reading Plan: Deuteronomy 2:1-3:29 Luke 6:12-38; Psalm 67:1-7; Proverbs 11:27

You, O Lord, are my help in times of trouble.

March 25 ~ A Day with Joni

How Long Until
We Get There?

He said to them, "But who do you say that I am?"
Peter answered Him, "You are the Christ."
— Mark 8:29

I was whining to a wise friend one day. I was telling her about a certain situation and set of circumstances I was enduring. I was complaining. I was certain God had looked the other way. Waah, waah, waah! You know what she said to me? "Just keep pedaling." What? I asked her to explain.

She recalled riding on the back of a bicycle built for two. She kept asking questions like, "Where are we going? Why are we going this direction? How much longer is this going to take?" Finally, the person in the front – called the Captain – turned around and simply replied, "Just keep pedaling." The person in the front seat knew where they were going, how to get there, and how long it would take. All they needed on a bicycle built for two, was two riders synchronized as they pedal. To stay on course, move properly and reach the place God has for us, we have to trust our Captain. Our answer may not come when we want it, and we may have to pedal uphill, but if we just keep peddling, we'll get there ... when we get there!

Today's Bible Reading Plan: Deuteronomy 4:1-49 Luke 6:39-7:10; Psalm 68:1-18; Proverbs 11:28

Heavenly Father – You are the Captain – my Captain. Will You help me be a better follower? Give me the grace and strength I need to pedal on, to persevere, trusting that You know the way and can get us there, by the best route possible. I pray in Jesus' name. Amen.

March 26

God Is Faithful

But the Lord is faithful, who will establish you
and guard you from the evil one.

— 2 Thessalonians 3:3

God is a God of timing, of intention, of purpose and design, and God is faithful. We are not wandering around aimlessly in a random evolutionary existence. God intentionally created us and breathed into us the breath of life, His breath.

Atheists deny the existence of God and say they have evolved from primordial slime, that there is no divine calling or purpose for their lives. For them, there is no sin, because there is no God; and since they believe there is no sin, they have no need of redemption, and so they do not need a Savior.

They miss out on the incredible loving relationship between God and man that has been obtained through Jesus Christ. They miss the astonishing experience of His love and faithfulness, as it plays out in their everyday lives. We who believe, however, know the power and depth of this beautiful relationship, today, and we look forward with hope to living with God eternally in the kingdom He is preparing for us.

Today's Bible Reading Plan: Deuteronomy 5:1-6:25
Luke 7:11-35; Psalm 68:19-35; Proverbs 11:29-31

With God all things are possible.

March 27

Do Not Fear Them

"Do not fear them, for the LORD your God,
He shall fight for you."

— *Deuteronomy 3:22*

The children of Israel were about to cross the Jordan into the Promised Land. Moses encouraged them, saying, *"The LORD your God has given you this land to possess it"* (Deuteronomy 3:18).

He continued by saying to Joshua, *"Your eyes have seen all that the LORD your God has done to these two kings. So shall the LORD do to all the kingdoms where you pass. Do not fear them, for the LORD your God, He shall fight for you"* (Deuteronomy 3:21-22).

What promise from God are you waiting to possess? Remember that God is fighting for you. No matter how oppressive or chaotic the circumstances may appear, God is overpowering the enemy. Whether you see the manifestation in the natural yet or not, trust that God has gone before you and has cleared the battlefield of the land mines planted by your adversary.

Be sensitive to the Holy Spirit and follow all of His instructions. God will use you to win the battle and put His enemy to shame.

Today's Bible Reading Plan: Deuteronomy 7:1-8:20 Luke 7:36-8:3; Psalm 69:1-18; Proverbs 12:1

Holy Spirit, give me courage and wisdom
in the heat of battle.

March 28

You Clothe Me with Strength

For You clothed me with strength for the battle;
You subdued under me those who rose up against me.

— Psalm 18:39

King David's son, Absalom, betrayed him. As David fled for his life, he cried out, *"LORD, how my foes have multiplied! Many rise up against me! Many are saying about my life, 'There is no help for him in God'"* (Psalm 3:1-2). In verse 3 David continues, proclaiming, *"But you, O LORD, are a shield for me, my glory and the One who raises up my head."* In verse 7 David implores God, crying out, *"Arise O LORD; save me, O my God!"*

David knew his help and strength would come from God alone. David was not a perfect man, but he remained faithful to the Lord God of Israel, and God considered David to be a man who was after His own heart (1 Samuel 13:14, Acts 13:22).

Whether you have experienced heartbreaking betrayal from a family member, coworker, neighbor or someone you thought was a friend, God will strengthen you, restore you and lift you from the depths of your despair. Trust God in all things.

Today's Bible Reading Plan: Deuteronomy 9:1-10:22 Luke 8:4-21; Psalm 69:19-36; Proverbs 12:2-3

Holy Spirit, strengthen me in the midst of conflict.
Help me to see You clearly in the heat of battle.

91

March 29

Built on the Rock

And I tell you that you are Peter, and on this rock I will build My church, and the gates of Hades shall not prevail against it.

— Matthew 16:18

Let me tell you the true story of a family who built their house on the Rock of Christ and kept trusting God, even in their darkest hour. First, the stock market crashed. Then their interior renovation business dried up and their car was repossessed. Finally, they lost their home. During Christmas, the whole family had to move in with a relative, into their small apartment.

They cried to God for help, and He turned things around miraculously. Now the husband has a job, and they have purchased another home. By God's grace and power, they have been restored, and the enemy has had to put back what he stole from them.

Jesus is the Rock (1 Corinthians 10:4). When we trust Him, we will not be disappointed. This family held on to Him with all they had, and He restored them completely. Whether you need healing in your body, deliverance from oppression or a relationship restored, Jesus is the answer to every problem.

Today's Bible Reading Plan: Deuteronomy 11:1-12:32 Luke 8:22-39; Psalm 70:1-5; Proverbs 12:4

Jesus truly is the answer for the ills of this world.

March 30

Annihilation of Evil Works

Whoever practices sin is of the devil, for the devil has been sinning from the beginning. For this purpose the Son of God was revealed, that He might destroy the works of the devil.

— 1 John 3:8

Jesus was anointed to bring liberty to the world. The word Christ (Messiah) literally means Anointed One. He was drenched in God's yoke-destroying, burden-removing anointing. The anointing does not merely break the yoke; it destroys the yoke upon your life.

There is a vast difference between breaking and destroying. If you break a glass, it is possible for it to be fixed. The actual Hebrew translation of the word *destroy* is *to cause to cease to be as though it never existed* or in a word, *annihilate*. Through the anointing, the forces of light bombard the forces of darkness that are arrayed against you and literally <u>annihilate</u> them!

Jesus came to annihilate the works of the devil. Whenever sickness, lack or strongholds have their icy tentacles wrapped around your life, they are lording or ruling over you. Anything that is trying to be lord in your life, other than Jesus, can be annihilated by the power of the Holy Spirit!

Today's Bible Reading Plan: Deuteronomy 13:1-15:23 Luke 8:40-9:6; Psalm 71:1-24; Proverbs 12:5-7

Jesus has annihilated the works of the enemy in my life!

March 31

Fight the Good Fight

Fight the good fight of faith. Lay hold on eternal life,
to which you are called and have professed a good profession
before many witnesses.

— 1 Timothy 6:12

Paul had forsaken all to follow Christ. But at every turn he suffered. He endured shipwreck, snakebite, stoning and was left for dead. Yet at the lowest point in his life, his faith was at its peak. Paul had fought the good fight. He had finished his course. He had kept the faith (2 Timothy 4:7).

If your faith can survive the greatest loss, then faith is your greatest commodity. Hold on to your faith, and faith will hold on to you. Paul never surrendered to the assaults against him. He knew there was a reward awaiting him. A crown of righteousness would be given to him from Jesus, his Righteous Judge.

When the daily battles of life are fierce and you are tempted to give up, remember your troubles today are producing for you an eternal glory that is far greater than anything you can imagine (2 Corinthians 4:17). You will finish strong!

Today's Bible Reading Plan: Deuteronomy 16:1-17:20 Luke 9:7-27; Psalm 72:1-20; Proverbs 12:8-9

I will finish my course and
receive my reward from my King!

APRIL

Fight with Fruit

So embrace, as the elect of God, holy and beloved, a spirit of mercy, kindness, humbleness of mind, meekness, and longsuffering. Bear with one another and forgive one another. If anyone has a quarrel against anyone, even as Christ forgave you, so you must do. And above all these things, embrace love, which is the bond of perfection.

— Colossians 3:12-14

April 1 ~ A Day with Joni

Ch-Ch-Changes

For I am the LORD, *I do not change…*
— Malachi 3:6

You know I don't like change. But I suppose subtle changes, the result of time and perspective, they're not so bad. I like the confidence that comes from experience. I like the assurance that troubling times won't last. I like the growth that has resulted from pain and the perspective that keeps me looking for the silver lining in the clouds. I've been through cloudy days, the rain, the thunder and lightning, and even a few hurricanes. Little orphan Annie was right: the sun will come out tomorrow.

Change comes with years, and years come with change. Since we'll never escape it, we might as well learn to ride those winds of change. Here's a beautiful truth: we don't face the winds of change alone. God is our anchor, our constant, our steady and invariable stability. We can feel like we're drowning in a sea of change, but know this: He is our next breath of forever.

Consider the words to this great old hymn: Because He lives, I can face tomorrow; because He lives all fear is gone. And remember, some change is not so bad after all.

Today's Bible Reading Plan: Deuteronomy 18:1-20:20 Luke 9:28-50; Psalm 73:1-28; Proverbs 12:10

My God; my Anchor; my Rock – as I face changes, help me to rest in the security of knowing You. You don't change. Big things or small, easy or trying, Your grace is enough. May I face this day with confidence and poise from Your throne and fountain! Amen.

April 2

The Fruit of Salvation

For the mountains may be removed,
and the hills may shake,
but My kindness shall not depart from you,
nor shall My covenant of peace be removed,
says the LORD who has mercy on you.

— Isaiah 54:10

No matter what you have done, God's covenant of mercy will never be removed from you. You may feel afflicted and battered by the storm. You may feel that your world is in such an upheaval that you cannot be comforted, but God can restore your foundation that is shaken and falling apart.

God is going to rebuild your crumbled foundation that used to be made of concrete with a foundation of precious stones. Great is your peace and the peace of your children. You are established in righteousness far from oppression and tyrants. God is about to remove people in your life who are consumers and polluters.

Let go of the piece of coal you're desperately holding onto, and let God give you a diamond. Jesus received the penalty for your sin and paid the price in full. Enjoy the fruit of salvation!

Today's Bible Reading Plan: Deuteronomy 21:1-22:30 Luke 9:51-10:12; Psalm 74:1-23; Proverbs 12:11

The fruit of salvation is the harvest
of God's covenant of peace.

April 3

The Heritage of God's Servant

*No weapon that is formed against you shall prosper,
and every tongue that shall rise against you in judgment,
you shall condemn. This is the heritage of the servants
of the LORD, and their vindication is from Me, says the LORD.*

— Isaiah 54:17

In Isaiah 54:7-9 God says for a small moment he forsook Israel, but with great mercy He would gather them back. In a little wrath, He briefly hid His face from His people; but with everlasting kindness He will have mercy on them, because He is their Redeemer, and He will never leave them again.

Like a husband returning to an abandoned wife, the Lord has come back to His chosen, and He is here to stay. Jesus has restored the relationship between man and God and is now the Bridegroom preparing eternity for His Bride.

No weapon that is formed against God's elect shall prosper. Stand back and watch God fight your battle. You are dwelling in the secret place of the Most High, and you will reap the fruit of His righteousness, because your righteousness is of Him.

Today's Bible Reading Plan: Deuteronomy 23:1-25:19 Luke 10:13-37; Psalm 75:1-10; Proverbs 12:12-14

*Jesus, thank You for my inheritance.
I will walk in your Spirit and reap an amazing harvest.*

April 4

Secret Service Christians

Then I heard a loud voice in heaven, saying:
"Now the salvation and the power and the kingdom of our God
and the authority of His Christ have come, for the accuser of our
brothers, who accused them before our God day and night,
has been cast down."

— Revelation 12:10

Satan is always accusing the people of God. If you have been busy working in the kingdom of God, you have probably been falsely accused, lied on and talked about. Don't let the accuser intimidate you and force you into hiding, so that you become a secret service Christian hiding out, keeping your faith undercover.

Jesus said if you're ashamed of Him, He will be ashamed of you. *For whoever is ashamed of Me and My words, of him will the Son of Man be ashamed when He comes in His own glory and in the glory of His Father and of the holy angels* (Luke 9:26).

The accuser will be cast down at the end of the age, but you don't have to die and go to heaven to receive your inheritance. When you acknowledge Jesus as your Savior, you receive the fruit of your confession: a relationship with God.

Today's Bible Reading Plan: Deuteronomy 26:1-27:26 Luke 10:38-11:13; Psalm 76:1-12; Proverbs 12:15-17

Because of You, Jesus, I have
a loving relationship with God.

April 5

The Reading of the Will

In Him also we have received an inheritance…according to the counsel of His own will, that we…after hearing the word of truth…were sealed with the promised Holy Spirit who is the guarantee of our inheritance…

— Ephesians 1:11-14

In the natural, a beneficiary doesn't die to receive an inheritance. Someone else has to die before the inheritance can be released. It is the same in the spiritual realm. Jesus died to release your inheritance. You don't have to die to receive your inheritance.

Jesus not only died to release your inheritance, but He was resurrected by the power of the Holy Ghost and attends the reading of His will every time you read His Word. God Almighty conquered the adversary of the souls of men on the cross of Christ. By the intermediary agency of the Holy Spirit, through you, God has not only conquered Satan, He controls him. Conquered is one thing, controlled is another.

You must be alert and vigilant, because the adversary is seeking to devour you. The fruit of your vigilance will be an unflappable faith controlled by the Holy Spirit.

Today's Bible Reading Plan: Deuteronomy 28:1-68 Luke 11:14-36; Psalm 77:1-20; Proverbs 12:18

Holy Spirit, thank You for keeping me alert and vigilant.

April 6

The Devil Is a Liar

You are of your father the devil, and you want to do the desires
of your father. He was a murderer from the beginning, and
does not stand in the truth, because there is no truth in him.
When he lies, he speaks from his own nature,
for he is a liar and the father of lies.

— John 8:44

Satan is an imitator and an imposter. He is a liar and the father of lies. Whatever he says to you, the exact opposite is true. If he says you are of no worth, that means you worth more than you could ever imagine.

Everything he says to you is a lie. If he says you have cancer, that means you are going to have a healing ministry. If the devil says you're going to go broke, you'd better get ready for financial prosperity.

When someone accuses you, you don't have to seek vengeance or fight with them. God wants you to love. Love is not weak. Love disarms the adversary, because it refuses to fight. You cannot fight someone who will not fight. You do not have to fight. God said stand still and see His salvation (Exodus 14:13). You fight with fruit, not physical weapons.

Today's Bible Reading Plan: Deuteronomy 29:1-30:20 Luke 11:37-12:7; Psalm 78:1-31; Proverbs 12:19-20

I will trust you, God, and I will not react in my flesh,
but I will wait on you, for you will always avenge me.

101

April 7

Fruit Must Be Pruned

For to those who are perishing, the preaching of the cross is foolishness, but to us who are being saved it is the power of God.

— 1 Corinthians 1:18

Trials and tribulations do the pruning work of the Holy Spirit so that you can bring the fruit of God to maturity. God is working from the outside in and then from the inside out.

Just because you were saved does not mean you are saved. You are at this moment in the state of being saved. When you read the Word of God and your mind is renewed, you are being saved.

Don't flirt with sin. You must stay strong in the Lord and the power of His might. When you are tempted, pray for strength. Ask the Holy Spirit to convict you of sin and convince you of righteousness.

If you do sin, allow the Holy Spirit to prune you. Repent, change the way you think and act. Turn back to Almighty God. If we turn back to God when we sin, the fruit of true repentance in the body of Christ will be revival!

Today's Bible Reading Plan: Deuteronomy 31:1-32:27 Luke 12:8-34; Psalm 78:32-55; Proverbs 12:21-23

Help me to recognize Your pruning work. Revive me, Holy Spirit! I long to see You move!

April 8 ~ A Day with Joni

WWLD?

Love suffers long ... bears all things ... and endures all things.

— 1 Corinthians 13:4-7

My feelings were hurt. Badly! What to do? Do I confront the offender? React? Respond in kind? You've experienced this too. I prayed for guidance. Do you know what I heard from the Lord? These words: "What would love do?" Not exactly the words I wanted to hear! I wanted God to say, "I will smite your enemies, and they are in big trouble for hurting you – they'll be sorry!"

Love? 1 Corinthians 13 came to mind. I've read it so many times, but never with this perspective – what *would* love do?

You know the passage. When I read "it bears all things; endures all things" I knew what I had to do – forgive. Love would do what Jesus, Love incarnate, would do. What would life look like if we made His love our aim?

Today's Bible Reading Plan: Deuteronomy 32:28-52 Luke 12:35-59; Psalm 78:56-64; Proverbs 12:24

My loving Father: You call me to love even my enemies, and to pray for those who spitefully hurt me. Will You give me the grace to always ask the question 'What would love do?' and then to do it? Fill my heart with compassion and forgiveness and love, I pray. Amen.

April 9

A Stumbling Block

But we preach Christ crucified, a stumbling block to the Jews and foolishness to the Greeks.

— 1 Corinthians 1:23

The cross is a stumbling block to the religious Jew and to the 21st century religious Christian, as well. The word translated *stumbling block* is the Greek word *skandalon.* It's where we derive our English word *scandal.* The true message of the cross has become scandalous to tradition-loving Christians.

The trendy and the intellectual religious leaders of our day stumble over the message of the cross. They don't want to preach this "bloody gospel." They have traded the true Gospel for a blood-less gospel.

The cross is the window into the heart of God. It points the way to the help man needs to rise out of the pit he has dug for himself, but pride keeps him from reaching to God for help. *Humble yourselves in the sight of the Lord, and He will lift you up* (James 4:10).

The fruit of humility is that you are now able to accept God's consolation and therefore be freed from the pit.

Today's Bible Reading Plan: Deuteronomy 33:1-29 Luke 13:1-21; Psalm 78:65-72; Proverbs 12:25

Holy Spirit, thank You for the fruit of humility.

104

April 10

The Perfect Sacrifice

But He emptied Himself, taking upon Himself the form
of a servant, and was made in the likeness of men.

— Philippians 2:7

The week of Passover begins at sunset this evening, and it commemorates God's deliverance of His people from slavery in Egypt. God told the Israelites to slay a lamb and put its blood on the doorpost and lentils of their homes. If the blood was not found on the home, the firstborn of that family would be slain by the death angel. (It is no coincidence the markings of the blood formed a cross.)

Jesus was crucified on Passover, and so it is not just a Jewish holiday, but a spiritual commemoration for followers of Christ, as well. Jesus is the Passover Lamb for all who believe in Him, both Jew and Gentile.

For He is our peace, who has made both groups one and has broken down the barrier of the dividing wall, by abolishing in His flesh the enmity, that is, the law of the commandments contained in ordinances, that in Himself He might make the two into one new man, thus making peace, and that He might reconcile both to God into one body through the cross, thereby slaying the enmity (Ephesians 2:14-16).

Today's Bible Reading Plan:
Deuteronomy 34:1-12-Joshua 1:1-2:24; Luke 13:22-14:6; Psalm 79:1-13; Proverbs 12:26

Jesus, thank You for Your perfect sacrifice.
Because of You, I have an intimate relationship with God.

April 11

The Furious Love of God

Greater love has no man than this:
that a man lay down his life for his friends.

— John 15:13

Calvary's cross is the place where the furious love of God intersects with our broken and shattered hearts. Never before and never since has love been on such open display as it was that day, when Jesus was swung up between heaven and earth. The pitiful Palestinian sun beat down into His open wounds until it felt as though the very flames of hell itself had embedded themselves in the flesh of the only begotten Son of God.

Women shrieked and men stood paralyzed. The earth shook, and it was as black as night at noonday. God was unsheathing His weapon. The love of Jesus was starkly, publicly exhibited for all to see.

The compassion of Jesus is the compassion of Almighty God. God loves you with a love so forceful, so powerful, that it becomes the wielded weapon in His hand to defeat every lie, accusation, sickness, bondage, torment and lack of your human soul. The fruit of God's love is power!

Today's Bible Reading Plan: Joshua 3:1-4:24
Luke 14:7-35; Psalm 80:1-19; Proverbs 12:27-28

Holy Spirit, help me to walk in the power of God's love.

April 12

Confidence in God

This is the confidence that we have in Him, that if we ask anything according to His will, He hears us. So if we know that He hears whatever we ask, we know that we have whatever we asked of Him.

— 1 John 5:14-15

God does not make mistakes. The only thing in the Bible that is not inspired is the punctuation. We read, "This is the confidence that we have in Him, that if we ask anything according to His will…" And so we dive out of faith, saying, "Lord, if it be thy will."

He looks back over the sapphire sill of heaven's gate and says to you, "Why don't you know my will?" This misunderstanding is all because a comma is wrongly placed. The emphasis is put on the wrong syllable. It should not read, "If we ask anything according to His will…" God says, "If we ask anything, according to His will He hears us." What does that mean? He willed to hear you. You have never prayed the prayer He did not hear and answer.

Be confident in God. He will hear and answer when you call, because He loves you and cares for you.

Today's Bible Reading Plan: Joshua 5:1-7:15
Luke 15:1-32; Psalm 81:1-16; Proverbs 13:1

*I will have confidence in my God,
for in Him I have everything I need.*

April 13

In the Beginning...

In the beginning God created the heavens and the earth.

— Genesis 1:1

God's identity and His plan for humanity is revealed in the very first word of the Bible. "In the beginning" is rendered in Hebrew as one word, B-R-A-SH-EE-T (English spelling: Beresheet). In Hebrew, each letter is a pictograph that represents a concept.

﬜ B is Bet, depicting a house.

ﬧ R is Resh, depicting a Head. (B and R together equal bar or son, as in Bar Mitzvah.)

א A is Aleph, depicted as an ox, representing God as a strong leader.

�ש SH is Shin, depicted as teeth gnashing to destroy.

﬩ EE is the Yod and looks like a hand and arm.

✝ T is Tau and resembles a cross and stands for the mark of a covenant.

These Hebrew letters put together read: "The Head of the house, the Son, God destroyed by His hand on a cross to secure the covenant." The entire Gospel message is revealed in the very first word of the Bible!

Today's Bible Reading Plan: Joshua 7:16-9:2 Luke 16:1-18; Psalm 82:1-8; Proverbs 13:2-3

Thank You, Lord, for Your incredible love that redeemed me from the very first day of creation.

108

April 14

You Are Never Forsaken

*About the ninth hour Jesus cried out with a loud voice,
"Eli, Eli, lama sabachthani?" which means,
"My God, My God, why have You forsaken Me?"*

— Matthew 27:46

When translated from the original text, the word *forsaken* includes such words as: what habitation, make plenteous, covenant, rejected refuse, pull up, loosen, draw, leave, rescue, restore, build, recollect the Rock.

The traditional translation is interpreted as: "Why have you rejected and left me?" Jesus' words take on a different meaning when using other words from the translation: "What plenteous habitation from the covenant. Rejected refuse [Jesus on the cross] will be pulled up, loosened [from the Earth], drawn [to the Father], leave [this world], will rescue, restore, and build. The Rock will be recollected.

I believe Jesus spoke words of victory. He moved from horrific crucifixion to triumph with words of conquest, not despair. He was and is a Warrior, not a victim. I believe He was telling His Father, "I am ready for the next leg of this journey. It is finished!"

Today's Bible Reading Plan: Joshua 9:3-10:43
Luke 16:19-17:10; Psalm 83:1-18; Proverbs 13:4

*Jesus, You were, are and will
forever be a victorious Warrior!*

April 15 ~ A Day with Joni

Hello, My Name Is...

I am my beloved's and my beloved is mine...
— Song of Songs 6:3a

We wear many labels. Some we've placed on ourselves. More often than not, others have labeled us – based on what we do, how we perform, or what others think of us. Labels have adhesive on them. They stick! If we're not careful, our true identities can quickly become lost in them.

Who does God say you are? You are His beloved! You are His dream come true! You began with a thought and were transformed into His likeness in the earth! You are so special that no one else has your fingerprints or your DNA – you are uniquely you. There is a place in God's heart that only you can fill.

If you were an only child, Jesus still would have died for you. That's how precious and valuable you are to Him. You have a Divine purpose, and no label applied on earth can take that from you. The only label that matters: You are God's beloved child!

Today's Bible Reading Plan: Joshua 11:1-12:24 Luke 17:11-37; Psalm 84:1-12; Proverbs 13:5-6

Gracious Lord: Your banner over me is love! I am thankful to be Your beloved child. Please remind me of this truth as I move through this day – wearing lesser labels that I and others have applied to my life. I am a child of God! I am a beloved child of God! In Jesus' name, Amen.

April 16

Feast of First Fruits Resurrection Day

*Early on the first day of the week, Mary Magdalene
went to the tomb while it was still dark and saw
that the stone had been taken away from the tomb.*

— John 20:1

The Feast of First Fruits celebrates the first harvest of the year: *Speak to the children of Israel, and say to them: When you have come into the land that I am giving to you and reap its harvest, then you shall bring a sheaf bundle of the first fruits of your harvest to the priest. And he shall wave the sheaf before the LORD so that you may be accepted. On the day after the Sabbath the priest shall wave it.* (Leviticus 23:10-11).

Here, a festival is established in the Old Testament that prophesies the resurrection of Jesus. He is the first fruits of God waved before the Father so that we may be accepted. Through Jesus, Jew and Gentile can have a relationship with God. *There is one body and one Spirit, even as you were called in one hope of your calling, one Lord, one faith, one baptism, one God and Father of all, who is above all, and through all, and in you all* (Ephesians 4:4-6). There is one body of Christ. Jesus, the first fruits of God's harvest, brought salvation to the entire world!

Today's Bible Reading Plan: Joshua 13:1-14:15
Luke 18:1-17; Psalm 85:1-13; Proverbs 13:7-8

*Because of Jesus, I am no longer alienated from the
citizenship of Israel and a stranger to God's covenant.*

April 17

Wait for the Promise

The former treatise have I made, O Theophilus, concerning all that Jesus began both to do and teach, until the day when He was taken up, after He had given commandments through the Holy Spirit to the apostles whom He had chosen, to whom He presented Himself alive after His passion by many infallible proofs, appearing to them for forty days, and speaking concerning the kingdom of God.
— Acts 1:1-3

The earthly ministry of Jesus was not over after His resurrection from the tomb. He now had to establish the direction of the church before ascending to heaven, and He did not leave until ten days before the Holy Spirit was to come indwell His faithful followers. He promised to never leave them nor forsake them; therefore, He did not ascend to heaven until it was nearly time for the Holy Spirit to indwell them.

There was a ten-day period after Jesus ascended that they would have to wait for the Holy Spirit, but they did not know at the time how long it would be. During those ten days, they had to remember and trust the words of Jesus and wait for the baptism, the immersion in His Spirit.

Today's Bible Reading Plan: Joshua 15:1-63
Luke 18:18-43; Psalm 86:1-17; Proverbs 13:9-10

Lord God, overwhelm me with Your presence today by baptizing me, immersing me in Your precious Holy Spirit.

April 18

Conclusion of Passover

"And look, I am sending the promise of My Father upon you. But wait in the city of Jerusalem until you are clothed with power from on high."
— Luke 24:49

Today marks the last day of Passover; however, this is not an ending. We are in the midst of counting down 50 days to Pentecost. In Leviticus 23:15-16, Israel received the following instruction: *You shall count seven full weeks from the next day after the Sabbath, from the day that you brought the sheaf bundle of the wave offering. You shall count fifty days to the day after the seventh Sabbath; then you shall offer a new grain offering to the LORD. You shall bring out of your habitations two wave loaves of two-tenths of an ephah. They shall be of wheat flour, baked with leaven. They are the first fruits to the LORD.*

This is another prophetic Feast. This Feast foretells of Pentecost, when the Holy Spirit would be poured out on the body of Christ, just as Jesus said and as the Father promised. In Christ, every moment of every day is a new beginning, because the Spirit of God dwells in us. We commemorate the Feasts of the Lord to honor Him corporately, but in reality we always have fellowship with God. His Spirit directs and guides us victoriously through each day, if we listen for His voice.

Today's Bible Reading Plan: Joshua 16:1-18:28
Luke 19:1-27; Psalm 87:1-7; Proverbs 13:11

Thank You, Holy Spirit, for filling me each day.

113

April 19

There Is One Fruit of the Spirit

But the fruit of the Spirit is love, joy, peace, patience, gentleness, goodness, faith, meekness, and self-control; against such there is no law.

— Galatians 5:22-23

God has given you one weapon in your spiritual arsenal with which to combat the principalities and powers of darkness. Even though the Bible says the weapons of our warfare are not carnal, in reality you only need one weapon.

Just like the last book of the Bible is Revelation, not Revelations, there is one fruit of the Spirit, not fruits. The fruit of the Spirit is love. People mistakenly think there are nine fruits listed in Galatians 5:22-23. Joy, peace, patience, gentleness, kindness, meekness and faith, are all expressions of love, the fruit of God's love working in and through you.

God is love. The outworking of God's love is that the fruit of His love manifests through your recreated human spirit. The Holy Spirit is your tutor, guide and Helper in the process of producing the fruit of God's love through your spirit.

Today's Bible Reading Plan: Joshua 19:1-20:9 Luke 19:28-48; Psalm 88:1-18; Proverbs 13:12-14

Holy Spirit, help me to love as God loves.

114

April 20

Love

Love is patient...kind...does not envy...does not boast...is not proud...does not dishonor others...is not self-seeking...not easily angered...keeps no record of wrongs. Love...always protects...trusts...hopes...perseveres. Love never fails.
— 1 Corinthians 13:4-8 (NIV)

Fruit is a food for consumption and presupposes life. God created every herb and every fruit tree bearing fruit after its kind with its seed in itself, perpetual life.

Fruit must be pruned, which is not pleasant. God cuts and trims you so that you will bring forth more fruit for His consumption. Jesus said, *"I am the vine, you are the branches. He who remains in Me, and I in him, bears much fruit"* (John 15:5).

Parents bear children so that their children will love them. God, as well, created you so that you would love Him. God wanted the fruit of your love so desperately that He climbed on the cross and gave His life for you.

Someone asked one of my children one day, "Would you ever do this?" "No," they replied "Well, wouldn't you want to just try?" "Yeah." "Well, why wouldn't you do it?" "Because it would hurt my dad." Let's not grieve our Father.

Today's Bible Reading Plan: Joshua 21:1-22:20 Luke 20:1-26; Psalm 89:1-13; Proverbs 13:15-16

Holy Spirit, produce the fruit of Your love in me today.

April 21

Joy Is Love's Awareness

But may all those who seek refuge in You rejoice; may they ever shout for joy, because You defend them; may those who love Your name be joyful in You.

— Psalm 5:11

You may think of joy as happiness, but joy is not an emotion. It is a supernatural expression given to us by the indwelling of the Holy Spirit.

Joy is a deep and abiding sense of contentment, providing a foundation for our lives in Christ. Unlike fragile happiness, which withers in times of testing, joy grows and blossoms in the hard soil of tough times.

The Bible is replete with examples of those who continued to rejoice even in the face of persecution. For example, the apostle Paul wrote his letter to the Philippians while he was imprisoned, yet his letter is one of joy, exhorting the people of Philippi to rejoice (Philippians 4:4).

True joy results when you give yourself to God, wholly and completely, and yield to His will and purpose. True joy is the gift of knowing that your loving heavenly Father holds your future in His hands. True joy is becoming aware of your Father's love.

Today's Bible Reading Plan: Joshua 22:21-23:16 Luke 20:27-47; Psalm 89:14-37; Proverbs 13:17-19

Holy Spirit, make me keenly aware of God's love, and fill my heart and spirit with joy!

116

April 22 ~ A Day with Joni

Greater Than...

Your way, O God, is holiness; what god is as great as our God?
— Psalm 77:13

Who is so great as our God? No one. Nothing can be compared to Him. He is supreme over all. What's really interesting about this Bible verse is where it's found – in Psalm 77. There, the psalmist writes of confusion and discouragement. It seemed as if God had turned a deaf ear to his cries. He poured out his heart. Have you ever felt like that? Wondered, God, are you there? Are you listening? I know I have!

But you see, in the midst of such uncertainty, the man or woman of God has this truth to cling to: there is no one like our God! It is to be expected that there will be things within God's bigger picture we cannot understand. Often we will have to wait for God's plan to unfold more fully to appreciate His presence and providence throughout. This knowledge – of God's ultimate greatness – ought to influence us today and every day, serving as foundation for life, faith and hope. What do you say?

Today's Bible Reading Plan: Joshua 24:1-33
Luke 21:1-28; Psalm 89:38-52; Proverbs 13:20-23

Father, these things I know: You are Author and Finisher. You never leave me nor forsake me. You neither slumber nor sleep. Will You help me to trust in You today – Your greatness over and above all? Grant me renewed faith; the assurance of things hoped for and the conviction of things not seen.

117

April 23

Peace Is Love's Assurance

And the peace of God, which surpasses all understanding, will protect your hearts and minds through Christ Jesus.

— Philippians 4:7

Everyone is searching for peace: peace of mind, inner peace, world peace. But as born-again believers, we want to know the peace that Jesus promised us in John 14:27: *"Peace I leave with you. My peace I give to you. Not as the world gives do I give to you. Let not your heart be troubled, neither let it be afraid."*

The peace of God is an inner calm we experience only when we put everything – our lives, our worries, our future – in His hands and fully trust Him for the result. When we face trials, we know He is in control. *"I have told you these things so that in Me you may have peace. In the world you will have tribulation. But be of good cheer. I have overcome the world"* (John 16:33)

When we utterly submit to His will for us, we can rest in Him knowing that our sins are forgiven, that we are reconciled to God and that soon we will leave this earth to share forever in His glorious kingdom!

Today's Bible Reading Plan: Judges 1:1-2:9
Luke 21:29-22:13; Psalm 90:1-91:16; Proverbs 13:24-25

Holy Spirit, cultivate the fruit of peace in me today so that I can experience the true peace promised by Jesus.

April 24

Patience Is Love's Attribute

Therefore be patient, brothers, until the coming of the Lord.
Notice how the farmer waits for the precious fruit of the earth
and is patient with it until he receives the early and late rain.
You also be patient. Establish your hearts, for the coming of the
Lord is drawing near.

— James 5:7-8

In the biblical sense, patience requires an entirely new attitude toward life and toward our dealings with others. As we face the difficulties of life, we must remember that as born-again believers our faith is rooted in the belief that we will spend eternity walking heaven's streets of gold.

Once we realize every situation on earth is just temporary, it changes our attitude. No matter what difficulties life throws our way, we can persevere and endure. *Blessed is the man who endures temptation, for when he is tried, he will receive the crown of life, which the Lord has promised to those who love Him* (James 1:12).

Patience toward others is grounded in the fruit of love – the kind of love that puts others' needs above your own and does not seek personal gain.

Today's Bible Reading Plan: Judges 2:10-3:31
Luke 22:14-34; Psalm 92:1-93:5; Proverbs 14:1-2

> *Holy Spirit, cultivate love's attribute of*
> *patience in me today. No matter what is*
> *thrown my way, let patience abound.*

April 25

Kindness Is Love's Activity

But when the kindness and the love of God our Savior toward mankind appeared, not by works of righteousness which we have done, but according to His mercy He saved us, through the washing of rebirth and the renewal of the Holy Spirit...

— *Titus 3:4-5*

As a Christian, once you are grafted into the vine of Jesus Christ, you begin to see yourself bearing the fruit of love. The way you look and act will begin to change as you become more like your Father in heaven.

Love's activity is kindness. Kindness mellows a harsh disposition. It is the divine attribute that makes God loving yet righteous. It doesn't take away from God's goodness, but rather, it makes God's goodness accessible to us. Kindness is the patient love of God that would allow Him to humble Himself and leave the portals of heaven to meet us where we were, so He could gently share His love with us.

By bearing God's kindness through your life, you will be sharing the love and patience that God bestowed upon mankind (Ephesians 2:1-9). It is not human nature to love those who are unloving or to put the needs of others first. Kindness is love's activity alive and working within your heart.

Today's Bible Reading Plan: Judges 4:1-5:31 Luke 22:35-53; Psalm 94:1-23; Proverbs 14:3-4

> *Holy Spirit, help me to be active in showing God's love through kindness to strangers and to those who are unloving toward me.*

April 26

Goodness Is Love's Ambiance

Who is wise and understanding among you? Let him show
his works by his good life in the meekness of wisdom.

— James 3:13

God has given us all good things and one of the best ways we can thank Him is by being good and doing good works. Goodness is defined as moral excellence, virtue and excellence of quality. Goodness is not just appearing to be good; it is the essence of a person's character.

However, we will never be good on our own. As sinful humans, we can only be good through the work of the Holy Spirit. If we are to be good, we must spend time with the source of all goodness: God. Do not engage in evil activities but seek to honor the Lord in your words, actions and even your thoughts.

Psalm 23:5-6 says, *You prepare a table before me in the presence of my enemies; You anoint my head with oil; my cup runs over. Surely goodness and mercy shall follow me all the days of my life, and I will dwell in the house of the LORD forever.*

If we give love, love will be returned to us. If we espouse good, then good will come to us. Be active in doing good, in thinking good and in being good, through the work of the Holy Spirit in you.

Today's Bible Reading Plan: Judges 6:1-40
Luke 22:54-23:12; Psalm 95:1-96:13; Proverbs 14:5-6

> *Holy Spirit, surround me in an*
> *atmosphere of God's goodness today.*

April 27

Faithfulness Is Love's Abundance

If we are faithless, He remains faithful;
He cannot deny Himself.

— *2 Timothy 2:13*

There are times we actually think we are the ones hanging onto God. The truth is that God is the One hanging onto us! He is the faithful One.

That's why we sing: "Great is Thy faithfulness! Morning by morning, new mercies I see. All I have needed Thy hand hath provided; great is Thy faithfulness, Lord, unto me!"

It is of the LORD's mercies that we are not consumed; His compassions do not fail. They are new every morning; great is Your faithfulness (Lamentations 3:22-23).

You can trust God, for He is faithful. If we allow His Spirit to cultivate the fruit of love in our lives, He actually increases our ability to trust and have faith in Him. As the Holy Spirit reminds us of the promises God has already fulfilled in our lives, we have faith to trust Him even more.

Faithfulness to God is the fruit of love's abundance, and it increases as we draw closer to Him.

Today's Bible Reading Plan: Judges 7:1-8:17
Luke 23:13-43; Psalm 97:1-98:9; Proverbs 14:7-8

Lord, thank You for your faithfulness that
saturates me in Your abundant, overwhelming love.

April 28

Meekness Is Love's Attitude

With all humility, meekness, and patience,
bearing with one another in love.

— *Ephesians 4:2*

When we are told that meekness is love's attitude, what does it mean? Meekness is directly associated with God's kindness. Because God is kind, He is meek. Meekness flows directly from God's disposition.

In the movies, Jesus is depicted as a sad, long-faced fellow who slowly walks around and softly touches people, as if that is meekness, but that's not meekness at all. Meekness is controlled power. Meekness is having the hands of a carpenter, hammering large planks of wood together, yet gently cradling a baby in those powerful arms.

Just think of the wonder of these statements: *Jesus reached out His hand and touched him...and immediately his leprosy was cleansed* (Matthew 8:3) or *He touched her hand, and the fever left her* (Matthew 8:15). This was more than just a carpenter touching these people. It was the God who created the heavens and the earth. That's the power of God's love in gentle action, and that's love's attitude of meekness alive in you!

Today's Bible Reading Plan: Judges 8:18-9:21
Luke 23:44-24:12; Psalm 99:1-9; Proverbs 14:9-10

Holy Spirit, let God's powerful love
flow gently through me.

April 29 ~ A Day with Joni

Life's Dash

So all the days of Methuselah were nine hundred and sixty-nine years, and he died.
— Genesis 5:27

Do you suppose Methuselah ever got tired of living? Do you think he might of rolled over one morning in his seven hundredth year and said, "I'm just too tired to get up"? Do you think he had trouble bridging the generation gaps? Think he was conversant with the Generation Xers and Millennials in his day? Was he hip? How did he keep up with his great, great, great, great grandchildren?

He lived a lot of years, and yet we really know nothing of him or his lasting impact on the world beyond his mind-boggling lifespan. Perhaps you've heard someone share this observation before, but it bears repeating: When you look at a headstone in a cemetery there are two dates – birth and death – separated by a dash. What goes into your dash, that's what matters!

A life measured by its length alone is a life truly unmeasured. Be careful that your life is not reduced to the marking of time. Every day should count for more than its passing.

Today's Bible Reading Plan: Judges 9:22-10:18
Luke 24:13-53; Psalm 100:1-5; Proverbs 14:11-12
O Lord, life is truly a gift from You. You have ordained all my days and even chosen the place of my habitation. I praise You that You both love me and have a purpose for my life. May I realize today's portion of that purpose and make the most of this day? In Jesus' name.

April 30

Self-Control Is Love's Crowning Achievement

For this reason make every effort to add virtue to your faith; and to your virtue, knowledge; and to your knowledge, self-control; and to your self-control, patient endurance; and to your patient endurance, godliness; and to your godliness, brotherly kindness; and to your brotherly kindness, love. For if these things reside in you and abound, they ensure that you will neither be useless nor unfruitful in the knowledge of our Lord Jesus Christ.

— *2 Peter 1:5-8*

There is no other sporting event like the Olympics. It thrills our senses as we watch the top athletes in the world going head to head in competition.

That is what self-control is all about. That is what the apostle Paul was describing when he said, *"Do you not know that all those who run in a race run, but one receives the prize? ... Everyone who strives for the prize exercises self-control in all things ... I bring and keep my body under subjection..."* (1 Corinthians 9:24-25, 27)

Self-control is love's crowning achievement that rises from within and calls us to live a holy life with God's power in control.

Today's Bible Reading Plan: Judges 11:1-12:15
John 1:1-28; Psalm 101:1-8; Proverbs 14:13-14

*Holy Spirit, crown me with self-control
that I might run this race today in victory!*

MAY

Gifts from the Spirit of God

There are various gifts, but the same Spirit. There are differences of administrations, but the same Lord. There are various operations, but it is the same God who operates all of them in all people. But the manifestation of the Spirit is given to everyone for the common good. To one is given by the Spirit the word of wisdom, to another the word of knowledge by the same Spirit, to another faith by the same Spirit, to another gifts of healings by the same Spirit, to another the working of miracles, to another prophecy, to another discerning of spirits, to another various kinds of tongues, and to another the interpretation of tongues. But that one and very same Spirit works all these, dividing to each one individually as He will.

— 1 Corinthians 12:4-11

May 1

Serve His Gifts to Others

As everyone has received a gift, even so serve one another with it,
as good stewards of the manifold grace of God.

— 1 Peter 4:10

Giving is the very heartbeat of the Father, beating passionately for humanity down through the ages. In a single gift, God gave everything He had so we would have everything we need. God Almighty proved His love for you when He gave His only Begotten Son.

As God loves us, we should love one another. God even gives us gifts so that we can serve one another. When we love with the love of God, we will serve one another with our resources, rather than heap them to ourselves. In Matthew 22:36-40, Jesus teaches His disciples the two greatest commandments: love God and love each other.

You are the apple of God's eye and He loves you so much. He was willing to give His only Son to die for you because you are the object of His affection. You have the assurance of knowing that nothing can separate you from His love. Pass His love on!

Today's Bible Reading Plan: Judges 13:1-14:20
John 1:29-51; Psalm 102:1-28; Proverbs 14:15-16

Father, thank You for loving me so much that
You gave me the gift of Your only Son, Jesus Christ.

May 2

Diversity of Gifts

We have diverse gifts according to the grace that is given to us...

— Romans 12:6a

As believers in Jesus Christ, every gift we give and receive is a reminder of the gift of God's Son.

The Lord has poured out His abundant blessing upon us like an open faucet. He is our source of strength, health and vitality. He brings prosperity, joy, peace and security.

God has given us a variety of gifts to perfect the body of Christ. The Holy Spirit distributes God's gifts so that His people are blessed. The gifts that are given by the Holy Spirit include wisdom, knowledge, faith, healings, miracles, prophecy, discerning of spirits, tongues and interpretation of tongues. These are all distributed by God's Spirit for the good of the body.

We serve a God who delights in giving gifts to those who serve Him. That is why you can always be sure that the good things in your life come from the Lord. He loves you with an everlasting love.

Today's Bible Reading Plan: Judges 15:1-16:31 John 2:1-25; Psalm 103:1-22; Proverbs 14:17-19

*I praise You, Giver of life, and thank You
for every good and perfect gift today and every day!*

May 3

Irrevocable Gifts

For the gifts and calling of God are irrevocable.

— *Romans 11:29*

What has the Lord called you to do? The anointing follows the calling, and His gifts and callings are without repentance. Other translations say they are *irrevocable.* In other words, God will not take them back. God gives no refunds. He operates on a *no exchange* policy.

If you are not anointed to do a given work, stay away from it. Otherwise, you will find yourself working in the flesh, and your ability will be limited to your own strength.

Find your place in the body of Christ and fill it. No task God has called you to do is too small or too great. If you have stepped out of God's calling, don't worry, He will always help you step back into your *topos* or position of opportunity. He never gave you a gift that He ever asked you to return. He loves you and desires to see you fulfill your divine purpose in Him.

Today's Bible Reading Plan: Judges 17:1-18:31 John 3:1-21; Psalm 104:1-23; Proverbs 14:20-21

I am anointed and appointed by You, Lord. You have given me gifts to accomplish Your calling upon my life.

May 4

Live to Love

"If you then, being evil, know how to give good gifts to your children, how much more will your heavenly Father give the Holy Spirit to those who ask Him?"

— Luke 11:13

God wants us to recognize our responsibility to operate in all the gifts of the Spirit and also expects us to validate those gifts by living a lifestyle that glorifies Him, and that means loving our brother even when our brother is unlovable.

God gives us gifts so that we can express His love to one another. 1 Corinthians 13:1-3 stresses that the gifts are nothing without love. 1 Corinthians 13:4-8 describes what love is and is not. The entire 13th chapter of Corinthians is to demonstrate how we are to serve one another in love.

Rejoice today in a love so deep and sure that death could not extinguish it. God's love stretches from time eternal and reaches out to you with grace and mercy. That same love has been shed abroad in our hearts by the Holy Spirit. Determine to reach out to someone today with the love of Jesus.

Today's Bible Reading Plan: Judges 19:1-20:48 John 3:22-4:3; Psalm 104:24-35; Proverbs 14:22-24

Holy Spirit, thank You for equipping me today with God's love and His gifts to serve in His body.

May 5

Live to Serve

I urge you therefore, brothers, by the mercies of God, that you present your bodies as a living sacrifice, holy, and acceptable to God, which is your reasonable service of worship.

— *Romans 12:1*

The Word of God teaches us not to think more highly of ourselves than we ought (Romans 12:3). When God gives us gifts, we have to be aware that the enemy will try to get us to use those gifts to exalt ourselves and not God.

Sometimes we get so excited about receiving the "exceedingly abundantly" part of Ephesians 3:20 that we forget to give to God what He asks for in verse 21. To God be the glory in the church and in Christ Jesus forever. We have to be careful not to focus so much on receiving that we forget to give to God what He alone deserves.

By staying in constant communication with the Holy Spirit, He is able to keep us grounded and rooted in the love of Christ (Ephesians 3:17). When we operate in the gifts for the purpose of expressing God's love, then God is exalted and people are drawn to Him, not just the gift.

Today's Bible Reading Plan: Judges 21:1-25
Ruth 1:1-22; John 4:4-42; Psalm 105:1-15; Proverbs 14:25

Holy Spirit, teach me to serve so that God alone is glorified.

May 6 ~ A Day with Joni

Where Are You, Lord?

We know that all things work together for good
to those who love God...
— Romans 8:28

The doctor said the word cancer, and – I admit it – the question formed immediately: "Where are You, Lord?" The thoughts of losing my husband, the devastation to our family...

Perhaps for you it was a diagnosis, or a teenage child slipping away. Maybe a career blow or some other major life change – whatever your crisis, I know you can relate. We've all had "Where are You, Lord?" moments.

I don't wish anyone to go through these experiences. But I can tell you this: If, in those most desperate moments you can quiet your heart and pray for renewed faith, you'll see that God never checks out on you. Beloved, know this: He is in the early stages of transforming your heartache to a heart-song. He is always making something glorious out of something hideous. God is working, and He is working all things for your good.

Today's Bible Reading Plan: Ruth 2:1-4:22
John 4:43-54; Psalm 105:16-36; Proverbs 14:26-27

Heavenly Father, it is difficult to read the words "all things work together for good" when such difficulty arises in my life. Will You meet me in my distress? Reveal Your presence to me in such a way as I cannot miss it. I need You. And I know You are there.

May 7

The Gift of the Kingdom

"Do not be afraid, little flock, for it is your Father's good
pleasure to give you the kingdom."

— Luke 12:32

There are many things to be anxious about in today's world, but Jesus assured us that we do not have to worry about the things of the world. (Luke 12:22).

Our Creator will always take care of us. He has, after all, prepared an entire kingdom for us. We are to remain watchful servants, awaiting His return, so that we can enjoy His kingdom unabated for eternity.

As we live out our daily lives in this age, it is a rehearsal for the age to come. Each day is a preparation for the kingdom to come. How can we be defeated when God has equipped us with the fruit of His love and the gifts to operate in that love?

Each day, you will be challenged by the enemy, as he tries to entice you to walk contrary to the love of God. Remain a faithful and wise steward of the gifts God has given you, for to whom much is given, of him much shall be required (Luke 12:48).

Today's Bible Reading Plan: 1 Samuel 1:1-2:21
John 5:1-23; Psalm 105:37-45; Proverbs 14:28-29

Thank You, Lord, for calling me into your kingdom!

May 8

God Does Not Withhold Good

For the LORD God is a sun and shield; the LORD will give favor and glory, for no good thing will He withhold from the one who walks uprightly.

— Psalm 84:11

God does not withhold good; however, there is one caveat. He does not withhold good from those who walk uprightly before Him. How do we walk uprightly before Him? By accepting the free gift of His Son and becoming the righteousness of God in Christ.

In Psalm 84, we see a portrait of David, a man after God's own heart, describing the dwelling place of God and declaring that those who dwell in God's house are blessed. God's dwelling place is not just a physical place we will enjoy for eternity, it is a spiritual place we can get to today where the enemy cannot harm us.

David says he would rather dwell one day in the courts of God than a thousand elsewhere and that he would rather be a doorkeeper in the house of God than to dwell in the tents of wickedness (Psalm 84:10).

God withholds no good thing. He did not even withhold the gift of His only begotten Son. God gave His all!

Today's Bible Reading Plan: 1 Samuel 2:22-4:22 John 5:24-47; Psalm 106:1-12; Proverbs 14:30-31

I will dwell and abide in God's goodness today.

May 9

Your Life Is a Ministry Outreach

For in Him we live and move and have our being...
— Acts 17:28a

Without the Holy Spirit, we are as chariots without horses to pull them, like branches without sap. We are withered. In Him we live, move and have our being.

Once the apostle Paul met Jesus on the road to Damascus (Acts 9:1-6), Paul's life became an outreach to the body of Christ. Even while Paul was in prison, he served the church by writing letters of inspiration, reassurance and encouragement, which are part of the New Testament we read today.

Although Paul needed comfort, he placed the needs of the body of Christ above himself and became a comfort to those around Him and to us today through his writings (2 Corinthians 1:3-4). Paul gave us marvelous letters written in ink, but the Holy Spirit has made you a walking, breathing letter alive with God's love.

You are a living letter to be read and known by all. You are the letter of Christ written on human tablets of the heart (2 Corinthians 3:2-3).

Today's Bible Reading Plan: 1 Samuel 5:1-7:17
John 6:1-21; Psalm 106:13-31; Proverbs 14:32-33

Holy Spirit, I rely totally on You today to make my life an outreach to those who are hurting and lost.

135

May 10

A Second Passover

There were men who were unclean by the dead body of a man, so they could not keep the Passover on that day, and they came before Moses and before Aaron on that day. And those men said to him, "We are defiled by the dead body of a man. Why are we kept back, that we may not offer an offering of the LORD at its appointed time among the children of Israel?"

— Numbers 9:6-7

Today is Pesach Sheni, the second Passover. Numbers 9:6-7 describes a scenario where there were men who could not keep the Passover because in the carrying out of their duties, they had become defiled. The men pleaded with Moses to give them an opportunity to give their Passover offering to the Lord.

Moses went before the Lord and inquired what should be done in this situation. God instructed Moses to speak to the children of Israel and tell them that anyone who was defiled or on a long journey during Passover could celebrate the Passover the next month.

It's good to know that if you miss an opportunity with God, He will give you another chance.

Today's Bible Reading Plan: 1 Samuel 8:1-9:27
John 6:22-42; Psalm 106:32-48; Proverbs 14:34-35

Thank you, Lord, for giving me another chance.

May 11

The Word of Wisdom

But the wisdom that is from above is first pure, then peaceable, gentle, open to reason, full of mercy and good fruits, without partiality, and without hypocrisy.

— *James 3:17*

Wisdom is the ability to successfully use knowledge. You can have a lot of knowledge, but it won't do you any good if you don't have the wisdom to effectively use that knowledge.

Just as knowledge and wisdom are different, the word of wisdom is different from the word of knowledge. We will cover the word of knowledge tomorrow.

The word of wisdom is a manifestation gift and is the working of the Holy Spirit that reveals things to you that you could not know. For example, a word of wisdom from the Holy Spirit could reveal to you what job you should take or the location you should live in.

As with all the gifts of the Spirit, the word of wisdom is manifested for the benefit of the body of Christ and to display the glory of God. A word of wisdom could be revealed to you by the Holy Spirit for your benefit or for the benefit of another.

Today's Bible Reading Plan: 1 Samuel 10:1-11:15 John 6:43-71; Psalm 107:1-43; Proverbs 15:1-3

Holy Spirit, give me wisdom today to make the right decisions.

137

May 12

The Word of Knowledge

Then you shall know that I am the LORD…

— Ezekiel 6:13a

Knowledge is the accumulation of facts; however, true knowledge is knowing the Lord Jesus Christ. As mentioned yesterday, wisdom is needed to be able to use knowledge effectively.

The word of knowledge is also a manifestation gift of the Holy Spirit that reveals things to you that you could not know. For example, a word of knowledge from the Holy Spirit could reveal something about your health that you would otherwise not know. Also, a word of knowledge could reveal a specific event that is about to happen, good or bad, that you would have no way of knowing.

The word of knowledge is also manifested for the benefit of the body of Christ and is displayed to glorify God. A word of knowledge, as with a word of wisdom, could be revealed to you by the Holy Spirit for your benefit or for the benefit of another.

Today's Bible Reading Plan: 1 Samuel 12:1-13:23
John 7:1-30; Psalm 108:1-13; Proverbs 15:4

Thank You for the knowledge I need to make wise choices.

May 13 ~ A Day with Joni

How Long?

O LORD, how long shall I cry, and You will not hear?
— Habakkuk 1:2

"How long?" Have you ever prayed that prayer? Have you wept as you've cried out to God? Have you ever felt as though He's not hearing you? This prayer of Habakkuk reveals his heart in all honesty. And there are times in my life when I can totally relate. In times like these we need to be reminded that God never sleeps. He is never idle, absent, ignorant, ambivalent, or insensitive to what we're going through. His purposes, though perfect, are often beyond our ability to see or understand. But they are glorious.

Nobody understood the cross when Jesus died. Yet in that dark hour, the greatest gift was given; the greatest love displayed. God answers Habakkuk's prayer a couple verses later. He says, "Look among the nations and watch; wonder and be amazed! For I am doing a work in your days that you would not believe, though it were told you" (1:5).

What is God doing in the midst of your suffering? You probably wouldn't believe it if He told you.

Today's Bible Reading Plan: 1 Samuel 14:1-52
John 7:31-53; Psalm 109:1-31; Proverbs 15:5-7

O Lord, hear my prayer. You know I long for answers, clarity, understanding. But You also know what I need, what I can handle, and what's best. Help me to trust You with whatever this is. I know You've got it. Amen.

May 14

Gifts of Healings

He said to her, "Daughter, your faith has made you well.
Go in peace, and be healed of your affliction."

— Mark 5:34

No healing is a small thing, but some healings also require a miracle. You can pray for someone to receive a healing, but it won't manifest, because they also need a miracle. Someone whose neck is broken and their spinal cord is severed in the natural needs a healing and a miracle, because there is no way for the spinal cord to reattach itself in the natural.

The Holy Spirit can heal someone who has been paralyzed their entire life with a healing and a miracle. When praying for someone in that condition, there needs to be a suspension of natural law.

Sometimes when praying for healing, you should also pray for deliverance, because the person may be in a weakened condition and is susceptible to spiritual oppression and depression. Sometimes the Holy Spirit has to manifest all three: healing, miracle, deliverance.

Healing is a gift from the Holy Spirit, and God should be glorified. As with all the gifts, do not worship the gift; worship the Giver who is God.

Today's Bible Reading Plan: 1 Samuel 15:1-16:23
John 8:1-20; Psalm 110:1-7; Proverbs 15:8-10

Lord God, You are the Giver of every perfect gift.

May 15

The Gift of Miracles

*There are various gifts, but the same Spirit…
to another the working of miracles.*

— 1 Corinthians 12:4, 10

As mentioned yesterday, a miracle is the suspension of a natural law. God can manifest a miracle in any area of your life – healing, finances, relationships. Whatever you need, God can supply a miracle to turn your darkness into light.

The working of miracles is a powerful manifestation of the Holy Spirit that can have an impact on someone for many years. It will not only impact the one who received the miracle, but it will also impact those who witness it or even hear about it.

A perfect example of such a miracle happened to a young man at World Harvest Church when he was just a baby. He was born without a brain, only a brain stem. God manifested a miracle in this baby and placed within him a fully functioning brain. Today, he is a vibrant, healthy young man who serves in the church and gives all honor and glory to God.

Today's Bible Reading Plan: 1 Samuel 17:1-18:4 John 8:21-30; Psalm 111:1-10; Proverbs 15:11

Holy Spirit, perform a miracle in my life, today that will give God glory and honor and go beyond anything I could ever ask or imagine.

141

May 16

Prophecy

For no prophecy at any time was produced by the will of man,
but holy men moved by the Holy Spirit spoke from God.

— 2 Peter 1:21

Prophecy is for instruction, comfort, building up and encouragement. Someone who is operating in the gift of prophecy will speak words that express God's love.

Revelation 19:10 says that *the testimony of Jesus is the spirit of prophecy.* The Old Testament points to the coming of Jesus, and the New Testament does the same. Prophecy has not ceased, because we now look forward to the second coming of the Messiah.

Any comfort or encouragement we give when we prophesy should point the receiver of the prophecy to Jesus, for prophecy will always point people to Him.

1 Corinthians 14:1 instructs us to pursue love and earnestly desire the spiritual gifts and especially desire the gift of prophecy. The one who prophesies speaks to people for their edification and exhortation and comfort.

Today's Bible Reading Plan: 1 Samuel 18:5-19:24
John 8:31-59; Psalm 112:1-10; Proverbs 15:12-14

Holy Spirit, help me to speak prophetic words today that point to Jesus and comfort the one to whom I prophesy.

May 17

Discerning of Spirits

Beloved, do not believe every spirit, but test the spirits to see whether they are from God, because many false prophets have gone out into the world.

— 1 John 4:1

Today, many false prophets and false religions are in the world. Even in Christianity, false teachings are offered to entice people from the true faith.

Jude warns in verse 4 that there are men who have secretly crept in, who are marked for condemnation, who are ungodly men, who pervert the grace of God into immorality and who deny the only Lord God.

We see that in abundance today, where people use the grace of God as an occasion to sin. Some believe that they can live any way they want, because God will forgive them, and everything will be okay. They do not realize they are missing an abundant life in Jesus, because their lifestyle creates many distractions that prohibit them from drawing near to Him.

Jude's letter ends with encouragement to the saints then and now that God is able to keep us from falling and present us blameless before Him with rejoicing.

Today's Bible Reading Plan: 1 Samuel 20:1-21:15 John 9:1-41: Psalm 113:1-114:8; Proverbs 15:15-17

Holy Spirit, do not let me be deceived. Give me Your gift to discern the spirits I may encounter today.

May 18

The Gift of Tongues

When the day of Pentecost had come, they were all together in one place. Suddenly a sound like a mighty rushing wind came from heaven, and it filled the whole house where they were sitting. There appeared to them tongues as of fire, being distributed and resting on each of them, and they were all filled with the Holy Spirit and began to speak in other tongues, as the Spirit enabled them to speak.

— Acts 2:1-4

Speaking in tongues and interpretation of tongues are New Testament gifts first given by the Holy Spirit on the day of Pentecost to facilitate the quick spread of the Gospel to the nations. Another purpose of the gift of tongues is as a prayer language between you and God.

The Message Bible says in 1 Corinthians 14:1-3 that you are sharing intimacies between you and God when you speak in tongues. It is a private prayer language to communicate with God. The spiritual benefit is that you may well be thwarting the plan of the adversary as you manifest the mysterious gift of tongues. No one else may understand this heavenly language, but God knows, and He acts. Tongues plus interpretation equals the gift of prophecy.

Today's Bible Reading Plan: 1 Samuel 22:1-23:29 John 10:1-21; Psalm 115:1-18; Proverbs 15:18-19

Holy Spirit, allow Your heavenly language to flow powerfully through me by way of the gift of tongues.

May 19

Interpretation of Tongues

So, when you pray in your private prayer language, don't hoard the experience for yourself. Pray for the insight and ability to bring others into that intimacy.

— 1 Corinthians 14:13 (MSG)

Paul instructs the church not to speak in tongues without giving the interpretation. Paul says, *So if you speak in a way that no one can understand, what's the point of opening your mouth? There are many languages in the world and they all mean something to someone. But if I don't understand the language, it's not going to do me much good. It's no different with you. Since you're so eager to participate in what God is doing, why don't you concentrate on doing what helps everyone in the church* (1 Corinthians 14:9-12 MSG)?

Paul firmly believes that the Holy Spirit's manifestation of spiritual gifts is for the benefit of the entire assembly (1 Corinthians 12:7). He does not say you should never speak in tongues. He stresses, however, that there should be an interpretation of the tongue when the saints assemble in a group, so that all can enjoy the revelation God is giving to the body of Christ.

Today's Bible Reading Plan: 1 Samuel 24:1-25:44 John 10:22-42; Psalm 116:1-19; Proverbs 15:20-21

Holy Spirit, give us the gifts of tongues and interpretation, as we assemble together, the body of Christ, so that we can receive revelation from God.

May 20 ~ A Day with Joni

Home Recipe

Let everyone come to know your gentleness.
— Philippians 4:5a

Building a family is the greatest building project of all. Sticks, bricks, steel, glass, and concrete are all child's play when compared to the complex nature of molding a marriage and shaping a child.

God is life's Master Builder, but He has entrusted spouses and parents with very important work. And He's identified a crucial tool for these callings: gentleness. You might have thought the job called for muscle and pressure, but in the home gentleness can accomplish what brute force cannot!

We're told to love our spouses, to respect and submit to one another. We're told to admonish our children, but not to exasperate them. To serve as examples before them. To impress our faith upon them (see Deuteronomy 6:4-10). These are all tasks accomplished with gentleness.

Husbands and wives, moms and dads, we don't need bigger hammers or tighter grips – just more love and gentleness.

Today's Bible Reading Plan: 1 Samuel 26:1-28:25
John 11:1-54; Psalm 117:1-2; Proverbs 15:22-23

Gracious Heavenly Father, You are loving and kind. You are patient and forgiving. You are merciful and gracious. Will You cultivate more of those attributes in me? May my gentleness and kindness increase in my home, and be evident to all – especially to my spouse and children!

May 21

The Gift of Teaching

My brothers, not many of you should become teachers, knowing that we shall receive the greater judgment.

— James 3:1

Teaching is a double-edged sword. Although the body of Christ desperately needs this gift, there are those who will try to exploit the teaching gift for their own benefit. *For the time will come when people will not endure sound doctrine, but they will gather to themselves teachers in accordance with their own desires, having itching ears, and they will turn their ears away from the truth and turn to myths* (2 Timothy 4:3-4).

The teaching gift manifested by the power of the Holy Spirit instructs the saints in sound doctrine and biblical truth. Jesus said in Matthew 5:19, *"Whoever, therefore, breaks one of the least of these commandments and teaches others to do likewise shall be called the least in the kingdom of heaven. But whoever does and teaches them shall be called great in the kingdom of heaven."*

There is a reward for those who teach the truth, but Jesus said those who do not teach the truth will be called least in the kingdom of heaven. Teaching must be done under the anointing of the Holy Spirit.

Today's Bible Reading Plan: 1 Samuel 29:1-31:13 John 11:55-12:19; Psalm 118:1-18; Proverbs 15:24-26

Holy Spirit, anoint me to speak the truth of God's Word.

147

May 22

The Gift of Exhortation

For our exhortation was not from deceit, nor from uncleanness, nor in guile. But as we were allowed by God to be entrusted with the gospel, even so we speak, not to please men, but God, who examines our hearts.

— *1 Thessalonians 2:3-4*

Through the gift of exhortation, the Holy Spirit can use you to encourage someone to press forward in Christ. *But exhort one another daily, while it is called "Today," lest any of you be hardened through the deceitfulness of sin* (Hebrews 3:13).

Exhortation provides a refreshing, comfort and consolation to another. Exhortation can also give admonition to someone who is straying away from God or not holding to sound doctrine. The gift of exhortation is given by the Holy Spirit to draw you nearer to God.

As we draw closer to God, we begin to look more and more like Him and less like us; therefore, others will also be drawn to Him.

Today's Bible Reading Plan: 2 Samuel 1:1-2:11
John 12:20-50; Psalm 118:19-29; Proverbs 15:27-28

Holy Spirit, grant me the gift of exhortation so that I can be a comfort to others.

May 23

The Gift of Generosity

Command those who are rich in this world that they not be conceited, nor trust in uncertain riches, but in the living God, who richly gives us all things to enjoy. Command that they do good, that they be rich in good works, generous, willing to share, and laying up in store for themselves a good foundation for the coming age, so that they may take hold of eternal life.
— 1 Timothy 6:17-19

In Acts 20:35, Paul says it is more blessed to give than to receive. If you have ever watched the face of someone you have been able to bless, you know this to be true. Whether with material resources or spiritually, being able to bless another person is a gift from God.

Paul said we must help the weak, and God blesses us to be a blessing. There are those that He blesses with exceedingly abundant resources so that they can be distributors of God's goodness and grace. We are not given wealth to heap it on ourselves. In the parable of Luke 12:16-21, Jesus admonished the man who, instead of distributing the resources God gave him, wanted to tear down his storehouses and build bigger ones to store more for himself. Let the goodness of God flow not just to you, but through you.

Today's Bible Reading Plan: 2 Samuel 2:12-3:39 John 13:1-30; Psalm 119:1-16; Proverbs 15:29-30

I repent of selfishness; Holy Spirit, release Your gift of generosity through me.

May 24

The Gift of Leadership

We have diverse gifts according to the grace that is given to us...he who rules, with diligence...

— Romans 12:6, 8

When taking a leadership role under the anointing of the Holy Spirit, a person is conscientious in their duties and focused on the task they have been given. Whether leading a congregation, a small home group or a large company, as a follower of Christ, you must take the role of a servant leader.

This type of leader enriches the lives of those he leads. Romans 12:3 comes to mind when I think of the gift of leadership:

For I say, through the grace given to me, to everyone among you, not to think of himself more highly than he ought to think, but to think with sound judgment, according to the measure of faith God has distributed to every man.

Jesus is the greatest servant leader. He serves those in His care every moment of every day. He leads by example, desiring that we are enriched by His leadership. If you are a leader, lead in love. If you are not a leader, pray for those who are in authority over you, that their leadership will reflect the love of Christ.

Today's Bible Reading Plan: 2 Samuel 4:1-6:23 John 13:31-14:14; Psalm 119:17-32; Proverbs 15:31-32

Holy Spirit, anoint leaders in our nation to be servant-leaders who lead in Your love and power.

May 25

The Gift of Mercy

We have diverse gifts according to the grace that is given to us...
he who shows mercy, with cheerfulness.

— Romans 12:6, 8

When someone is anointed by the Holy Spirit with the gift of mercy, they are filled with the compassion and grace of Christ to help those who are afflicted and in need of help. Not only is their heart filled with compassion for those in need, but when they have the opportunity to minister to someone in need, they do it with a spirit of joy and cheerfulness that lifts the needy person out of the pit of despair.

The gift of mercy is manifested by the Holy Spirit to bring light into darkness. *For You will cause my lamp to shine; the LORD my God will enlighten my darkness* (Proverbs 18:28).

This gift is not just pity where you feel sorry for someone in need. This gift empowers the recipient of the gift to spring into action at a moment's notice and make a difference in someone's life. They are able to put themselves in the shoes of the person in need and treat them as they would want to be treated. *Do unto others as you would have others do unto you.* (Luke 6:31).

Today's Bible Reading Plan: 2 Samuel 7:1-8:18 John 14:15-31; Psalm 119:33-48; Proverbs 15:33

Holy Spirit, let mercy flow through me like a river today.

May 26

The Gift of Song

Let the word of Christ dwell in you richly in all wisdom,
teaching and admonishing one another in psalms and hymns and
spiritual songs, singing with grace in your hearts to the Lord.

— *Colossians 3:16*

Music can affect the atmosphere surrounding you. Spiritual songs can break off a depression, set your heart to dancing, create an environment of worship and humble your heart in thanksgiving and gratitude for what God has done, is now doing and will do.

When we listen to music that invites the presence of God, there is a strong connection that builds a more intimate relationship with our Creator. Whether listening to music created by someone else or singing a song spontaneously prompted by the presence of the Holy Spirit, the gift of song can take a dark day and make it brighter.

When the saints gather together, music has a way of uniting the body of Christ and bringing us into one accord. It's hard to argue, or backbite, or gossip, or put someone down when you're lifting praise to God in sincere worship. Make listening to and singing songs of praise a part of your day.

Today's Bible Reading Plan: 2 Samuel 9:1-11:27
John 15:1-27; Psalm 119:49-64; Proverbs 16:1-3

Holy Spirit, give me songs of praise
in my heart today for God.

May 27 ~ A Day with Joni

Come, Follow

Jesus said to them, "Come, follow Me, and I will make you fishers of men." Immediately they left their nets and followed Him.
— Mark 1:17-18

Jesus said, "Come follow me." These men dropped everything and followed Him. Who among us could do that? I'm a planner. I like schedules, lists, and predictability. I could hear myself saying, "Now? Can I have a trip itinerary first? Where are we going? What should I wear? What should I pack? I've got a lot to think about, here. Drop everything? Seriously?"

When reading this passage, I am astonished these men dropped everything, and did it without delay. I started to prayerfully ask myself, "What is keeping me from dropping everything to follow Him? What am I unwilling to leave behind, either consciously or subconsciously?" He's been showing me – these things are nothing in comparison! Beloved, we can't say we're disciples with lip service. When we follow Him, and we follow what He is and who He is. We follow peace, we follow victory, we follow healing, we follow grace, and most importantly … we follow love. It's worth it. He's worth it. You coming?

Today's Bible Reading Plan: 2 Samuel 12:1-31
John 16:1-33; Psalm 119:65-80; Proverbs 16:4-5

Gracious Lord, thank You for loving me and for calling me to follow Jesus. Will You help me identify the things in my life which hinder my pursuit of You? I confess, they are temporal and lesser affections. I want to follow You with all my heart, today, tomorrow and always. Amen.

May 28

Walk in God's Glory

Therefore, whether you eat, or drink, or whatever you do,
do it all to the glory of God.

— *1 Corinthians 10:31*

When you get a revelation of God through spending time in His Word, in prayer, in praise and in worship, then you will begin to see the Father in His fullness, in His glory, in His demonstration, in His magnificence and in His beauty.

The Lord can anoint you, and equip you with His gifts and use you to show His glory and power to those who are lost and those who are hurting.

The Glory of God became flesh through Christ and dwelt among us (John 1:14). Jesus endured temptation and great persecution to ensure that salvation would be available to all men and heaven could be gained.

He now becomes the Christ in you, the hope of glory (Colossians 1:27). The glory of God dwells in you, giving you blessed assurance and hope beyond the scope of human limitation.

Today's Bible Reading Plan: 2 Samuel 13:1-39 John 17:1-26; Psalm 119:81-96; Proverbs 16:6-7

Jesus, thank You for paying the price
so the glory of God could dwell in me richly.

May 29

Memorial Day

Render to all what is due them: taxes to whom taxes are due,
respect to whom respect is due, fear to whom fear is due, and
honor to whom honor is due.

— *Romans 13:7*

Today, on Memorial Day, we honor those in the military who paid the ultimate price of freedom with their lives. We honor those who deserve honor.

Without their faithful service, it is possible we would not have the freedom to worship the Lord Jesus Christ, Jehovah Joshua Messiah in this great nation.

Psalm 27:3-4 declares, *Though an army should encamp against me, my heart will not fear; though war should rise against me, in this will I be confident. One thing I have asked from the LORD, that will I seek after—for me to dwell in the house of the LORD all the days of my life, to see the beauty of the LORD, and to inquire in His temple.*

Whether in war or times of peace, the Holy Spirit abides in the spirit of the believer, and we see the glory of the Lord in our daily lives, because we have made Him our dwelling place, and He has made us His dwelling place. We are the temple of the Holy Spirit.

Today's Bible Reading Plan: 2 Samuel 14:1-15:22 John 18:1-24; Psalm 119:97-112; Proverbs 16:8-9

> *Jesus, thank You for the freedoms we enjoy.*
> *What You did at Calvary set us free forever.*

May 30

Shavuot Begins at Sundown

*You must observe the Feast of Weeks,
the first fruits of the wheat harvest...*

— *Exodus 34:22a*

Shavuot is also known as the Feast of Weeks. This is the second pilgrimage festival of the year. Israel was instructed by God to count 50 days from Passover, which is seven weeks or seven Sabbaths, plus one day, at which time they reap the wheat harvest. Israel also commemorates this day because it is believed it was 50 days after Israel left Egypt on the first Passover that God gave the Ten Commandments (Torah) at Mount Sinai.

The correlation for believers in Christ is that 50 days after the Passover crucifixion of Jesus, the Holy Spirit was poured out. The written Word was given 50 days after the very first Passover in Egypt, and the Spirit of the living Word was poured out 50 days after the Passover crucifixion of Jesus. This is no coincidence.

We are now blessed with the gifts of the Holy Spirit to benefit the body of Christ and give God glory!

Today's Bible Reading Plan: 2 Samuel 15:23-16:23 John 18:25-19:22; Psalm 119:113-128; Proverbs 16:10-11

*Thank You, Holy Spirit, for baptizing us
in God's love and power.*

May 31

Holy Ghost Power!

But ye shall receive power, after that the Holy Ghost is come upon you: and ye shall be witnesses unto me both in Jerusalem, and in all Judaea, and in Samaria, and unto the uttermost part of the earth.

— Acts 1:8 (KJV)

When Jesus said, "It is finished," He didn't mean it was over. Back to heaven He went with a tag-team handoff to the Holy Spirit of God. From the four Gospels to the Book of Acts you take the great theological leap to where the God in Christ becomes the Christ in you.

Jesus needed Holy Spirit empowerment, and so do we! Acts 10:38 records *how God anointed Jesus of Nazareth with the Holy Spirit and with power, who went about doing good and healing all who were oppressed of the devil, for God was with him.*

If you are going to be a conqueror, you <u>must</u> be filled with the Holy Ghost! When you are immersed in Him, you are given supernatural power, grace, and ability. Invite Him to fill and transform you today.

Today's Bible Reading Plan: 2 Samuel 17:1-29
John 19:23-42; Psalm 119:129-152; Proverbs 16:12-13

Jesus, baptize me in Your Spirit.
Empower me to live in Your presence daily.

157

JUNE

Healing Is the Children's Bread

But He answered, "I was sent only to the lost sheep of the house of Israel." Then she came and worshipped Him, saying, "Lord, help me." But He answered, "It is not fair to take the children's bread and to throw it to dogs." She said, "Yes, Lord, yet even dogs eat the crumbs that fall from their masters' table." Then Jesus answered her, "O woman, great is your faith. Let it be done for you as you desire." And her daughter was healed instantly.

— Matthew 15:24-28

June 1

Shavuot Ends at Sundown

'In the last days it shall be,' says God,
'that I will pour out My Spirit on all flesh…'

— Acts 2:17a

This evening at sundown marks the close of Shavuot, the Festival of Weeks. Corporately, we have celebrated when God gave the Ten Commandments (Torah) at Mount Sinai 50 days after the first Passover and when He then wrote those Commandments on our hearts by pouring out His Holy Spirit 50 days after Jesus was crucified on Passover.

Now we can individually continue in the anointing of the Holy Spirit, filled with His fruit (His character) and His gifts (His power). For believers in Christ, it is not the end of the celebration. We are just beginning.

Make each day count. Every day we walk with Jesus, filled with His life-giving Spirit, it is a celebration! Renew us today, Holy Spirit, so that we can continue in your refreshing, giving glory to Almighty God for His many great and wonderful gifts!

Today's Bible Reading Plan: 2 Samuel 18:1-19:10 John 20:1-31; Psalm 119:153-176; Proverbs 16:14-15

Holy Spirit, thank You for a life filled with celebration!

June 2

Healing in the Covenant

But now He has obtained a more excellent ministry, because He is the Mediator of a better covenant, which was established on better promises.

— Hebrews 8:6

God established many covenants with His people throughout the Old Testament but they always fell short. Adam was the first to fall after he reached for a piece of forbidden fruit. God cut covenant with Abraham but he was a habitual liar. David was a covenant man; yet, he fell prey to lust and murder. Again and again mankind broke their end of the covenant with God. They failed to measure up to the requirements for righteousness because of sin.

So God made a covenant between Himself and His only Son, Jesus Christ. God put His own reputation on the line and took an oath in His own name (Hebrews 6:13). At that moment, perfection entered into covenant with perfection.

After the failure of the first Adam, God made a promise for all future generations. But there was still a price to be paid, and it was the price of blood, which would offer healing and restoration to all mankind.

Today's Bible Reading Plan: 2 Samuel 19:11-20:13 John 21:1-25; Psalm 120:1-7; Proverbs 16:16-17

I rejoice because I am a partaker of greater promises!

June 3 ~ A Day with Joni

Go and Tell

I cried to the LORD with my voice,
and He answered me from His holy hill. Selah
— Psalm 3:4

I remember being in elementary school music class as we prepared for the annual Christmas concert. We were to sing, "Go Tell It on the Mountain."

Still too young to have developed the concept of metaphors, I remember thinking the song lyric so strange: Why in the world would God want us to climb a mountain to tell people Jesus was born? That seemed like a lot of trouble when we could just pick up the phone, or proclaim it on television or in the newspapers. Of course, I get the words and the meaning to this song now. The glorious birth of our Savior should be told, celebrated – shouted from the mountaintops. But my friend, I have another thought for you. Our Lord's salvation should all the more be proclaimed from the depths. That's where we often cry out to Him – from the valleys between life's mountainous occasions – and He answers. That's a telling testimony: I cried out and He heard my call!

If you're there today, cry out to Him. He will hear and answer you. When you've found Him in the valley, go tell it!

Today's Bible Reading Plan: 2 Samuel 20:14-21-22 Acts 1:1-26; Psalm 121:1-8; Proverbs 16:18

Almighty God: The psalmist asked, How are they increased that trouble me? I can often relate. Thank You for hearing my cries. Thank You for your abiding presence, "over the hills and everywhere." May I celebrate Your goodness and proclaim Your faithfulness today and always.

June 4

Pentecost

When the day of Pentecost had come, they were all together in
one place. Suddenly a sound like a mighty rushing wind came
from heaven, and it filled the whole house where they were sitting.
There appeared to them tongues as of fire, being distributed and
resting on each of them, and they were all filled with the Holy
Spirit and began to speak in other tongues, as the Spirit enabled
them to speak.

— *Acts 2:1-4*

Today is the Christian observance of Pentecost. Because Jewish festivals are observed according to the lunar cycle and Christian observances are set by the Gregorian calendar, Shavuot and Pentecost rarely fall on the same date.

The day's significance, however, does not change. It still commemorates when the Holy Spirit was poured out for the purpose of empowering the body of Christ. On Pentecost, God spoke life to the church in much the same way He spoke at creation. When God speaks to us, His Spirit reverberates in our human spirit. We can then speak the oracles of God and allow His message to reverberate in the hearts and spirits of others.

Today's Bible Reading Plan: 2 Samuel 22:1-23:23 Acts 2:1-47; Psalm 122:1-9; Proverbs 16:19-20

Holy Spirit, rain on us and reign in us.

June 5

Forgiveness & Healing

...who forgives all your iniquities,
who heals all your diseases...

— *Psalm 103:3*

All through the Bible, forgiveness and healing are found hand-in-hand in relation to the redemptive work of Jesus. I like to call it Calvary's double cure.

In one instance, as Jesus was teaching to a packed house in the town of Capernaum, four men brought their paralytic friend to the Master to be healed. But as the crowd overflowed into the street, the men didn't give up. When they saw they couldn't get in through the front door, they climbed up onto the house, dug a hole in the roof, and lowered the invalid on a cot right in front of Jesus!

Moved by their faith, Jesus declared, "Son, your sins are forgiven!" The Scribes began to murmur, "Who does He think He is? He's not God! He can't forgive sins!" Knowing their thoughts, He asked, "Why do you question whether it is easier to say your sins are forgiven or take up your bed and walk?" Then Jesus went further and told the paralytic man, "Arise! Take up your bed and go home." (Mark 2:1-11).

Today's Bible Reading Plan: 2 Samuel 23:24-24:25 Acts 3:1-26; Psalm 123:1-4; Proverbs 16:21-23

By faith, I appropriate Calvary's double cure.

163

June 6

Let Go of Religion

Then Jesus said to the crowds and to His disciples, "The scribes and the Pharisees sit in Moses' seat. Therefore, whatever they tell you to observe, that observe and do, but do not do their works. For they speak, but do nothing. They fasten heavy loads that are hard to carry and lay them on men's shoulders, but they themselves will not move them with their finger."

— *Matthew 23:1-4*

The challenge for the religious leaders of Jesus' day was His ability to forgive sins not His ability to heal. Today, most people believe Jesus forgives sins but they doubt His power to heal. The truth is He is the one who forgives all our sins *and* who heals all our diseases.

The miraculous began between Christ and the cross. Jesus' blood left a crimson stain on a tree, initiating God's plan of redemption from our sin *and* sickness.

God loves you and it is His desire to see you completely whole – spirit, soul and body – and living victoriously in Him. Jesus' name is far greater than every sin, sickness, and disease in your life today and every day.

Today's Bible Reading Plan: 1 Kings 1:1-53
Acts 4:1-37; Psalm 124:1-8; Proverbs 16:24

I receive the blessings of salvation and healing in Jesus' name and for Your glory, Lord!

June 7

The Balm in Gilead

Is there no balm in Gilead? Is there no physician there? Why then has not the health of the daughter of my people recovered?

— Jeremiah 8:22

Looking toward the region of Gilead, a land known for its medicinal ointments to heal wounds, Jeremiah lamented the approaching Chaldean invasion. He cried, "Is there no balm in Gilead?"

Now Jeremiah wondered if the balm was strong enough to heal the putrefying wound of his people's sins. For the harvest was past. The summer was over. Still they had not turned to God (Jeremiah 8:20).

Isaiah, grieved over the wounding sins of the people, said, *Why should you be beaten again, that you revolt more and more? The whole head is sick, and the whole heart faint* (1:5).

What could be done? Punishment did not seem to be the answer. Instead God enlisted mercy.

Today's Bible Reading Plan: 1 Kings 2:1-3:2
Acts 5:1-42; Psalm 125:1-5; Proverbs 16:25

Lord, thank You there is still a balm in Gilead, which heals the sin-sick soul.

June 8

The Eternal Balm

*If you remain in Me, and My words remain in you,
you will ask whatever you desire, and it shall be done for you.*

— John 15:7

In the distant future, there was One coming who possessed the cure for our sin-sick souls. Jesus is the Great Physician, and His blood is the balm in Gilead. The Savior came to bind up the brokenhearted. He came to mend shattered dreams. He came to heal and restore.

In Matthew 4:23, we see the love of God being demonstrated through Jesus as He moved throughout Galilee.

Jesus went throughout all Galilee teaching in their synagogues, preaching the gospel of the kingdom, and healing all kinds of sickness and all sorts of diseases among the people.

Whether you need healing from physical sickness, forgiveness of sin, or restoration in your life, your pain is no match for the balm of Jesus. The Master will apply His anointing on the hurting areas of your life that only He can heal.

Today's Bible Reading Plan: 1 Kings 3:3-4:34
Acts 6:1-15; Psalm 126:1-6; Proverbs 16:26-27

There is a balm in Gilead that makes the sinner whole!

June 9

The Great Physician

Is anyone sick among you? Let him call for the elders of the church, and let them pray over him, anointing him with oil in the name of the Lord. And the prayer of faith will save the sick, and the Lord will raise him up. And if he has committed any sins, he will be forgiven.

— James 5:14-15

"*Those who are well have no need of a physician, but those who are sick...*" (Mark 2:17). This was Christ's response as He moved among the lower dregs of society. Jesus was following divine orders, and He was well qualified for the task.

Jesus, the Great Physician, was sent to those who were sin-infected, spiritually bound and physically sick. There were many who, since time immemorial, suffered from sin's debilitating effects. He was in high demand, for He cured everyone He saw and His success rate was 100 percent!

Entrust your life to Jesus. He will never disappoint you. Whatever you encounter, today, the struggle is over. Turn it over to Jesus. He has never lost a battle.

Today's Bible Reading Plan: 1 Kings 5:1-6:38
Acts 7:1-29; Psalm 127:1-5; Proverbs 16:28-30

I submit to the loving hands of my Great Physician to make me whole – spirit, soul and body.

June 10 ~ A Day with Joni

Our God of Hope

*Now may the God of hope fill you with all joy and peace in
believing, so that you may abound in hope,
through the power of the Holy Spirit.*
— *Romans 15:13*

God of hope – that's a beautiful title, isn't it? Hope isn't just something God doles out, but rather it is Who He is. Hope is an inherent element of our God's essence – one of His attributes!

And when He is your God, you can rest in every perfection of His nature. By calling Him the God of Hope, the Bible makes it clear: God is hope's source.

Heavenly hope is so much higher than the hope this world expresses. "I hope it doesn't rain tomorrow" is typical of how people view hope – a wish without any degree of certainty.

Is biblical hope so fickle? Not at all! Hope is certain because it is founded upon our unchanging God and His unfailing promises. You, believer, have hope!

Where is your heart today? What trials and tribulations assail you? Pray this verse! "May the God of hope fill you ..." for He is hope's source. And He will do it.

Today's Bible Reading Plan: 1 Kings 7:1-51
Acts 7:30-50; Psalm 128:1-6; Proverbs 16:31-33

You are the God of hope – moreover, my God of hope! I so need Your joy and peace today. Will You fill me to overflowing? Will You raise my eyes above the circumstances of this life, this day, to a clearer vision of You and things eternal? You Lord are the source of my hope! Amen.

June 11

Our Passover, Our Healer

For even Christ, our Passover, has been sacrificed for us.

— 1 Corinthians 5:7b

All the Feasts of Israel are symbolic of some aspect of the ministry of Jesus, but perhaps none of them are as easily recognizable as Passover. The Passover meal was first initiated when Moses was about to lead more than six million Israelites from Egyptian captivity. It was the last divine intervention by God's hand before their exodus (Exodus 12:3-14).

The Passover was more than just a final meal before their departure. It was the occasion for the healing power of God to flow through the weak and sick Israelites among them (Psalm 105:37). The Lord Jesus Christ is our type of sacrificial Passover. He gave His life so we could be redeemed from the bondage of sin and sickness. His sacrifice provided for our healing as well as freedom from sin.

God's healing power is still available to all who believe in the sacrifice of Jesus. Reach out, receive your healing touch from the hand of the Passover Lamb.

Today's Bible Reading Plan: 1 Kings 8:1-66
Acts 7:51-8:13; Psalm 129:1-8; Proverbs 17:1

Thank You, Jesus, for being my Passover Lamb.

169

June 12

Better Promises, Better Blood

Through this oath Jesus became the guarantor
of a better covenant.

— Hebrews 7:22

Jesus was the ultimate Sacrifice. When He shed His blood on the cross – as the veins of God Himself were emptied – at that moment, Jesus, the God-man acting on behalf of humanity, entered into a far superior covenant with the Almighty than had existed before.

God made a covenant of grace. It was no longer a covenant born of ritual necessary for the ongoing shedding of innocent animals' blood. It was a covenant born of relationship and faith whereby Jesus became the Guarantee of a better way and where His guiltless blood was shed only once for the total removal of sins.

This is the great exchange. In covenant with us, we exchange our death for Jesus' life; disease for His healing; poverty for His wealth; weakness for His strength; bondage for His freedom. Choose Jesus, the Guarantee of this Better Covenant, and receive a reprieve from God's judgment – or reject Jesus and suffer eternal separation from His love. Choose Jesus!

Today's Bible Reading Plan: 1 Kings 9:1-10:29
Acts 8:14-40; Psalm 130:1-8; Proverbs 17:2-3

I thank You, God, for Your covenant
guaranteed through the shed blood of Jesus.

June 13

Grace to Preach

To me, the very least of all saints, this grace was given, to preach to the Gentiles the incomprehensible riches of Christ...

— Ephesians 3:8

In my book *Culturally Incorrect,* I wrote, "Much of the church's present impotence and failure is due to a fundamental understanding about what it really means to be a Christian, after all..."

What do I mean? The Gospel many preach is but a mere shadow of the real thing. We have replaced the deep things of God with a one-dimensional facsimile. Many believers understand the message of salvation, but few fully comprehend the true doctrine of healing, atonement, sanctification, deliverance or prosperity.

They are busy serving the Lord but have no real personal relationship with Him. Despite their outward Sunday morning attire, they are inwardly and outwardly a verifiable stranger to the actual character of the Christ they claim they serve.

Jehovah Joshua Messiah deeply desires an intimate relationship with you, not just religious exercises you execute to appease Him.

Today's Bible Reading Plan: 1 Kings 11:1-12:19
Acts 9:1-25; Psalm 131:1-3; Proverbs 17:4-5

Today, I choose to lay aside the superficial trappings of religion for a deep, intimate relationship with Christ.

June 14

Tell Your Problem
How Big Your God Is

For My thoughts are not your thoughts, nor are your ways My ways, says the LORD. For as the heavens are higher than the earth, so are My ways higher than your ways, and My thoughts than your thoughts.

— Isaiah 55:8-9

We need to be reacquainted with the infiniteness of God. Our vision of Him has become too weak, too small and too timid. When we see the immensity of His Person, then no problem, no demonic power is too big. When we truly know the *endless treasures* available to us, then fear's grip will loose its icy tentacles from our hearts.

Paul had this revelation, and from the time of his Damascus Road conversion sought to show the world the depth and limitless riches of Christ. Like Paul, the Lord is looking for believers who are passionate for His presence. He is looking for those who know Him beyond a weekly encounter. He is looking for those who are on a quest to know Him intimately.

Today's Bible Reading Plan: 1 Kings 12:20-13:34 Acts 9:26-43; Psalm 132:1-18; Proverbs 17:6

Holy Spirit, plunge me into a deep intimacy with God.

June 15

Healing Waters Run Deep

Then he brought me back to the door of the temple; and water was flowing out from under the threshold of the temple eastward, for the front of the temple faced east; the water was flowing down from under from the right side of the temple, south of the altar... And it was a river that I could not pass over, for the water had risen, enough water to swim in, a river that could not be passed over.

— Ezekiel 47:1, 5b

God gave Ezekiel an incredible picture of the future of the church through a vision of a pure river of life. In the vision a "man," or Jesus, pressed Ezekiel to go farther into the waters. As he did, they flowed from heaven and first covered his ankles before rising to conceal his knees and loins.

Finally, the river rose to depths so great that it overflowed its banks making it unsurpassable. Everywhere it flowed from the throne of God it gave life and healing to all it touched.

The body of Christ is not getting weaker and weaker. She will continue to increase in power, strength, authority and glory as we move toward the Lord's return.

Today's Bible Reading Plan: 1 Kings 14:1-15:24 Acts 10:1-23; Psalm 133:1-3; Proverbs 17:7-8

God, help me not to settle for the shallow waters of religion.

June 16

Holy Spirit Outpouring

And it will be that, afterwards, I will pour out My Spirit on all flesh; then your sons and your daughters will prophesy, your old men will dream dreams, and your young men will see visions. Even on the menservants and maidservants in those days I will pour out My Spirit.

— Joel 2:28-29

Jesus gave the promise of the Holy Spirit for all believers. He would be a river of life spilling over from the depths of their being to a lost and hurting world (John 7:38-39). His power will continue to increase as we move further into the depths of God's presence toward Jesus' imminent return.

What Ezekiel witnessed was so powerful that even he could not fathom the coming outpouring of God's glory. I believe what the Church has experienced up until now is just a trickle, just ankle deep, in the river of God's glory. Continue to wade out into the deep and experience the overflowing abundance of His presence.

Today's Bible Reading Plan: 1 Kings 15:25-17:24 Acts 10:24-48; Psalm 134:1-3; Proverbs 17:9-11

I want to wade out into the floodtide of Your presence!

June 17 ~ A Day with Joni

Extravagant Worship

While He was in Bethany in the house of Simon the leper, as
He sat at supper, a woman came with an alabaster jar of
ointment, a very costly spikenard. She broke the jar and poured
the ointment on His head.
— Psalm 19:1

She threw caution to the wind – I don't like to do things that draw attention. She was emotional – I hate to wear my emotions so visibly. But here is her devotion to the Lord on display, a testimony still, thousands of years later.

This woman poured out her heart for everyone to see. It causes me to ask myself a rather uncomfortable question, "Have I ever done anything like that for Jesus?" Do I give my all, my very best to demonstrate my love for Him? Have I ever drawn the criticism of others because of my devotion to Jesus? Is my expression of worship extravagant, or is it reserved before watching eyes? Some called it a wasteful display, but Jesus said that what she did would be remembered forever. And it is!

My dear friend, I've learned that the greatest days in life are lived outside of our comfort zone. Don't be so afraid to get outside of yours. Take a look at this woman today and ask yourself, "Have I ever done anything like that for Jesus?"

Today's Bible Reading Plan: 1 Kings 18:1-46 Acts 11:1-30; Psalm 135:1-21; Proverbs 17:12-13

Jesus, I love You! Let my love for You be a visible, tangible expression and testimony. Give me courage – reckless abandon, even – to live my love out loud. Be pleased, I pray, in my thoughts, words and deeds, today and every day. Amen.

June 18

He Sent His Word

He sent His word and healed them
and delivered them from their destruction.

— Psalm 107:20

Our bodies belong to the Lord. The same Spirit that raised up Christ from the dead dwells in you right now and is alive in your mortal body. Your body is the temple, the dwelling place of the Holy Spirit. Your body has to recognize and realize it has no choice but to obey the living Word of God. God's Word was sent to heal and deliver you from all your destruction.

Jesus was wounded for your transgressions and bruised for your iniquities. The chastisement of your peace was laid upon Him and with His stripes you were and are healed (Isaiah 53:3, 1 Peter 2:24). God has restored your health and healed all your wounds (Jeremiah 30:17).

The power of God in the believer is so mighty that one day you're going to be walking through the grocery store past the frozen peas and carrots and people will be healed. Believe the Word of God and walk in His power!

Today's Bible Reading Plan: 1 Kings 19:1-21
Acts 12:1-23; Psalm 136:1-26; Proverbs 17:14-15

Holy Spirit, make the Word of God alive in me!

June 19

The Spirit of Life

*For the law of the Spirit of life in Christ Jesus
has set me free from the law of sin and death.*

— *Romans 8:2*

Sickness is nothing but limited death and a trespasser in your life. By the power of the Holy Spirit, you can enforce the boundaries of the kingdom of the living God and of His Christ, and the enemy has to take his hands off of God's property.

When you plead the blood of Jesus, the enemy has to flee! Galatians 3:15-19 says that those who belong to Christ are Abraham's seed, according to the covenants of promise, and you are able to be a partaker of the inheritance of the saints.

You are able, capable and worthy, according to your birthright from heaven, to receive the healing power of God and to have everything restored to you. When you receive restoration, expect it back even greater and more blessed than it was before the enemy stole from you. You are a child of the King!

Today's Bible Reading Plan: 1 Kings 20:1-21:29
Acts 12:24-13:15; Psalm 137:1-9; Proverbs 17:16

*Lord God, thank You for restoration of
everything the enemy stole and even greater!*

June 20

Worldly Wealth Cannot Satisfy

The blessing of the LORD makes rich,
and He adds no sorrow with it.

— Proverbs 10:22

Worldly wealth carries sorrow with it. Continue to fix your eyes on Jesus. Although our nation seems to be rocking and reeling under a heavy weight of materialism and darkness, God is now, has always been, and will forever be our refuge and strength and our very present help in times of trouble (Psalm 46:1).

The spiritual attacks on our country cannot be fixed in the natural, no matter what politician makes promises to fix what's wrong with America. These are perilous times, times we do not have an answer for. The political system will not fix America's ills.

Righteousness exalts a nation, and we need to walk in righteousness, because sin is a reproach to any people (Proverbs 14:34). *When the righteous are in authority, the people rejoice; but when the wicked rule, the people mourn* (Proverbs 29:2). If we, as followers of Christ, live our everyday lives to honor Him, we will set an example for our nation.

Today's Bible Reading Plan: 1 Kings 22:1-53
Acts 13:16-41; Psalm 138:1-8; Proverbs 17:17-18

Holy Spirit, help me live daily for Christ so that
I can be an example of His righteousness to our nation.

178

June 21

Authority to Heal

He called His twelve disciples to Him and gave them authority
over unclean spirits, to cast them out, and to heal all kinds of
sickness and all kinds of disease.

— Matthew 10:1

Years ago, my mother had breast cancer. The doctors told her, "We're going to have to remove your breasts." She replied, "I'm going to hear my son preach in South Bend, Indiana, first. If I have cancer when I get back to Columbus, you can do the surgery."

I am not against doctors. I have used doctors myself. I believe doctors are a gift from God. One of the disciples, Luke, was a physician. I am just sharing with you what happened to my mother.

When my mother went to the conference, Dr. Lester Sumrall, T.L. Osborn and I prayed for her and laid hands on her. There was a doctor in the congregation who told my mother, "You must go back to the doctor today. God has healed you." My mother went to the doctor, they did the exam and there was no cancer. Then the doctor in Columbus did another exam, and there still was no cancer. The cancer never came back.

Today's Bible Reading Plan: 2 Kings 1:1-2:25
Acts 13:42-14:7; Psalm 139:1-24; Proverbs 17:19-21

Jesus, thank You for the delegated authority
You have given us over unclean spirits
and to heal sickness and disease.

June 22

You Are an Overcomer

They overcame him by the blood of the Lamb and by the word of their testimony, and they loved not their lives unto the death.

— *Revelation 12:11*

According to Revelation 12:11, the way to overcome the adversary is through the blood of the Lamb, speaking your testimony and not loving your life more than you love God. You may be in a very difficult place, today, but the test you're going through is going to produce an amazing testimony of the goodness and faithfulness of God.

During my battle with cancer, I had to endure excruciating pain, and I had third degree burns from the radiation treatments. I went through six months battling panic attacks and trepidation. But the Holy Spirit equipped me to fight off the fear with faith.

In the end, my struggle with vocal cord cancer yielded a remarkable testimony of God's amazing love and faithfulness to me and to my family. I have a testimony that I am now sharing with the world of how God healed me and restored me with a seven times greater anointing than I had prior to the cancer.

Today's Bible Reading Plan: 2 Kings 3:1-4:17
Acts 14:8-28; Psalm 140:1-3; Proverbs 17:22

Holy Spirit, give me boldness to share my testimony so that others can witness God's goodness.

June 23

Utterance of the Spirit

And they were all filled with the Holy Ghost, and began to speak with other tongues, as the Spirit gave them utterance.

— Acts 2:4 (KJV)

When I had cancer on my vocal cord, I could not utter a word, and I would go to my study to pray, read the Word and meditate for hours on end. As I spent time in God's presence, I would lay hold to the truth of God's Word and claim every promise I could find.

Because I could not even utter a sound, one of my favorite verses during this time was Acts 2:4, that the Holy Spirit gave them utterance. If you study it out in the original text, it actually reads, "as the Holy Spirit enabled them to express their original selves."

When you speak in that heavenly language, that's actually the original you, the real you speaking. That is the pre-fall you expressing to God your prayers, desires and entreaties in a language you do not understand, unless the Holy Spirit gives you the interpretation.

When you pray in that heavenly language each day, it sets the atmosphere for your day.

Today's Bible Reading Plan: 2 Kings 4:18-5:27
Acts 15:1-35; Psalm 141:1-10; Proverbs 17:23

Holy Spirit, refresh my prayer language today so that I can do battle in the spiritual realm throughout the day.

June 24 ~ A Day with Joni

Grace Sufficient

But after you have suffered a little while, the God of all grace, who has called us to His eternal glory through Christ Jesus, will restore, support, strengthen, and establish you.

— 1 Peter 5:10

Does anyone have a trouble-free life? If you do, please let me in on your secret!

In reality, life is filled with experiences and some of them we're not going to like. We are the sum total of what we've been through – the good and bad.

Life's difficulties leave a lasting impression that molds us into the people that we are. While we're going through tough times, we need the gentle voice of God reminding us that while we were promised trials and tribulations, we were promised a Savior to be with us along the way.

Do you hear that, friend? What you're going through has a purpose and an accompanying promise. He will provide grace sufficient. Look to Him in faith.

Today's Bible Reading Plan: 2 Kings 6:1-7:20
Acts 15:36-16:15; Psalm 142:1-7; Proverbs 17:24-25

O Father, suffering hurts. I wouldn't choose this, but I can choose to look to You in the midst of it, to keep Your promise and to accomplish Your purpose. Give me strength, Lord! And be glorified in me.

June 25

Father, Son, Spirit

*There are three who testify in heaven: the Father,
the Word, and the Holy Spirit, and the three are one.*

— *1 John 5:7*

The Father, the Son (the Word), and the Holy Spirit are three distinct personalities, all agreeing in one, totally separate and totally one.

As we gain a closer, more personal relationship with the Holy Spirit, we will have a deeper revelation of God.

The Holy Spirit is the Paracletos, the One called alongside us to help. We will meet Jesus in the air, but the Holy Spirit is here with us now. He is the One who gives us power to live right, wisdom to make the right choices, discipline to live healthy lives, to have healthy relationships, to prosper every day and thereby glorify God.

The Holy Spirit is teaching us how to live and operate in the kingdom of God.

Today's Bible Reading Plan: 2 Kings 8:1-9:13
Acts 16:16-40; Psalm 143:1-12; Proverbs 17:26

> *Holy Spirit, thank You for showing me how to
> live practically each day in the kingdom of God.*

June 26

God Will Heal Your Wounds

For I will restore health to you,
and I will heal you of your wounds,
says the LORD,
because they called you an outcast, saying,
"This is Zion whom no man cares for."

— *Jeremiah 30:17*

God promises to heal all of your wounds: in your physical body, your mind, that torment, fear, your finances, your family. The goodness of God is without measure.

God will restore you and those you love, because He is no respecter of persons (Acts 10:34). There is no partiality with God (Romans 2:11). You can be among the walking wounded, and God will restore your health and heal your wounds.

God does not change. *For I am the LORD, I do not change; therefore you, O sons of Jacob, are not consumed* (Malachi 3:6). He is your Healer yesterday, today and forever. He will not stop loving you, and He will not stop helping you.

Today's Bible Reading Plan: 2 Kings 9:14-10:31 Acts 17:1-34; Psalm 144:1-15; Proverbs 17:27-28

Lord, thank You for restoring my health
and healing my wounds today and every day.

June 27

The Afflictions
of the Righteous

*Many are the afflictions of the righteous,
but the LORD delivers him out of them all.*

— Psalm 34:19

If you've had many afflictions, it testifies of your righteousness. Healing is in the atonement of Jesus. According to His Word, Jesus was wounded for my transgressions, bruised for my iniquities, and the chastisement of my peace was laid upon Him, and with His stripes I am healed (Isaiah 53:5).

Stand firmly on the Word of God. God's Word is not defined by your experience, but His Word will define your experience. You can stand on the Word when there is nothing to stand on.

Jesus already conquered the adversary of your soul. The enemy is controlled, cast down, cast out and cast away. The Holy Spirit gives you the strength to resist the devil in word and deed.

You can go through your day dancing, shouting and praising God, because the enemy has already been defeated!

Today's Bible Reading Plan: 2 Kings 10:32-12:21 Acts 18:1-22; Psalm 145:1-21; Proverbs 18:1

Lord, I will praise you at all times! No matter what afflictions come, you have called me righteous.

185

June 28

Repairer of the Breach

Those from among you shall rebuild the old waste places;
you shall raise up the foundations of many generations;
and you shall be called, the Repairer of the Breach,
the Restorer of Paths in which to Dwell.

— Isaiah 58:12

Sickness and disease comes from the curse. Jesus is your Healer. The thief came to steal, kill and destroy, but Jesus is the life giver (John 10:10). Jesus gives us life sufficient in quantity and superior in quality.

The devil has no power. He tried to steal my voice, but the power of the Holy Spirit raised me up again. I am a repairer of the breach, and my voice will be heard. Followers of the Lord Jesus Christ, Jehovah Joshua Messiah, are called to rebuild the old waste places, and raise up the firm foundation of God, and restore the paths of righteousness, for His name's sake.

As you go through your daily activities today, remember you are charged by God to rebuild the old waste places. Call on the Holy Spirit to show you what you can do to be a vessel of restoration with family, friends, coworkers and those in your neighborhood.

Today's Bible Reading Plan: 2 Kings 13:1-14:29 Acts 18:23-19:12; Psalm 146:1-10; Proverbs 18:2-3

Holy Spirit, give me the words to say to those I encounter today so that I can be a vessel of Your restoration and love.

186

June 29

Valley of the Shadow of Death

Even though I walk through the valley of the shadow of death,
I will fear no evil; for You are with me...

— Psalm 23:4

I know what it's like to walk through the valley, and I know what it's like to come out of the valley and get to the mountaintop. I know what it's like to get my shout back.

Because of the anointing of the Holy Spirit, I have faith for anything. The valley of the shadow of death could not hold me, because the Spirit of God propelled me forward. Sickness failed and fear failed.

Jesus is the vine, and we are the branches that bear much fruit (John 15:5). Only the kingdom of God has a right to operate in our lives. Jesus is praying that our faith will not fail (Luke 22:32). If Jesus is praying for our faith, how can our faith ever fail?

The anointing of the Holy Spirit empowers us and strengthens us to do mighty exploits for God!

Today's Bible Reading Plan: 2 Kings 15:1-16:20
Acts 19:13-41; Psalm 147:1-20; Proverbs 18:4-5

Holy Spirit, propel me forward and establish
God's kingdom in every area of my life.

June 30

The Enemy Is Defeated!

God anointed Jesus of Nazareth with the Holy Spirit and with power, who went about doing good and healing all who were oppressed by the devil, for God was with Him.

— *Acts 10:38*

You may be in a great battle. I know what that's like. Because of my battle with vocal cord cancer, I know what it's like to walk the floor at night. I know what it's like to be in constant pain. I know what it's like to extend my faith to its very limits. I know what it's like to be at a point where you cannot even pray. You just have to trust.

I know my journey isn't necessarily the same as yours, but in many ways you and I are on the same journey. Though my battles may be different, we are on a walk of faith together. There are things you have to believe and trust God to do in your life. We all need the Holy Spirit to anoint us and equip us for the journey.

The enemy attacks, but God gets the victory every time. Trust Him today and every day to equip you for the battle.

Today's Bible Reading Plan: 2 Kings 17:1-18:12
Acts 20:1-38; Psalm 148:1-14; Proverbs 18:6-7

Holy Spirit, lead me through this day in victory!

JULY

It Is God's Will That You Prosper

Beloved, I wish above all things that thou mayest prosper and be in health, even as thy soul prospereth.

— 3 John 2 (KJV)

July 1 ~ A Day with Joni

Gossip? Don't Do It.

The words of a talebearer are as wounds, and they go down into the innermost parts of the belly.

— Proverbs 26:22 (KJV)

I offer this as food for thought today because the Bible is filled with verses on taming the tongue and using our words to speak life and not death. There is enough negativity in the world, and as Christians we need to be using our words wisely.

We are a light in a dark place. The world needs our example, but first we have to stop hurting each other. Our words should reflect the character of the One we claim to serve; He heals and loves and forgives. His words to us are laced with tenderness and mercy because we are His beloved.

Just think of how He feels when we hurt someone He loves, and we use our words as the weapon to do so.

Today's Bible Reading Plan: 2 Kings 18:13-19:37 Acts 21:1-17; Psalm 149:1-9; Proverbs 18:8

Father, forgive me. I have used my words to hurt others. I have entertained, and even furthered gossip. You call me to a higher love. Please help me to measure what I say against that higher standard. And may my words be healing instead of hurting; life-giving! Amen.

July 2

Two Masters

"No servant can serve two masters. Either he will hate the one and love the other, or he will be loyal to the one and despise the other. You cannot serve God and wealth."

— Luke 16:13

There are many things that can lord over us, today: our job, kids, hobbies, clubs. Anything that diminishes your ability to spend quality time with God is a master over you.

For example, don't let your job take your attention away from God, to the point you think it is your skill and ability that make you successful. Every good and perfect gift comes from God (James 1:17).

God and God alone gives us knowledge, wisdom, understanding, skill and ability to have success each day in every area of our lives.

Give the Lord the honor He is due. Do not lose sight of where your help comes from. *I will lift my eyes to the hills, from where does my help come? My help comes from the LORD, who made heaven and earth* (Psalm 121:1).

Before you start your day, establish early in the morning who you serve and who your Master will be that day.

Today's Bible Reading Plan: 2 Kings 20:1-22:2
Acts 21:18-36; Psalm 150:1-6; Proverbs 18:9-10

Jehovah Joshua Messiah, you are the Lord of my life!

191

July 3

God and Money

"No one can serve two masters. For either he will hate the one and love the other, or else he will hold to the one and despise the other. You cannot serve God and money."

— *Matthew 6:24*

You cannot serve God and money. You must <u>never</u> serve money. Turn it around and declare, "Money will serve me."

There is no shortage of money in the world; it's just in the wrong hands. The gross US federal government debt at the end of 2016 was projected to be more than 19 trillion dollars, according to the FY17 Federal Budget. A trillion is a thousand billion. Again, there is no shortage of money.

God is absolutely powerful, because He is absolutely holy. His value is based on the singular fact that He is the only one of Him. The more there is of a thing, the less value it has. God, in reality, places no value on money.

God wants you to serve Him, because He is the one and only God. He wants you to make the trillions of green paper bills floating around out there serve you.

Today's Bible Reading Plan: 2 Kings 22:3-23:30 Acts 21:37-22:16; Psalm 1:1-6; Proverbs 18:11-12

Holy Spirit, by Your wisdom and power, show me how to make money serve me today.

July 4

Your True Independence Day

"The Spirit of the Lord is upon Me, because He has anointed
Me to preach the gospel to the poor;
He has sent Me to heal the broken-hearted,
to preach deliverance to the captives
and recovery of sight to the blind,
to set at liberty those who are oppressed;
to preach the acceptable year of the Lord."

— Luke 4:18-19

Today is Independence Day, the day the United States commemorates its freedom from the British. Although we are grateful for the freedoms we enjoy in our country, followers of Christ know true freedom and liberty is found in the Lord Jesus Christ. *Now the Lord is the Spirit. And where the Spirit of the Lord is, there is liberty* (2 Corinthians 3:17).

The Holy Spirit leads us into all truth, and it is the truth you know that <u>makes</u> you free (John 8:32 KJV). Your life will be changed in an instant when the Lord sets you free from bondage. No matter what has you bound today – sickness, lack, oppression, grief or relationship issues – the Spirit of the Lord can <u>make</u> you free! Turn to the Lord, for He is your true liberty!

Today's Bible Reading Plan: 2 Kings 23:31-25:30 Acts 22:17-23:10; Psalm 2:1-12; Proverbs 18:13

Jehovah Joshua Messiah, thank You for true freedom.

193

July 5

Be Faithful with Little

"He who is faithful in what is least is faithful also in much.
And he who is dishonest in the least is dishonest also in much."

— Luke 16:10

When God can trust you with what He has already given you, He will then bless you with more, because you have proven yourself to be a good steward.

Jesus addresses two issues in the parable of the dishonest steward in Luke 16:1-13: faithfulness and honesty. The employee in this parable used his employer's resources for his own gain. The employer required the employee to give a complete audit of his books. This employee had been unfaithful and dishonest with what his employer entrusted to him.

God has given us stewardship over His kingdom on earth. He has entrusted a marvelous task to His people, not so we can enrich ourselves, but so we can prosper His kingdom. When we help the poor, assist a neighbor in distress, provide food and clothing to the needy, we are God's vessel of outreach. Look for ways to enrich someone else materially or spiritually. When you are faithful with what you have, God will increase His kingdom in you.

Today's Bible Reading Plan: 1 Chronicles 1:1-2:17 Acts 23:11-35; Psalm 3:1-8; Proverbs 18:14-15

Lord, increase Your kingdom in me today.

July 6

The Good Steward

"So if you have not been faithful in the unrighteous wealth, who will commit to your trust the true riches?"

— Luke 16:11

In this parable, Jesus talks about a crooked manager who wastes his master's resources. His master calls him in to give an account of his stewardship. The man was found lacking in his duties and was fired.

The fired manager immediately devises a plan to get money for himself, so that he won't be in poverty. He begins stealing from his master's clients by having the clients pay less than they owe directly to him. You would think the master would be outraged, but he actually commends the crooked manager for acting so shrewdly. Jesus says the sons of this world are wiser in their own generation than the sons of light.

Jesus explains in Luke 16:8-9 (MSG) that the manager knew how to look after himself. *"I want you to be smart in the same way—but for what is right—using every adversity to stimulate you to creative survival...so you'll live, really live, and not complacently just get by on good behavior."* Jesus wants us to live the kingdom life in every way so that we are living testimonies to His goodness.

Today's Bible Reading Plan: 1 Chronicles 2:18-4:4 Acts 24:1-27; Psalm 4:1-8; Proverbs 18:16-18

Lord, give me power to use adversity to glorify You.

July 7

True Prosperity Comes from God

I pray for good fortune in everything you do, and for your good health—that your everyday affairs prosper, as well as your soul!

— 3 John 2 (MSG)

Prosperity does not just refer to financial prosperity or material things. You can prosper in other ways: in your family life, in your friendships, in your relationship with God.

The Holy Spirit gives us many things that help us to prosper in our daily lives: wisdom, understanding, revelation, discernment, truth, skill, ability and so much more. We can be blessed with prosperity that is tangible or intangible. When you see your family filled with joy, that is prosperity you cannot place a price on. When you give spiritual comfort to someone who is hurting, that is prosperity that doesn't provide financial benefit, but it gives great fulfillment.

A prosperous journey is a journey that is blessed by God in every area of your life.

Today's Bible Reading Plan: 1 Chronicles 4:5-5:17 Acts 25:1-27; Psalm 5:1-12; Proverbs 18:19

Holy Spirit, show me true prosperity today. Prosper me as God wants me to prosper.

July 8 ~ A Day with Joni

Are You a Connector?

The eye cannot say to the hand, "I have no need of you," nor the head to the feet, "I have no need of you."

— 1 Corinthians 12:21

Do you draw people together, or push them apart?

Unity in the body of Christ is so important. The health of the body suffers when vital connections are broken. The very fact that the metaphor of a body is used of the church – think of it! When one part of the body ceases to function as part of the whole, we call it a handicap!

Within the body, we are all different; we are supposed to be different; our glory and giftings shine through our differences. But rather than withdraw in the face of our diversity, we must all become keepers of the connections. The more connectors a church has, the healthier her fellowship.

What role do you play in the church where unity is concerned? Are you a connector? Do you draw people together, or push them apart?

Today's Bible Reading Plan: 1 Chronicles 5:18-6:81 Acts 26:1-32; Psalm 6:1-10; Proverbs 18:20-21

You are the Head of the Church, Lord. You've placed me in the body and given me a vital role to play. Will You help me to appreciate more fully the important roles others play, to be a connector and not a defector where relationships are concerned? Lord, bless Your church – and use me to bless others, I pray.

July 9

Weep and Howl
for Your Misery

And a final word to you arrogant rich: Take some lessons in lament. You'll need buckets for the tears when the crash comes upon you. Your money is corrupt and your fine clothes stink. Your greedy luxuries are a cancer in your gut, destroying your life from within. You thought you were piling up wealth. What you've piled up is judgment.

— James 5:1-3 (MSG)

This is a very stern warning to those who rely on money for their satisfaction and who put their faith in wealth. James says they will need <u>buckets</u> for the tears they will shed when the crash comes.

James goes on to say that the workers who have been exploited and cheated are crying out for judgment. He says explicitly that the groans of the workers who have been used and abused are a roar in the ears of the Master Avenger.

God cares deeply how we treat each other. Jesus tells us to treat others as we would like to be treated. *Here is a simple rule of thumb for behavior: Ask yourself what you want people to do for you; then grab the initiative and do it for them!* (Luke 6:31 MSG).

Today's Bible Reading Plan: 1 Chronicles 7:1-8:40 Acts 27:1-20; Psalm 7:1-17; Proverbs 18:22

Holy Spirit, point out opportunities for me to grab the initiative and treat someone with kindness and love today.

198

July 10

The Great Transfer

Meanwhile, friends, wait patiently for the Master's Arrival.
You see farmers do this all the time, waiting for their valuable
crops to mature, patiently letting the rain do its slow but sure
work. Be patient like that. Stay steady and strong. The Master
could arrive at any time.

— James 5:7-8

Do not focus on the temporal wealth of this world, but focus instead on the lasting, eternal reward that is awaiting you. When God blesses you, use the resources He gives you to build His kingdom, not your own. The Lord Jesus Christ could come at any time.

Will He find you faithfully managing the resources He has blessed you with, or will He find you squandering it on yourself? *"I tell you, He will avenge them speedily. Nevertheless, when the Son of Man comes, will He find faith on the earth?"* (Luke 18:8)

God wants you to prosper, and He blesses you with many good things to enjoy; however, don't keep it all for yourself. Look beyond yourself to see where God may want you to bless someone else. The Lord doesn't just give to you; He also gives through you.

Today's Bible Reading Plan: 1 Chronicles 9:1-10:14 Acts 27:21-44; Psalm 8:1-9; Proverbs 18:23-24

Thank You, Lord, for blessing me to be a blessing.

July 11

Bless Me Indeed!

Then Jabez called on the God of Israel, saying, "Oh, that You would indeed bless me and enlarge my territory, that Your hand might be with me, and that You would keep me from evil, that it may not bring me hardship!" So God granted what he asked.

— 1 Chronicles 4:10

God blessed Jabez and enlarged his territory merely because Jabez asked God to do so. It shows that the Lord has compassion on His people when they call out to Him.

Jabez also asked that God would protect him from evil. Jabez knew that provision and protection came from God. We would do well to acknowledge God for every good thing we receive.

There is no God but Jehovah Joshua Messiah, the Lord Jesus Christ. When we acknowledge His sovereignty and power and love, it creates a connection and relationship like no other.

I pray the Holy Spirit will make you aware of His presence in your life today and every day. The God of the universe wants to connect deeply with you.

Today's Bible Reading Plan: 1 Chronicles 11:1-12:18 Acts 28:1-31; Psalm 9:1-12; Proverbs 19:1-3

Jehovah Joshua Messiah, Lord Jesus Christ, I submit to You and acknowledge You as Sovereign over all things.

July 12

Do You Serve Money?

For the love of money is the root of all evil. While coveting after money, some have strayed from the faith and pierced themselves through with many sorrows.

— 1 Timothy 6:10

There are four indicators that you serve money, instead of money serving you:

1) Rather than working 40 hours a week for God, to serve Him, you work 40 hours a week at a job you hate for money.

2) You spend more than 30% of your monthly income on debt.

3) You use your savings or credit card cash advance to pay bills, to finance a lifestyle you cannot afford.

4) There is conflict in your home over money.

Ask the Holy Spirit to open opportunities for you to serve God, not just work at a job you hate because you have to. You can serve God on your job, but it doesn't have to be a job you hate. You can love the work you do for Him, whether it be as a waitress, CEO, pastor, teacher or housewife. Then live contentedly within the resources God gives you.

Today's Bible Reading Plan: 1 Chronicles 12:19-14:17 Romans 1:1-17; Psalm 9:13-20; Proverbs 19:4-5

Holy Spirit, place me in the vocation for which God has designed me to serve Him.

201

July 13

The Supply of God

Consider the ravens: They neither sow nor reap, they have neither storehouses nor barns. Yet God feeds them. How much more valuable are you than birds?

— *Luke 12:24*

God does not want you to go in debt to finance a lifestyle you cannot afford. Debt is never your way out. The existence of your need does not indicate the lack of supply.

I'm sure you've heard it said that a penny saved is a penny earned. If you save a penny, and then tomorrow save two pennies, and the third day save three pennies and so on, at the end of 365 days you will have saved $667.95, and the largest investment you will make on any day is $3.65. You can also do a weekly plan of saving one dollar per week. The first week save one dollar, week two save two dollars, week three save three dollars and so on. At the end of 52 weeks, you will have saved $1,378, and the largest investment in any week will be $52.

By being patient and having faith in God, you can live debt free. There is no lack of supply when you trust God.

Today's Bible Reading Plan: 1 Chronicles 15:1-16:36 Romans 1:18-32; Psalm 10:1-15; Proverbs 19:6-7

Holy Spirit, grant me patience and perseverance to do things God's way.

July 14

The Proof of Ownership

For every wild animal of the forest is Mine,
and the cattle on a thousand hills.

— *Psalm 50:10*

The proof of ownership is the ability to convey. You do not own your car if you cannot convey the title without paying off a car loan first. If you have a mortgage, you cannot sell your house and convey title until you first pay off the mortgage. Debt is not your system; it is financial slavery. Possessions are not bad, but do not make them your master. *But seek first the kingdom of God and His righteousness, and all these things shall be given to you* (Matthew 6:33).

You must break the mindset that poverty is a virtue. Poverty is a curse. The other end of the spectrum is greed. Greed is a compulsion that you have to have what you want now. You need instant gratification and cannot wait until you have saved for what you want. The lottery is not God's way, either. *Ill-gotten gain gets you nowhere; an honest life is immortal* (Proverbs 10:2 MSG). *Easy come, easy go, but steady diligence pays off* (Proverbs 13:11 MSG). If you are diligent in doing things God's way, He will bless you richly.

Today's Bible Reading Plan: 1 Chronicles 16:37-18:17 Romans 2:1-24; Psalm 10:16-18; Proverbs 19:8-9

Holy Spirit, help me to wait.

July 15 ~ A Day with Joni

Go, Preach

He said to them, "Go into all the world,
and preach the gospel to every creature.
— Mark 16:15

I got saved in the seventies. It was during what was called the Jesus movement. It was all about winning the lost. We shared our faith, anywhere, everywhere, all the time. Somehow, in the current *Me, Myself, and I* movement, we've lost this emphasis – this passion – to see the lost come to faith.

Go! Preach the gospel! These were the last words of Jesus before His ascension. He didn't tell us to sit in our church pews and drink coffee while we listen to a "please make me feel good" message.

If we love Him, we'll love those He loves. If we love Him, we'll do what He told us to do. He knew the secret of life, peace, and joy was wrapped up in our obedience to fulfill His plan; to Go!

As a disciple, it's time to be fishers of men again. We were lost and now we're found. Someone helped us get there so we need to return the favor!

Today's Bible Reading Plan: 1 Chronicles 19:1-21:30 Romans 2:25-3:8; Psalm 11:1-17; Proverbs 19:10-12

Heavenly Father, this is Your plan A – and there is no plan B. You called me to be Your witness, to testify of Your love, Your grace, the good news. Give me opportunities today to share. Give me the courage to seize these opportunities as they arise. Help me tell them about You. Amen.

July 16

You Have Need of Patience

*For you need patience, so that after you have done
the will of God, you will receive the promise.*

— *Hebrews 10:36*

When you first create a budget, the first 90 days is critical. You will want to stop 90 times in 90 days. There is nothing your flesh is going to like about your budget. If what you want to buy is not a matter of life and death, do not buy it. If you can live without it and live, that is an indicator you can have it and die. Crucify your flesh; be disciplined in your finances.

In the first month, it is going to seem like your budget is not working. The second month, you will probably still need to make some major adjustments. When you started your budget, you did not know where your money was going; now that you've started the process, you begin to see where you need to tweak and make modifications. By the third month, you will be able to tell that a budget is making a significant difference in your financial stability. It probably took a long time to get in the mess you're in. It will take time to get out. Do not give up.

Today's Bible Reading Plan: 1 Chronicles 22:1-23:32
Romans 3:9-31; Psalm 12:1-8; Proverbs 19:13-14

*Holy Spirit, give me the wisdom and patience
to achieve financial stability.*

July 17

Excuses, Excuses, Excuses

The man said, "The woman whom You gave to be with me, she gave me fruit of the tree, and I ate." Then the LORD God said to the woman, "What have you done?" And the woman said, "The serpent deceived me, and I ate."

— Genesis 3:12-13

There are three main excuses people give for not keeping a budget:

1) People are afraid of what they'll find out about their spending habits. Some will find they're spending so much money eating out, they could actually make a mortgage payment.

2) Some think a budget is too restrictive. They want to be free to spend their money the way they want to spend it. They think they'll never be able to have fun. How much fun is it to have overdue bills and bill collectors calling you?

3) Budgets have been used as a paper club to beat people, such as your spouse, to shame them for making the smallest mistake in the budget or for spending money where they shouldn't.

Ditch the excuses, create a budget and stick to it.

Today's Bible Reading Plan: 1 Chronicles 24:1-26:11 Romans 4:1-12; Psalm 13:1-6; Proverbs 19:15-16

Holy Spirit, help me to face me and stop making excuses.

July 18

If You Do Not Work, You Do Not Eat

For when we were with you, we commanded you that if any will not work, neither shall he eat.

— 2 Thessalonians 3:10

In a two-spouse home, meaning a husband and wife, a husband may feel condemned if he feels he is not making enough money. A man's drive is to work. The feminization of our culture has driven the work ethic out of men. My wife tells me virtually every day of my life, "You are a man; you are made to work."

A man is a hunter-provider. If men do not work, something goes wrong inside of them and creates conflict in the home because he is allowed to lay around on the couch and do nothing. Lazy, without a miracle, is incurable. Lazy is a lifestyle.

Barring some type of debilitating disability, men are made to work. When men get in their place, the culture will be vastly different.

Today's Bible Reading Plan: 1 Chronicles 26:12-27:34 Romans 4:13-5:5; Psalm 14:1-7; Proverbs 19:17

Lord, help men to find their position in You.

July 19

Three Reasons Budgets Fail

Moreover it is required in stewards that a man be found faithful.

— 1 Corinthians 4:2

There are three reasons why your budget may not work:

1) When you create your budget, you leave things out, such as cosmetics or hobbies. It is imperative that you start keeping receipts and keep a record of every expenditure to learn where your money is being spent.

2) You overcomplicate your budget. Keep it simple by starting with one page.

3) You don't live according to the budget you've created. Developing the math for your budget is not the most important thing; your behavior is the most important thing. Self-denial and self-control are paramount.

If you watch out for these pitfalls, you will be able to stick with your budget and change the way you view money, and you will begin to make money work for you instead of you working for money.

Today's Bible Reading Plan: 1 Chronicles 28:1-29:30 Romans 5:6-21; Psalm 15:1-5; Proverbs 19:18-19

Holy Spirit, help me change
my behavior regarding spending.

July 20

Four Necessities

But if any do not care for their own,
and especially for those of their own house,
they have denied the faith and are worse than unbelievers.

— 1 Timothy 5:8

There are four basic necessities the head of a household should provide for those of their house:

1) Food – eat at home most times. Do not eat out five nights a week. It is a waste of money and probably unhealthy. If you work or go to school, take a packed lunch from home on most days.

2) Shelter – rent or mortgage. Never pay rent unless you have to. It is the worst investment you can make.

3) Clothing – you are not required to provide the most expensive clothing or the latest trend in clothing. Do not try to provide Christian Louboutin red bottom shoes on a Payless budget.

4) Transportation – vehicles, gas, bus fare, bicycle, whatever your budget can afford. Do not take a taxi to work every day when you only live a mile from your place of employment.

Provide these four fundamentals for your household, and you will be doing God's will.

Today's Bible Reading Plan: 2 Chronicles 1:1-3:17 Romans 6:1-23; Psalm 16:1-11; Proverbs 19:20-21

Lord God, thank You for providing for my household.

July 21

Miraculous Provision

Then it shall be when the LORD your God brings you into the land which He swore to your fathers, to Abraham, Isaac, and Jacob, to give you great and fine cities, which you did not build, and houses full of all good things which you did not fill, and hewn cisterns which you did not dig, vineyards and olive trees which you did not plant, and you eat and are full, then beware lest you forget the LORD who brought you out of the land of Egypt, out of the house of bondage.

— Deuteronomy 6:10-12

Over the last few days, I have been teaching you about saving and budgeting. These are good biblical fundamental principles. God can, however, as you obey His principles, bless you to live in houses you did not build full of good things you did not have to buy.

Some people have faith to believe they're going to live in heaven and walk around on streets of gold, but they can't believe God for one little band of gold to put on their finger.

Today's Bible Reading Plan: 2 Chronicles 4:1-6:11 Romans 7:1-13; Psalm 17:1-15; Proverbs 19:22-23

Thank You, Holy Spirit, for faith to believe the impossible.

July 22 ~ A Day with Joni

One Day at a Time

Therefore, take no thought about tomorrow,
for tomorrow will take thought about the things of itself.
Sufficient to the day is the trouble thereof.
— Matthew 6:34

We've heard it a million times as a cliché, in a song or as an overused piece of advice that carries little weight. But if we really think about it, it's an answer to the questions we often ask: "How do I do this?" "How can I get through this?" "How do I get over this?" "How do I heal from this?" One day at a time!

If we're honest, we don't want to be told that something is going to take time. Process might as well be a four-letter word. We want it now! But taking life one day at a time allows us to make the most out of God's plan for this day. We can make the most out of our relationships. We can make the most out of this day's lessons and experiences. Today, you can allow God to continue unfolding His plan and His story for your life. When you focus on the present, you can trust the God who heals your past and holds your future. You can do this, get over this, get through this, and heal from this – one day at a time.

Today's Bible Reading Plan: 2 Chronicles 6:12-8:10
Romans 7:14-8:8; Psalm 18:1-15; Proverbs 19:24-25

O Lord, I thank You that Your mercies are new each morning. You've ordained each of my days. And this is the day You have made! Help me to rest in You this day – to trust in Your process – for You have my very best interests at heart. In Jesus' name.

July 23

Put God in Control

Put GOD in charge of your work,
then what you've planned will take place.

— Proverbs 16:3 (MSG)

Although one million dollars will pass through the hands of 64% of the people in America, 70% of them will end up living on Social Security. Sometimes we dig a hole so deep, we think we can never climb out; but when you're in a pit, the only way out is up.

The singular difference between you and a person who is much wealthier than you is information. The information you need is contained in God's Word. Determine in your heart to believe the Bible, because the only part of the Bible that works for you is the part you believe.

Jesus provided everything you need through His sacrifice on the cross. Through His blood shed on Calvary, you have salvation, healing, deliverance, prosperity, wholeness and completeness.

Ask God to give you a vision and then answer His call and walk in that vision. *Where there is no vision, the people perish...* (Proverbs 29:18).

Today's Bible Reading Plan: 2 Chronicles 8:11-10:19 Romans 8:9-25; Psalm 18:16-36; Proverbs 19:26

Holy Spirit, give me a vision, lest I perish.

July 24

The Power of Agreement

"Again I say to you, that if two of you agree on earth
about anything they ask, it will be done for them
by My Father who is in heaven."

— *Matthew 18:19*

Most couples are rarely in agreement, but the moment you are married, your everyday life becomes 10,000 times more spiritually powerful through the power of agreement. *A threefold cord is not quickly broken* (Ecclesiastes 4:12). One can chase a thousand and two puts ten thousand to flight (Deuteronomy 32:30).

Likewise, you husbands, live considerately with your wives, giving honor to the woman as the weaker vessel, since they too are also heirs of the grace of life, so that your prayers will not be hindered (1 Peter 3:7).

In households with a husband and wife, a budget needs to be created with both spouses. Chances are good that one or the other of the couple will be the better money manager, and that's okay. Just agree to that among yourselves. In a marriage relationship and covenant, there is no his and hers. Your decisions together determine your financial stability. Husband and wife must come into agreement.

Today's Bible Reading Plan: 2 Chronicles 11:1-13:22 Romans 8:26-39; Psalm 18:37-50; Proverbs 19:27-29

Holy Spirit, help husbands and wives
to walk in agreement.

July 25

Decisions Define Your Future

Then God said, "Let us make man in our image, after our likeness, and let them have dominion over the fish of the sea, and over the birds of the air, and over the livestock, and over all the earth, and over every creeping thing that creeps on the earth." So God created man in His own image; in the image of God He created him; male and female He created them.

— Genesis 1:26-27

Your decisions determine your financial stability. In Genesis 1:26-27, God forever surrendered His right to invade your marriage. In a marriage, the husband and wife have the ability to direct divine activity. If you don't like the atmosphere of your marriage, change it.

You are not a thermometer reacting to the elements; you are a thermostat creating your environment. It is your responsibility to create an environment for your family.

There is agreement or disagreement in the spirit realm, whether your mind picks it up or not. It is a spiritual principle. There are no standoffs.

Today's Bible Reading Plan: 2 Chronicles 14:1-16:14 Romans 9:1-24; Psalm 19:1-14; Proverbs 20:1

Renew marriages, Lord, so that Your kingdom can be established through spiritually strong families in agreement.

214

July 26

Money Is Only a Tool

Praise the LORD!
Blessed is the man who fears the LORD,
who delights greatly in His commandments.
His offspring shall be mighty in the land;
the generation of the upright shall be blessed.
Wealth and riches shall be in his house,
and his righteousness endures forever.

— Psalm 112:1-3

Wealth and riches are supposed to be in your house now, not after you get to heaven. A man was moving his family into a home that his parents had occupied. They moved the sofa from the wall and found a 1.2 million dollar painting in a $40,000 house.

Money is nothing more than a tool to accomplish God's will. Money doesn't mean anything to God except to be used for the purpose for which He intended it – that the Gospel be preached worldwide.

God gives you money, then asks for part of it back, then leaves you 90%, and He runs the world on 10%. Faithfulness, hard work, obedience, truthfulness and productivity lead to wealth.

Today's Bible Reading Plan: 2 Chronicles 17:1-18:34 Romans 9:25-10:13; Psalm 20:1-9; Proverbs 20:2-3

I agree with You, Lord, for Your plan for my finances.

July 27

Four Keys for Wealth

Bring all the tithes into the storehouse, that there may be food in My house, and test Me now in this, says the LORD of Hosts, if I will not open for you the windows of heaven and pour out for you a blessing, that there will not be room enough to receive it.

— *Malachi 3:10*

There are four keys to setting the environment for wealth in your home:

1) Determine that God's Word is the absolute final authority in your finances.

2) Determine financial family goals. If you are married, the goals should be determined by the husband and wife together.

3) Determine to live the faith life. Do not allow debt to tempt you to live a lifestyle that your faith cannot cover. Ask the Holy Spirit for persistence to drive the car you've got until it's paid off, and then take that payment, keep driving that car and four years later pay cash for a car.

4) Determine your willingness to adjust to change. Increased information creates the need for change. If you are not changing, you are not growing. The information you are receiving today will elicit change.

Today's Bible Reading Plan: 2 Chronicles 19:1-20:37 Romans 10:14-11:12; Psalm 21:1-13; Proverbs 20:4-6

Holy Spirit, fill me with knowledge and wisdom about finances.

216

July 28

Seven Myths About Debt

The rich rules over the poor,
and the borrower is servant to the lender.

— *Proverbs 22:7*

Here are seven myths about debt:

1) I'll help family or friends by lending them money. *The borrower is servant to the lender.* (Proverbs 22:7).

2) I'll help family or friends by cosigning a loan. *It's stupid to try to get something for nothing, or run up huge bills you can never pay* (Proverbs 17:18).

3) Gambling brings wealth. *Ill-gotten gain gets you nowhere; an honest life is immortal* (Proverbs 10:2 MSG).

4) Car payment – it is a lie that you will always have a car payment.

5) Get a 30-year mortgage and pay it off early. The truth is less than 1% pay off a 30-year mortgage early.

6) If I pay the credit card off every month, I will enjoy the benefits without debt. The truth is very few people are able to pay their credit card debt off at the end of every month.

7) Debt is a tool to create prosperity. As stated before, *The rich rules over the poor, and the borrower is servant to the lender* (Proverbs 22:7).

Today's Bible Reading Plan: 2 Chronicles 21:1-23:21
Romans 11:13-36; Psalm 22:1-18; Proverbs 20:7

Holy Spirit, help me to not be deceived regarding debt.

July 29 ~ A Day with Joni

Greater Than I Imagine

Now, Lord, what do I wait for? My hope is in You.

— Psalm 39:7

What are you waiting for? At times we may have a sense that we know, while at others we haven't a clue. Isn't it marvelous that our God is a God "able to do immeasurably more than all we ask or imagine"?

I think we often limit God by confining our hopes within the context of our past experiences or what we think is possible. But all things are possible with our God.

Let us believe that God has our very best interests at heart. Let us believe He knows what we need before we even ask. Let us believe He knows every thought upon our heart and every word before it crosses our lips. And let us live expecting that His answer to our pleas will be according to His love, grace, and mercy by which He is able to do immeasurably more than we can imagine.

Today's Bible Reading Plan: 2 Chronicles 24:1-25:28 Romans 12:1-21; Psalm 22:19-31; Proverbs 20:8-10

My hope is in You, Lord. I believe. Help my unbelief! Will You free my thinking from the shackles of my past experiences and what I think possible? You are so much greater. I wait upon You, Your plan, Your promise. In Jesus' name.

July 30

Ask, Seek, Knock

"Ask and it will be given to you; seek and you will find; knock and it will be opened to you. For everyone who asks receives, and he who seeks finds, and to him who knocks, it will be opened.

— Matthew 7:7-8

Have you ever misplaced your keys just to find you stuck them in your pocket? Maybe you misplaced a pair of glasses only to discover them right on top of your head. When we call upon the Lord, He will make those things visible that were once hidden. Your answer is right in front of you. The Lord did not set any conditions for calling on Him. Jesus only said, *"Ask and it will be given to you; seek and you will find; knock and it will be opened to you.* (Matthew 7:7).

If we know the Lord hears us, we can have steadfast confidence and assurance that He has already granted to us for our present possession those things we have asked Him for. You have never prayed the prayer that God did not hear and answer the moment you formed the words upon your lips. God will tell you everything you need to know when you take the time to cry out to Him.

Today's Bible Reading Plan: 2 Chronicles 26:1-28:27 Romans 13:1-14; Psalm 23:1-6; Proverbs 20:11

Thank You, Lord, that You always hear my cry and answer my prayer.

July 31

It's Time for Change

I will go before you and make the crooked places straight; I will break in pieces the gates of bronze and shatter the bars of iron.

— *Isaiah 45:2*

Lombard Street at Presidio Boulevard inside The Presidio in San Francisco, California, has earned the honor of being the most winding street in the world. The street was purposely designed to make very sharp turns to allow cars to navigate the hill's steep grade and be less of a hazard to pedestrians.

Lombard Street was strategically twisted for ease of travel. Can you imagine the deathtrap it would be if it were a steep, straight incline? Contrast this to Satan who has set crooked places to entrap us. He has devised a winding maze of deception to detour us from our heavenly purpose.

The Messiah came to make the crooked places straight. Jesus, the Anointed One, has gone ahead of us. He will break in pieces the barrier erected between God's provision and us. Your barrier is your benefit. Trust in the Lord. He will use your problem to propel you from where you are to where He wants you to be.

Today's Bible Reading Plan: 2 Chronicles 29:1-36 Romans 14:1-23; Psalm 24:1-10; Proverbs 20:12

Jesus, thank You for making my way straight and tearing down every obstacle between my destiny and me.

AUGUST

The Name
of the Lord

The name of the LORD is a strong tower;

the righteous run into it and are safe.

— Proverbs 18:10

August 1

There Is Power in His Name

And whoever calls on the name of the Lord shall be saved.

— Acts 2:21

Our English names for God do not carry the detail and nuance that the Hebrew names for God do. Learn to use these Hebrew names in prayer, praise and worship. Use them often and allow them to paint a more accurate and transforming picture of who God is. Calling on the name of the Lord will enrich your everyday, ordinary, sleeping, eating, going to work, walking-around life.

God declares in Numbers 6:22-27 that He will bless His people when they call on His name. Psalm 44:5 decrees that with God's name, you can trample those who rise up against you. We are to declare the excellence of God's name, according to Psalm 8:1. When Job was under attack from the adversary, He blessed the name of the Lord (Job 1:21).

Make calling on the name of the Lord a big part of your daily walk. Acknowledging Him as first and foremost above everything and everyone sets the tone for each and every day.

Today's Bible Reading Plan: 2 Chronicles 30:1-31:21 Romans 15:1-22; Psalm 25:1-15; Proverbs 20:13-15

Jehovah Joshua Messiah, I will glorify Your name!

August 2

El-Shaddai, God Almighty

When Abram was ninety-nine years old, the LORD
appeared to him and said, "I am Almighty God..."

— *Genesis 17:1a*

The only name by which Abraham had ever known God was Elohim. Elohim was the creator of all things. He was the One who established natural laws.

But in Genesis 17:1, God introduced Himself to Abraham by the Hebrew name, "El Shaddai: the All-Sufficient One" or "the God who is more than enough." Why? He told this 99 year-old man he was going to give him a son by which all the nations of the earth would be blessed. He was about to suspend the very laws He created. As El Shaddai, God reserves the right to reverse, suspend, prolong, or accelerate any natural law He has set in motion.

As the story goes, Sarah did conceive and Abraham became the father of many nations. When you get a revelation of El Shaddai, you will never stagger at the promises of God again. Like Abraham, you will be fully persuaded that what He promised He is also able to perform.

Today's Bible Reading Plan: 2 Chronicles 32:1-33:13 Romans 15:23-16:9; Psalm 25:16-22; Proverbs 20:16-18

My Father is El Shaddai,
the God who is more than enough for me.

August 3

YAHWEH, the Great I AM

And God said to Moses, "I AM WHO I AM," and He said … "This is My name forever, and this is My memorial to all generations."'

— *Exodus 3:14-15*

The letters in God's name tell a truly fascinating story. Everywhere in your Bible you see LORD in all capitals, it is God's personal name, Yahweh, which means I AM WHO I AM. The name Yahweh is embedded in your Bible almost 7,000 times, disguised as LORD. But there is an even greater revelation within the name of God when it is spelled out in ancient Hebrew pictographs. Yahweh is spelled Yod-Hey-Waw-Hey (YHWH). In Hebrew pictographs it is יהוה. (Hebrew is read right to left.)

The pictograph for Yod is a hand suspended in air. Hey resembles a window, meaning look or behold. Waw resembles a nail. When the letters of God's name are put together, the name YHWH יהוה declares, "The hand, behold; the nail, behold!" The Father's sacrifice of His Son, Jesus Christ, for our salvation is revealed in the very name of Yahweh! Behold the hand, behold the nail! In His name, God is saying – before anything was ever created – look to Jesus!

Today's Bible Reading Plan: 2 Chronicles 33:14-34:33 Romans 16:10-27; Psalm 26:1-12; Proverbs 20:19

Thank You for Salvation!

August 4

The Lamb of God

*Then Abraham lifted up his eyes and looked, and behind him
was a ram caught in a thicket by his horns. So Abraham went
and took the ram and offered him up as a burnt offering in the
place of his son.*

— Genesis 22:13

From Mount Moriah, you can see Golgotha, the
place of the skull, the site of Jesus' crucifixion in full
view. It is a foreshadowing of the just for the unjust.

It was to Mount Moriah that Abraham made the
three-day journey with his son, two servants, some
wood, and fire.

Yet they had no sacrifice.

When his son Isaac asked about the absence of an
offering, Abraham only responded, "God will provide
himself for a lamb." What Abraham did not disclose
was Jehovah had already told him to sacrifice his only
son, the promised heir from whom his descendants
and all nations of the earth were to be blessed.

Today's Bible Reading Plan: 2 Chronicles 35:1-36:23
1 Corinthians 1:1-17; Psalm 27:1-6; Proverbs 20:20-21

*I acknowledge that my need is
nothing but an illustration for You.*

August 5 ~ A Day with Joni

Ordinary to Extraordinary

But we have this treasure in earthen vessels…
— 2 Corinthians 4:7a

God never calls you to a task that fits. He always calls you beyond – to something beyond your strength, imagination, talent, and depth, because He wants you to trust him.

He delights in pouring living water from leaky clay pots. David didn't like much when he was tending sheep. It was God who called a shepherd to be king! Saul of Tarshish certainly didn't look like anybody's first choice to become missionary to the Gentiles. It was God who turned Saul into Paul!

What did Noah know of boat building? Zoo keeping? You get up in the morning and see an ordinary person in the mirror. That's wonderful! Your God calls ordinary people like you and me, forward to extraordinary ends. Don't dismiss God's voice calling you beyond "tasks that fit." Swallow. Take a breath. And say, "Here I am, Lord!" God always calls us to something greater than ourselves.

Today's Bible Reading Plan: Ezra 1:1-2:70
1 Corinthians 1:18-2:5; Psalm 27:7-14; Proverbs 20:22-23

You are Lord! You use the weak things of this world to confound the strong; the foolish things to confound the wise – it is all about You! I want to be about You. Give me courage to step forward when You call. Here I am, Lord. Send me.

226

August 6

Jehovah Shammah Is Present

After him was Shammah the son of Agee the Hararite. The Philistines had gathered into a troop, where the plot of the field was full of lentils, and the people fled before the Philistines. He took his stand in the midst of the plot of land, defended it, and defeated the Philistines. The LORD brought about a great victory.

— 2 Samuel 23:11-12

Shammah was an Israelite farmer who diligently tended the crops of his field. But every year at harvest time, the enemy showed up to steal his produce. This year, Shammah decided he would defend his property from the pillaging Philistines. The Philistines asked him who he thought he was. He took a step forward and shouted with a voice that reverberated off the mountains, "I am Shammah!"

Jehovah Shammah means *the Lord is there*, personally present. When Shammah announced his name, he was not telling his enemies who he was. He was telling them that the Lord of Hosts, the God of battles, had come to defend his field. Instead of shrinking from the conflict, we should run to the fight because God is with us. The Lord has anointed you to win.

Today's Bible Reading Plan: Ezra 3:1-4:23
1 Corinthians 2:6-3:4; Psalm 28:1-9; Proverbs 20:24-25

Praise God, for He is Jehovah Shammah!
I am never alone.

August 7

Jehovah Nissi My Banner

Then Moses built an altar and called the name of it,
The LORD Is My Banner…

— Exodus 17:15

Douglas MacArthur said, "It is fatal to enter any war without the will to win it." The Israelites faced an unprovoked attack from the Amalekites. When Moses held up his staff, Israel prevailed against their enemy; when he tired, then Amalek began to triumph. But Moses and the children of Israel never gave up. In the end, Israel prevailed, and Moses built an altar to God with the name Jehovah Nissi, which means "the Lord is our banner of victory."

Just as Moses and the Israelites won a great victory that day, Jesus did the same for us. As our Savior hung on an old rugged cross in mankind's darkest hour, even the disciples thought He was doomed to certain defeat. But His cry of "it is finished!" was a mighty declaration of victory for you and me.

God has given you the power to overcome every obstacle on the way to your victory. Don't give up! Persevere, trusting in the Lord, and you will prevail!

Today's Bible Reading Plan: Ezra 4:24-6:22
1 Corinthians 3:5-23; Psalm 29:1-11; Proverbs 20:26-27

I am promised victory, advancement and increase
because of what Christ has done for me.

August 8

Jehovah Shalom My Peace

Then Gideon built an altar for the LORD there and called it
The LORD Is Peace. Even to this day it stands in Ophrah of
the Abiezrites.

— Judges 6:24

Gideon was a young man living in a time when the Midianites oppressed his people. When the angel of the Lord appeared to him and called him a mighty man of valor, he retorted, "Are you talking to me?" He did not see himself the way God saw him. In his own eyes, he was from the weakest tribe and the runt of the litter. However, to the Lord, he was a mighty man. Facing such a momentous task, He soon discovered that Jehovah Shalom, the Lord of Peace, was with him.

Jesus' parting gift before His death was His peace (John 14:27). When you are filled with His Spirit, then His peace creates a sense of wellbeing and wholeness in spite of what is going on around you. This kind of peace is produced only by a supernatural knowledge, a revelation of God on a different level than perhaps you have ever known Him before.

Today's Bible Reading Plan: Ezra 7:1-8:20
1 Corinthians 4:1-21; Psalm 30:1-12; Proverbs 20:28-30

Lord, I praise You that You are my Peace,
my calm, restful assurance.

August 9

Sar Shalom, Prince of Peace

For He is our peace...

— Ephesians 2:14

It is easy to say you have peace when everything is going well. Yet in the middle of your greatest trials, you find out if you are truly relying on God's supernatural peace. When you are troubled on every side, distressed and cast down, you must be able to rest in the peace of God.

There is peace in the midst of your storm-tossed life. There is an anchor. There is a rock to build your faith upon. No matter what you may encounter, the Lord will be your Peace and He will bring you through to victory!

Jesus is the Prince of Peace, Sar Shalom, and He will sustain you through every trial and through every battle. Do not be afraid. The Lord is your wholeness and your completeness, and He is victorious!

Today's Bible Reading Plan: Ezra 8:21-9:15
1 Corinthians 5:1-13; Psalm 31:1-8; Proverbs 21:1-2

Jesus, my Prince of Peace, with You I have victory!

August 10

Jehovah Rapha My Healer

"For I am the LORD who heals you."

— Exodus 15:26b

After the Egyptian army was overthrown in the Red Sea, the Israelites encountered an obstacle they had not faced before. The water in the wilderness was contaminated and undrinkable. Moses cried unto the Lord, and God told him to cast a piece of wood into the water. Immediately, the bitter water became sweet. God showed Himself as Jehovah-Rapha, a Healer to the children of Israel, because He healed the waters.

Jesus revealed Himself as our Healer as He went to the cities and villages around Galilee *healing every sickness and every disease* (Matthew 9:35). When anyone was sick, they could depend upon Him for help and a cure.

God's desire for you is health. Healing is a benefit of salvation; but like salvation, it must be received by faith. Once you have a revelation of Jehovah Rapha – the Lord who heals all your diseases – then sickness and disease will never have power over you again.

Today's Bible Reading Plan: Ezra 10:1-44
1 Corinthians 6:1-20; Psalm 31:9-18; Proverbs 21:3

Lord, you are Jehovah Rapha, my Healer.

231

August 11

Jehovah Ropheka My Healer

God worked powerful miracles by the hands of Paul. So handkerchiefs or aprons he had touched were brought to the sick, and the diseases left them, and the evil spirits went out of them.

— Acts 19:11-12

Almighty God, Jehovah Ropheka, the eternally self-existent God who heals, gave me an incredible healing after the enemy attacked my vocal cord with cancer. Of all people to be attacked in that way, and of all the places I could have been attacked, who would have thought it would be me receiving this attack and in this way?

I am a preacher of the Gospel of Christ, and the enemy tried to silence my voice. Well, the enemy's plan did not succeed. I have been healed, and I am still preaching the Gospel of Christ with a seven times greater anointing than I had before!

If you are sick in your body, God is your Healer and your healing. Don't hesitate to call on Him to make you whole and complete. He is Jehovah Ropheka your Healer and Jehovah Shalom, the God who brings peace, wholeness and completeness, with nothing broken, nothing missing and nothing lacking.

Today's Bible Reading Plan: Nehemiah 1:1-3:14
1 Corinthians 7:1-24; Psalm 31:19-24: Proverbs 21:4

Because of You, Jehovah Joshua Messiah,
the enemy is defeated!

August 12 ~ A Day with Joni

My Will vs. His Will

Therefore, if any man is in Christ, he is a new creature. Old things have passed away. Look, all things have become new.

— 2 Corinthians 5:17

It's the epic battle of human history – man's will versus God's will. Let me ask you, Is your will David or Goliath?

The battle of wills is ongoing. In our humanness, we want what we want, and we want it now! Waaaahhh! We don't want to wait on the Lord. We want answers, blessings, and miracles like pulling up to a drive-through window. We want to have it our way!

It's human nature, but when we were born again, we were given a new nature – we were given His nature.

Our nature, the nature of self, has its own voice and will – this is what scripture refers to as the old things passed away. Behold the fresh and new you has come! It really is that simple. Stop wearing those old clothes! You've been given fresh, new garments!

Today's Bible Reading Plan: Nehemiah 3:15-5:13
1 Corinthians 7:25-40; Psalm 32:1-11

You make all things new – including my voice and my will. Father, help me to put off the old and to put on the new life and light You've provided. Help me reckon the old rubble, and the new, my garments of praise. In Jesus' name.

August 13

Jehovah Tsori My Strength

But the salvation of the righteous is of the LORD:
he is their strength in the time of trouble.

— Psalm 37:39 (KJV)

The name of God carries earth-shattering power. His name conveys His glory, His character and His irresistible strength.

God is strong when you are weak. It is through His strength that you can do all things (Philippians 4:13). Jehovah Tsori gives strength to the weary and power to the weak (Isaiah 40:29).

When you feel you cannot go one step further and your strength has completely failed, go to God and find strength.

Finally, my brothers, be strong in the Lord, and in the power of His might (Ephesians 6:10).

No matter what you face today, you can gain strength from Jehovah Tsori. He will not fail you. He will be your strong tower.

Today's Bible Reading Plan: Nehemiah 5:14-7:73
1 Corinthians 8:1-13; Psalm 33:1-11; Proverbs 21:8-10

Jehovah Tsori, You are my strength!

August 14

Jehovah Joshua

He said, "Neither, for I am the commander
of the army of the LORD. Now I have come."

— Joshua 5:14a

Just prior to the death of Moses, there was a changing of the guard. A new prophetic warrior was commissioned to take the children of Israel into the Promised Land. His name was Joshua, meaning, "Jehovah is salvation." He fulfilled his purpose and led the Children of Israel into the land, but they never fully drove out their adversaries.

Since the fall, man has been searching for peace and rest bearing the full weight of their sin, until an angel told a little virgin girl named, Mary, "You shall bear a son and call his name Jesus (Yeshua) Salvation!" His purpose was not to lead us into the Promised Land but into the land of promises!

Now you can ask in the name of Jesus, in the name of Salvation, for whatever you need. For at that name, all power is given to set the helpless captive free! Every pain, disease and sickness must bow to that name and forevermore surrender!

Today's Bible Reading Plan: Nehemiah 7:73-9:21
1 Corinthians 9:1-18; Psalm 33:12-22; Proverbs 21:11-12

I am an overcomer! With Jesus, the Captain of my
salvation, praying for me I will have freedom!

August 15

Jehovah Sabaoth
Lord of Hosts

This man went up out of his city annually to worship and to sacrifice to the LORD of Hosts in Shiloh.

— 1 Samuel 1:3a

From Samuel to Malachi, there are more than 200 references to the Lord of Hosts. Time and time again throughout the Old Testament, God's people petitioned Him for His help and praised Him for His deliverance.

As the Lord of Hosts, all power and authority in heaven and earth was given to Jesus (Matthew 28:18). He is the God of battles. The battle is not yours but the Lord's, and He never surrenders, and He never loses.

He is your burden bearer, Savior, Healer, Deliverer and victorious King! Don't hesitate to cry out to Him, today. There is no situation that you find yourself in today that is too small or too big for the Lord of Hosts to handle. He will hear and answer you, fight your battle, and He will be victorious!

Today's Bible Reading Plan: Nehemiah 9:22-10:39
1 Corinthians 9:19-10:13; Psalm 34:1-10; Proverbs 21:13

Lord God, I thank You that You are the Lord of Hosts, and You are with me. You are my refuge and strong tower.

August 16

Adonai My Lord

But Abram said, "Lord GOD, what will You give me, seeing I
am childless and the heir of my house is Eliezer of Damascus?"

— Genesis 15:2

When Abram called God "Lord" in this verse, the word in Hebrew is Adonai. Abram was recognizing God's complete rule and sovereignty over his life. Adonai comes from a root word meaning lord, sovereign, controller, master and owner.

Abram was not just calling God by a title. He was acknowledging God as supreme and that he was giving God complete control of his life. Abram was acknowledging that only God could do anything about his situation.

As we face obstacles in our lives, the first one we should turn to is God, the one who can take control and work all things together for good for those who love Him and are called according to His purpose (Romans 8:28).

Do not let the enemy intimidate you. He is not in control. Adonai Jehovah is in control, and He is sovereignly working on your behalf today and every day.

Today's Bible Reading Plan: Nehemiah 11:1-12:26
1 Corinthians 10:14-33; Psalm 34:11-22; Proverbs 21:14-16

Adonai, I give you full control of my life today!

August 17

Jehovah Goel My Redeemer

For I know that my Redeemer lives,
and He will stand at last on the earth…

— Job 19:25

Job had lost nearly everything. His cattle and children were gone. His houses were burned and boils covered his body. His wife pressed him to curse God and die. Yet standing in the midst of his ruined life, Job lifted his voice in praise!

Job had a revelation of whom he was serving and it was Jesus, his ever-living Redeemer. Job knew who He was without the help of a preacher, a prophet, a Sunday morning church service or a Christian program. He had a divine encounter with the One who would later invade Bethlehem's manger.

It is not enough to know what other people say about Jesus. You have to have an up-to-date revelation of Him for yourself, because He is risen and alive forevermore! When you do, regardless of what you encounter, you will have the faith to boldly proclaim, "I know my Redeemer liveth!"

Today's Bible Reading Plan: Nehemiah 12:27-13:31
1 Corinthians 11:1-16; Psalm 35:1-16; Proverbs 21:17-18

My Redeemer was resurrected
and He is alive forever in me.

August 18

Jehovah Rohi My Shepherd

The LORD is my shepherd…
Your rod and Your staff, they comfort me.

— Psalm 23:1, 4b

The Shepherd's staff had two purposes. Firstly, it was used as a weapon of protection against predators. In Israel, there are narrow passageways for the sheep to go through to find pasture. At the end of those narrow passages, predators waited to snatch the sheep as they came out the other side. So the shepherd passed through the passageway first, and with his rod and staff, he drove the animals away, so the sheep could safely follow him into the pasture.

Secondly, the crook was used to comfort and give security to the sheep. With it, the shepherd gently nudged wandering sheep back into place whenever they would stray away from the security of the sheepfold. The shepherd knew there were wild beasts waiting to kill any sheep that became lost and alone.

In much the same way, Jesus, as our Shepherd, went before us and drove back every enemy waiting to seize us. Do not fear, for Jehovah Rohi has preceded you into the future and prepared the way for you.

Today's Bible Reading Plan: Esther 1:1-3:15
1 Corinthians 11:17-34; Psalm 35:17-28; Proverbs 21:19-20

I trust Jehovah Rohi for comfort
and protection every day.

239

August 19 ~ A Day with Joni

Are You Ready?

Always be ready to give an answer to every man who asks you for a reason for the hope that is in you…
— 1 Peter 3:15b

Boy Scouts have nothing on moms. "Be prepared" is a motto to them. It's a way of life for us! Peter admonishes us to "always be ready to give a defense" of the gospel. Have you ever taken a few minutes to consider the most concise way you can share Christ with someone today should the opportunity arise?

We should be prepared! Our world is spiritually hungry. People are looking for answers. Only the gospel can truly satisfy. We have the message and we are surrounded with need. Shouldn't we prepare ourselves for those opportunities? Imagine before you two plates – on one all the ingredients that go into a loaf of homemade bread. On the other, a golden loaf, just out of the oven. Which is more appetizing?

Put the ingredients together. Think through what you'd say. Maybe write out your testimony. Be prepared. If someone needed a safety pin or a needle and thread in a pinch, chances are a mom could produce it in a heartbeat. What if someone needs Jesus – and they bump into you?

Today's Bible Reading Plan: Esther 4:1-7:10
1 Corinthians 12:1-26; Psalm 36:1-12; Proverbs 21:21-22

Almighty God, You know the day before me. You know every Divine encounter I will have. Lord, help me be prepared – to call to mind and memory quickly my testimony and to be able to articulate Your love. Then bump me into the people who need You. Prepare me – and use me, I pray.

August 20

Jehovah M'Kaddesh
My Sanctifier

Therefore, "Come out from among them and be separate, says the Lord. Do not touch what is unclean, and I will receive you."

— 2 Corinthians 6:17

There are three levels of sanctification. Positional sanctification occurs when a person accepts Jesus as their personal Savior, and they are translated from the kingdom of darkness into the kingdom of light.

Ultimate sanctification happens at the rapture of the church when the elect of God are separated from this world and united with Jesus.

Experiential sanctification is an ongoing process of submission and separation to the Holy Spirit's work in your life. Paul referred to it as presenting our bodies as a living sacrifice to God whereby we are not conformed to this world but transformed by the renewing of our minds (Romans 12:1-2).

Purity and power will be the mark of the end-time believer who completely surrenders to our Sanctifier. Consecrate yourself and you will see the miraculous.

Today's Bible Reading Plan: Esther 8:1-10:3
1 Corinthians 12:27-13:13; Psalm 37:1-11;
Proverbs 21:23-24

I take spiritual inventory of my life. May the Holy Spirit sanctify and cleanse my heart of all impurities.

241

August 21

Jehovah Kanna Is Jealous

…(for you shall not worship any other god, for the LORD,
whose name is Jealous, is a jealous God)…

— Exodus 34:14

God is jealous over us with a burning jealously. He does not want us to have divided interests. In the time of Moses, the Israelites were just as likely to worship Jehovah as Baal or Asherah. Today, more than likely, believers do not have physical idols in their homes, but they still may have an unholy alliance between God and the world.

The Father's jealousy aggressively pursued us with a love that climbed every mountain, bridged every chasm, went to the heights of the summit, and to the depths of despair. This kind of holy jealously is what caused the Father to send His own flesh and blood, Jesus Christ, to die, rise again, and redeem you and me back to a place where He could wrap His arms around us and say we belong to Him. The Lord loves you with an unconditional love, and He wants your unwavering devotion and love also.

Today's Bible Reading Plan: Job 1:1-3:26
1 Corinthians 14:1-17; Psalm 37:12-29; Proverbs 21:25-26

> *Today, I make the decision to serve You*
> *in singleness of heart. I will love the Lord*
> *with all my heart, mind, soul and strength.*

August 22

Jehovah Machsi My Refuge

Because you have made the LORD, who is my refuge,
even the Most High, your dwelling,
there shall be no evil befall you,
neither shall any plague come near your tent…

— Psalm 91:9-10

Under the Old Covenant, God dwelt in the Ark of the Covenant made by men. But when Jesus died and rose again, the Most High no longer dwelt in temples made with hands (Acts 7:48). Instead, He took up residence in the earthen vessels of His beloved children.

If God lives in you now, then so does His anointing; therefore, His anointing becomes your place of refuge because the Lord Jesus Christ is always present with you. Every time you encounter trials, begin to exercise your faith by calling on the name of Jehovah Machsi and declare, "God is my Refuge."

You are promised protection from the evil schemes of Satan. In your darkest hour of adversity, God will be your Refuge, and He will be your lifeline to bring you safely into a place of protection.

Today's Bible Reading Plan: Job 4:1-7:21
1 Corinthians 14:18-40; Psalm 37:30-40; Proverbs 21:27

Lord, You are my Refuge, and I trust in You alone!

August 23

Jehovah Magen My Shield

Behold, O God our shield,
and look upon the face of Your anointed.

— Psalm 84:9

There is a place in God you can get to where the evil one cannot touch you. Why? Jesus, Jehovah Magen, is your Shield! You are protected by the Anointed One and saturated in His anointing.

In Jehovah Magen, you have a mighty shield of faith. You can deflect the fiery darts of the wicked one, and you can stand and declare the powerful promises of God's Word from your mouth.

Jesus has given *you authority to trample on serpents and scorpions, and over all the power of the enemy. And nothing shall by any means harm you* (Luke 10:19). You are drenched in a powerful anointing, and you can escape sin's grasp.

Jesus is Jehovah Magen, your Shield! He shields you when the enemy plots his greatest onslaught against you.

Today's Bible Reading Plan: Job 8:1-11:20
1 Corinthians 15:1-28; Psalm 38:1-22; Proverbs 21:28-29

Jesus, You are my Shield. You surround me
with Your presence and the evil one touches me not.

August 24

Jehovah Ma'oz My Fortress

O LORD, my strength and my fortress,
and my refuge in the day of affliction...

— Jeremiah 16:19a

Our God is a mighty fortress against every attack of the adversary. As we stand unwaveringly in Jehovah Ma'oz, the church is a fortified garrison holding fast and raising the standard of God.

We are fortified by the anointing of the Holy Spirit, and we will not be defeated!

We belong to God, and we are impenetrable to the alien armies of the antichrist. We are heavily protected by Jehovah Ma'oz, our mighty fortress!

The LORD is good, a stronghold in the day of distress; and He knows those who take refuge in Him. (Nahum 1:7).

We will not bow, and we will not bend under the weight and intensity of the battle. Victory belongs to our God alone!

Today's Bible Reading Plan: Job 12:1-15:35
1 Corinthians 15:29-58; Psalm 39:1-13;
Proverbs 21:30-31

Jehovah Ma'oz, my mighty fortress will stand forever!

August 25

Jehovah HaMelech Olam
Lord King Forever

The LORD is King forever and ever;
the nations perished from His land.

— Psalm 10:16

Many perceive Jesus much the same as the pictures you might remember from Sunday school. He has long brown hair and a beard, wears a long flowing robe and sandals. Add to this a yellow glowing light around His head, and show Him holding a little lamb. However, we do not serve a baby wrapped in swaddling clothes and laid in a manger. We serve the King of kings and Lord of lords, with the keys of death and hell in His hand!

Jesus is returning not as a suffering servant but as a reigning King! God is passionately calling His church to abandonment, so that we may usher in the greatest harvest of souls the world has ever seen, before our Savior's soon return. Consequently, Jesus must be Lord of all or not Lord at all.

Is Jesus ruling in every area of your life? Have you submitted to His lordship?

Today's Bible Reading Plan: Job 16:1-19:29
1 Corinthians 16:1-24; Psalm 40:1-10; Proverbs 22:1

I yield to the sovereignty of Jesus, my Lord and King.

August 26 ~ A Day with Joni

A Look in the Mirror

Charm is deceitful, and beauty is vain,
but a woman who fears the LORD, she shall be praised.
— Proverbs 31:30

There are pros and cons to getting older, let's face it. Well, speaking of faces, that's one of the cons. Sometimes, I look in the mirror and study my face like a science project and ask myself, "What the heck happened? Where did the pretty young lady go?"

And mirrors? Have you been in a dressing room lately? What's the deal with the three-way fat mirrors? Honestly, I don't want to see myself at every angle. Certain body parts aren't where they used to be, and I don't need nor want to see it all showcased!

As I reflect on my younger years, I marvel at how age has changed me. I am more serious, but comfortable, much like my shoes. I used to wear stilettos and didn't care that they hurt my feet. Now, I try on shoes for comfort, not looks, and … "Ahh!"

Wisdom comes with age, my friend! And I realize, now, as the scriptures declare, charm and beauty are fleeting. What matters – and what lasts – is my relationship with my God. It never goes out of style. It never gets old. It just gets sweeter and sweeter with age!

Today's Bible Reading Plan: Job 20:1-22:30
2 Corinthians 1:1-11; Psalm 40:11-17; Proverbs 22:2-4

Your Word declares that gray hair is splendor. I don't want to think about that! But it is true, Lord – aging offers us a chance to see wisdom's fruit in our lives. Draw me close, I pray. May my beauty be seen in my devotion to You! Amen.

August 27

Jehovah Misqabbi
My High Tower

For You have been a refuge for me,
and a strong tower from the enemy.

— Psalm 61:3

Jehovah Misqabbi is a High Tower, where we can safely run when we are overwhelmed by our circumstances. When we hasten to God, He will do more than merely provide a hiding place from our adversary, He will set us on high. In the Tower of the Lord, the invading enemy army looks like ants from the height of where we stand. On the walls of the High Tower, we are lifted high above the fiery darts of temptations, trials, slander, separation and sickness. From this precipice, we are hidden in the name of Jehovah Misqabbi, secure from all harm.

When you get off base, you can always run back to Jehovah Misqabbi. There is safety in His presence. There is security in His name.

Today's Bible Reading Plan: Job 23:1-27:23
2 Corinthians 1:12-2:11; Psalm 41:1-13; Proverbs 22:5-6

You are my High Tower I run to;
You set me safely on high.

August 28

Jehovah 'Ori My Light

The LORD is my light and my salvation; whom will I fear? The LORD is the strength of my life; of whom will I be afraid?

— Psalm 27:1

Jehovah 'Ori is your light. When you walk with Him, His light shines in you and through you. Jesus said, *"You are the light of the world. A city that is set on a hill cannot be hidden"* (Matthew 5:14).

Unless God shines through you, you cannot shine; however when you exhibit His light, you will affect the people around you.

Even a small ray of light can pierce the darkness; but if a light is turned off and hidden away, it is of no use. Instead, *"Let your light so shine before men that they may see your good works and glorify your Father who is in heaven"* (Matthew 5:16).

Let Jehovah 'Ori light your path and illuminate your life. *God is light, and in Him is no darkness at all … But if we walk in the light as He is in the light, we have fellowship one with another, and the blood of Jesus Christ His Son cleanses us from all sin* (1 John 1:5, 7).

Today's Bible Reading Plan: Job 28:1-30:31
2 Corinthians 2:12-17; Psalm 42:1-11; Proverbs 22:7

> *Jehovah Ori, shine brightly through me and pierce the darkness of this chaotic, dark world.*

August 29

Jehovah Perazim
My Breakthrough

So David came to Baal Perazim, and David defeated them there. He said, "The LORD has breached my enemies before me like bursting tides." Therefore, he named that place Baal Perazim.

— 2 Samuel 5:20

Often, we are so busy trying to make it day to day that we do not seem to gain any spiritual ground. We seem to blindly accept the wall of problems the enemy has erected against us instead of bursting through.

Rather than bow to the dictates of a spiritual oppressor, we need to destroy the barrier Satan has erected between God's promises and us through the power of His Word, because we serve Jehovah Perazim, the Lord of the Breakthrough!

Rest today knowing the Lord is the Master of the Breach. The battle is not yours but His. The anointing can break you through every stronghold your adversary has raised against you. You can burst forth into a greater dimension in God than you ever believed was even possible.

Today's Bible Reading Plan: Job 31:1-33:33
2 Corinthians 3:1-18; Psalm 43:1-5; Proverbs 22:8-9

Jesus, You are the Lord of my breakthrough.

250

August 30

Jehovah Sel'l My Rock

The LORD is my pillar, and my fortress, and my deliverer;
my God, my rock, in whom I take refuge;
my shield, and the horn of my salvation, my high tower.

— Psalm 18:2

Jesus asked the disciples, "Who do men say that I am?" (Matthew 16:13) Jesus was not asking His disciples these questions because He was having doubts about who He was. He knew exactly who He was, who His Father was and what His mission was. The reason He asked His disciples these questions was He was building something, not a physical building but a people, a church, called by His name!

Peter saw through the eyes of the Spirit. He had a revelation, or revealed knowledge, that Jesus was in fact God Himself, wrapped in humanity. All power in heaven and earth was given unto Him because He was the Son of Man.

The "Rock" Jesus referred to was a revelation of who He was, and His Church would be built as the result of receiving this revealed knowledge of Him. Upon this rock of revelation the very gates of hell would not prevail.

Today's Bible Reading Plan: Job 34:1-36:33
2 Corinthians 4:1-12; Psalm 44:1-8; Proverbs 22:10-12

Jesus, You are my Rock and my Salvation!

August 31

Jesus (Yeshua) My Savior

"She will bear a Son, and you shall call His name JESUS,
for He will save His people from their sins."

— *Matthew 1:21*

The name of Jesus is the English transliteration of the Hebrew name Yeshua. If you look up word H3444 in Strong's Concordance, it is yeshuwah and the definition is literally salvation, healing, deliverance, help, aid, victory, prosperity, security and well-being. The name Jesus describes every name of Jehovah.

When the angel of the Lord appeared to Joseph, he told him that he and Mary were to name the child Jesus (Yeshua), which literally means Salvation. Yeshua was not a random name. The Father named His Son Salvation, because Yeshua was going to save His people from their sins.

If we were to translate the word salvation into Hebrew, it would be Yeshua. Jesus is a transliteration, a conversion and matching of similar Hebrew letters to English letters. But if we were to do a strict translation of Yeshua into English, it would be Salvation. Salvation is His name! When you call on Jesus, you're calling on Salvation. Speak His name often today!

Today's Bible Reading Plan: Job 37:1-39:30
2 Corinthians 4:13-5:10; Psalm 44:9-26; Proverbs 22:13

I have power in Your mighty name, Yeshua!

SEPTEMBER

Repentance Is a Good Thing

Therefore repent and be converted, that your sins may be wiped away, that times of refreshing may come from the presence of the Lord, and that He may send the One who previously was preached to you, Jesus Christ, whom the heavens must receive until the time of restoring what God spoke through all His holy prophets since the world began.

— Acts 3:19-21

September 1

A Way of Life

Do you despise the riches of His goodness,
tolerance, and patience, not knowing that
the goodness of God leads you to repentance?

— *Romans 2:4*

Repentance is not a negative message, but one of covenant blessing. When you allow your heart to indulge in lust, pride, rebellion or selfishness, you cut yourself off from His covenant.

Sin does not destroy God's love for us; He loves us with a love that is incorruptible (Romans 5:8), but you can go to hell with God still loving you. Just as confession is more than lip service to God, salvation is more than forgiveness of your sins. It is a lifestyle in which you choose to become God's own possession. The only way you can ever enter into His covenant and stay in that covenant is to love Him with all your heart and have no idols before Him.

If God is not first in everything, you need to change your mind about God and turn toward God. Then and only then will your heart be free to abandon itself to loving Him.

Today's Bible Reading Plan: Job 40:1-42:17
2 Corinthians 5:11-21; Psalm 45:1-17; Proverbs 22:14

Holy Spirit, convict me of sin and
convince me of righteousness so that
I live my life wholly and completely for God.

September 2 ~ A Day with Joni

Family Resemblance

He must increase, but I must decrease.

— *Psalm 19:1*

This is His plan. We are to cultivate God's nature in us. He is to become more prominent; we must grow less so.

How do you become like someone? An actor studies a person, spends time with that person, and works at developing and adopting his or her mannerisms and behaviors in order to capture that persona for their audience.

That's not a bad metaphor. We want to develop and adopt our God's persona. We need to spend time with and study Him to grow in His likeness. And, make no mistake, the watching world is our audience. They want to see God.

His will more evident; my self-will shrinking. His love growing; my selfishness diminishing. His mercy, grace, forgiveness and hope embodied before their eyes – Imagine if we bore such a strong resemblance to our Father the world could see Him in and through us!

Today's Bible Reading Plan: Ecclesiastes 1:1-3:22
2 Corinthians 6:1-13; Psalm 46:1-11; Proverbs 22:15

Almighty God, I am thankful You created me in Your image. I want to more clearly and strongly bear Your likeness, Your character, Your heart. Will You draw me closer? Impress more of You upon me, I pray. In Jesus' name.

September 3

The Gift of Repentance

...and saying, "Repent, for the kingdom of heaven is at hand."
For this is he who was spoken of by the prophet Isaiah, saying:
"The voice of one crying in the wilderness: 'Prepare the way of
the Lord; make His paths straight.'"

— Matthew 3:2-3

Repentance does not mean making a slight change in course. It is a 180-degree turn. You cannot turn away from something without turning toward something. God not only delivers you <u>from</u>, He delivers you <u>to</u>. When He delivered the children of Israel, He delivered them <u>from</u> Egyptian bondage and <u>to</u> the Promised Land. When we repent, we turn away from our former ways, leaving them behind, as we turn to live for God.

Imagine that God has set before you a dish of dog food and a T-bone steak. He points to the dog food and says, "That is what you have been eating." Then he points to the steak and says, "This is what you can have. The choice is yours."

Today's Bible Reading Plan: Ecclesiastes 4:1-6:12
2 Corinthians 6:14-7:7; Psalm 47:1-9; Proverbs 22:16

Thank you, Lord God, for the gift of repentance.

September 4

Labor Day

For you shall eat the fruit of the labor of your hands;
you will be happy, and it shall be well with you.

— *Psalm 128:2*

During this Labor Day, we thank those who work every day, laboring in jobs all across our nation, jobs that enrich our lives: waiters and waitresses who serve those who are hungry, factory workers who help produce the goods that we consume, truck drivers who make sure those goods get to their destination, those who work in offices and make our lives run a little smoother, and many, many more.

We thank the millions of people who labor and keep our nation running strong and who contribute to the prosperity and well-being of our country. But we know the source of it all is Almighty God who has truly blessed us with the many things we enjoy each and every day.

God has abundantly provided for us here in America. We know without a doubt that it is our heavenly Father who provides every good and perfect gift from above (James 1:17).

Today's Bible Reading Plan: Ecclesiastes 7:1-9:18
2 Corinthians 7:8-16; Psalm 48:1-14; Proverbs 22:17-19

Holy Spirit, help me to recognize and appreciate
the unsung heroes in the workforce,
who make my day run a little smoother.

September 5

Believe the Gospel

…saying, "The time is fulfilled, and the kingdom of God is at hand. Repent and believe the gospel."

— *Mark 1:15*

True repentance means you change the way you think and act. Repentance is not just saying you are sorry for something or feeling bad that you did something wrong. If I repent of vulgar language, I change my mind about vulgarity. I no longer think it is clever or funny to be vulgar. It becomes repulsive to me, and I change my behavior.

The Holy Spirit convicts us when we do something that offends our Lord. He makes us aware of the harm it does, especially to our brothers and sisters in the kingdom. We no longer live under the old way of doing things. We have been born again and are being changed day by day into the image of our King!

When God delivers you, He will never deliver you from something good to something bad. He is a God of increase, not decrease. When He delivers you, you will always take a turn for the better! This is why the Bible says that it is the goodness – not the meanness – of God that leads you to repentance.

Today's Bible Reading Plan: Ecclesiastes 10:1-12:14 2 Corinthians 8:1-15; Psalm 49:1-20; Proverbs 22:20-21

Holy Spirit, thank you for renewing my mind each day.

258

September 6

Turn to God

...if My people, who are called by My name, will humble
themselves and pray, and seek My face and turn from their
wicked ways, then I will hear from heaven, and will forgive
their sin and will heal their land.

— *2 Chronicles 7:14*

When we individually repent and begin living our lives to bring glory and honor to Almighty God, then we, as a nation, can turn back to God. When we, as believers, turn from pornography, the pornographers will go out of business.

When we, as believers, denounce racism, the nation will reject racism. Sunday morning is still the most segregated day of the week, as Christians segregate into one racial group or another as they head off to their houses of worship.

When we, as believers, do not have the same percentage of divorces as the world, we will begin to build strong, godly families.

We who are called by God's name need to humble ourselves, pray, seek His face and turn from evil. Then He will hear us, forgives us and heal our land.

Today's Bible Reading Plan: Song of Songs 1:1-4:16
2 Corinthians 8:16-24; Psalm 50:1-23; Proverbs 22:22-23

Jehovah Joshua Messiah, we turn to You to heal our land.

September 7

You Have a Choice to Make

See, I am setting before you today a blessing and a curse: the blessing if you obey the commandments of the LORD your God, which I am commanding you today, and the curse, if you will not obey the commandments of the LORD your God, but turn from the way which I am commanding you today, to go after other gods which you have not known.

— Deuteronomy 11:26-28

The choice seems very obvious between blessing and cursing, but to some it is not such an obvious choice. To some it is not clear that the life of a child begins in the womb and that it is a blessing to bring life into the world. They don't consider it a curse to snuff out that child's life in its mother's womb.

To some it is not clear that homosexuality is an abomination to God. *If a man lies with another man as with a woman, both of them have committed an abomination. They shall surely be put to death. Their blood guilt shall be upon them.* (Leviticus 20:13). The enemy deceives people into thinking it is just an alternative lifestyle.

Our Creator knows what true blessing is, because it is He who created us, and He is trying to extend to us the way of abundant life.

Today's Bible Reading Plan: Song of Songs 5:1-8:14 2 Corinthians 9:1-15; Psalm 51:1-19; Proverbs 22:24-25

Holy Spirit, reveal to me each day the true blessings of God.

260

September 8

Choose Life

I call heaven and earth to witnesses against you this day, that I have set before you life and death, blessing and curse. Therefore choose life, that both you and your descendants may live…

— Deuteronomy 30:19

When we seek the Holy Spirit, He gives us wisdom to make the right choices each day. God gave Adam and Eve everything and gave them one very important instruction: *"Of every tree of the garden you may freely eat, but of the tree of the knowledge of good and evil you shall not eat, for in the day that you eat from it you will surely die"* (Genesis 2:16-17).

But Satan, as he always does, tried to thwart God's plan and said: *"You surely will not die! For God knows that on the day you eat of it your eyes will be opened and you will be like God, knowing good and evil"* (Genesis 3:4).

Adam and Eve made the mistake of thinking life would be better if they knew the difference between good and evil themselves. People are still making that mistake today, thinking they know what is right or wrong, based on their desires. We must repent, change the way we think and act, so that we believe God, not the enemy and our own lustful flesh.

Today's Bible Reading Plan: Isaiah 1:1-2:22
2 Corinthians 10:1-18; Psalm 52:1-9; Proverbs 22:26-27

Holy Spirit, help me bring glory and honor to Jehovah Joshua Messiah by the choices that I make each day.

261

September 9 ~ A Day with Joni

Victim or Victor

But thanks be to God, who gives us the victory
through our Lord Jesus Christ!
— 1 Corinthians 15:57

To be a victim is to always point the finger and to blame another. I prefer, regardless of the circumstances, the word victor. I am a victor. That word conveys strength, determination, fortitude, and good old fashion grit. We are not victims of anything; we are victorious! We made it through one valley after another and, once again, we can breathe. We rise, ready for the next challenge.

Victims look to everyone else to rescue and repair. Victors depend on God. Victors are endowed, while victims are enabled and entitled.

Victims long for happiness. Victors rely on joy because it brings strength. Happiness depends on happenings – and is fleeting. Joy, on the other hand, always has a source, and we know who that source is.

We get happy but we have joy. What words are you using in your heart today? Victim? Victor? Perspective really does make a big difference.

Today's Bible Reading Plan: Isaiah 3:1-5:30
2 Corinthians 11:1-15; Psalm 53:1-6; Proverbs 22:28-29

You are Jehovah Nissi – the Lord my banner! Victory is in You! Lord, please help me remember this truth today, especially as I encounter difficulties. Your plans cannot be thwarted. Grant me the joy of my salvation, found resting in You, victorious, this day and always. Amen.

September 10

New Beginnings

In the beginning God created the heavens and the earth.

— Genesis 1:1

The very first page of the Bible can change your mind. In fact, the very first line can change your mind. The first four words alone can revolutionize your entire walk with God!

"In the beginning God…" He is already in the second that has not yet occurred. When that second arrives, He will already be there waiting for you. Before any defeat, distress, sorrow, pain or discouragement, God is there, and He is in control.

Every second brings an opportunity for a new beginning. Allow Him to take control of that second, and the next, and the next. Allow God to become bigger than the pain you felt in the last moment, and in that moment you will begin anew with Him. Make every day matter by giving Him control of every second of every day.

Today's Bible Reading Plan: Isaiah 6:1-7:25
2 Corinthians 11:16-33; Psalm 54:1-7; Proverbs 23:1-3

Lord God, I give my days, moments and seconds to You so that You can receive glory and honor in my daily life.

September 11

Who Will You Believe?

And without faith it is impossible to please God,
for he who comes to God must believe that He exists
and that He is a rewarder of those who diligently seek Him.

— *Hebrews 11:6*

Sometimes when we are confronted by the cares of the world, we find ourselves believing in a god who is different from the God of the Bible. We may account for the sad and bewildering moments of our lives by deciding God is not who He says He is.

Change your mind! Believe in Him! Believe He is exactly who He has revealed Himself to be. The God of the Bible always hears and answers your prayers. The God of the Bible does not fail. The God of the Bible does not cower in the presence of the devil and will never leave nor forsake you.

He is the God of victory. He is the God of battles, the Lord of Hosts. He never surrenders, never has surrendered, and never will surrender.

In the next second He can lift your burden, and in the next minute He can heal your body. He can give you the miracle you have been believing for your entire life, if you will only take Him at His Word.

Today's Bible Reading Plan: Isaiah 8:1-9:21
2 Corinthians 12:1-10; Psalm 55:1-23; Proverbs 23:4-5

Lord Jesus Christ, You are the
God who is awesome in power!

September 12

Renew Your Mind

...that you put off the former way of life in the old nature, which is corrupt according to the deceitful lusts, and be renewed in the spirit of your mind; and that you put on the new nature, which was created according to God in righteousness and true holiness.

— Ephesians 4:22-24

God's will for us is to prosper and be in health in every aspect of our being: in our spirit, soul and body (3 John 2).

Our soul is comprised of our intellect (or our mind), our will and our emotions. God wants us to be prosperous and in perfect health in every one of these areas. There is no aspect of our lives for which He hasn't already made provision.

In order to prosper in our soul, our mind, will and emotions, we must renew our mind by the Word of God (Romans 12:1-2).

Believers must change their way of thinking concerning blessing and health as part of the total salvation package for which Jesus suffered and died to provide the body of Christ.

Today's Bible Reading Plan: Isaiah 10:1-11:16
2 Corinthians 12:11-21; Psalm 56:1-13; Proverbs 23:6-8

Holy Spirit, help me change my way of thinking about God's will on health and prosperity.

September 13

Perfect Love

There is no fear in love, but perfect love casts out fear,
because fear has to do with punishment.
Whoever fears is not perfect in love.

— 1 John 4:18

Perfect faith cannot exist where there is doubt regarding God's will for prosperity and healing.

Fear will keep you from stepping into the untapped realm of God's blessing and trap you into a prolonged present where the vicious cycle of lack never ends.

But where the will of God is known, faith comes alive and fear dies: the Father's will is total prosperity and complete health.

Therefore guard your minds, be sober, and hope to the end for the grace that is to be brought to you at the revelation of Jesus Christ (1 Peter 1:13).

Do not be afraid to trust in God's love for you. His desire is to bless you, not to curse you. *For all the promises of God in Him are "Yes," and in Him "Amen," to the glory of God through us* (2 Corinthians 1:20). All the promises of God are yes and amen!

Today's Bible Reading Plan: Isaiah 12:1-14:32
2 Corinthians 13:1-14; Psalm 57:1-11; Proverbs 23:9-11

Thank you, Jehovah Joshua Messiah,
for all of Your many promises which
you have already willed to give to Your children.

September 14

You Are Not Stuck

Isaiah the prophet called to the LORD, and He made
the shadow go back ten steps on the stairs of Ahaz.

— *2 Kings 20:11*

As mentioned previously, repent means to turn. You are not stuck in your circumstances. You can turn to God and receive deliverance.

There is a divinely ordained moment in time, destined by God to change everything in your life. For Hezekiah, it came when Isaiah delivered the message of his impending death.

Hezekiah could have thrown up his hands and accepted his fate. Instead, he turned his face toward the wall and prayed. God heard Hezekiah's prayers and added fifteen years to his life. God has everything under control, even time. As a sign to Hezekiah, God made the sun stand still and changed time forever.

It was not God's best for Hezekiah to die. He had more for him to do. In the next fifteen years, he delivered Jerusalem from evil King Sennacherib; and, he had a son through whom would continue the lineage of the Messiah.

Today's Bible Reading Plan: Isaiah 15:1-18:7
Galatians 1:1-24; Psalm 58:1-11; Proverbs 23:12

You are the God who steps into my present
and changes my future forever for your glory.

267

September 15

Turning Changes You Forever

"The people who sat in darkness saw great light.
And on those who sat in the land of the shadow of death,
light has dawned."

— *Matthew 4:16*

At the intersection of a timeless God with temporal man, you will find the point of transition where now becomes forever. The same thing happened at Calvary. When our Lord died on the cross, all that had been undone by the curse of sin and separation changed forever. Salvation brought restoration of humanity's relationship to God – a return to the original state of affairs.

When you turn from darkness to light, there is a great awakening! You are no longer comfortable with the status quo. You become uncomfortable with an entire generation of so-called believers who are completely ill-equipped to engage the culture outside our church doors.

I believe your time has come. You stand at the crossroads where God's super invades your natural, and you are forever changed by the hand of the Lord.

Today's Bible Reading Plan: Isaiah 19:1-21:17
Galatians 2:1-16; Psalm 59:1-17; Proverbs 23:13-14

Holy Spirit, let Your supernatural power
invade my life in dynamic demonstration today!

268

September 16 ~ A Day with Joni

Resolve

I will arise and go to my father...
— Luke 15:18

You know the story of the prodigal son. He comes to this point where he makes a foundational resolution – he decides to return home, "I will arise and go."

Beloved, two words are necessary for change: *I will*.

Think about it. The prodigal would have missed out on the restored relationship with his father if he hadn't resolved to return home. Daniel would have never risen to power had he not resolved to honor God over Nebuchadnezzar. Blind Bartimaeus would not have been healed had he not resolved – against the insistence of the crowd – to cry out to Jesus.

Spiritual indecision is a jailer. Don't run from resolute faith. Run to it! Set goals, seek the help of the Lord, step out in faith, and celebrate the victory. Or ... you can just keep feeding the pigs and dreaming of what might have been. The apostle Paul said, "I can do all things through Christ who gives me strength." People who trust the Lord saying, "I can" and "I will" become, by His grace, people who say "I am" and "I did."

Today's Bible Reading Plan: Isaiah 22:1-24:23
Galatians 2:17-3:9; Psalm 60:1-12; Proverbs 23:15-16

My Heavenly Father, grant me a growing faith today. I want to experience Your strength in my weakness. I don't want to miss out on the very best You have in store for me, today and every day. Thank you, Lord.

September 17

Always & Forever

"I am the Alpha and the Omega,
the Beginning and the End," says the Lord,
"who is and who was and who is to come, the Almighty."

— *Revelation 1:8*

Life is filled with variables. All around us everything is changing. Technology changes at such a drastic pace that your computer and mobile devices are already outdated within a few months. Fads and fashions come and go. Our bodies age with every tick of the clock. Seasons, circumstances, feelings and fortunes can change without notice. The Lord Jesus Christ, however, remains the same perfect, loving, faithful God. *Every good gift and every perfect gift is from above and comes down from the Father of lights, with whom is no change or shadow of turning.* (James 1:17).

God is eternal. He has no beginning of days nor ending of life. When the earth was without form and when darkness covered the earth, God existed. Men change, doctrines change, ideals change, but God never changes! He was, is and will forever be perfect!

Today's Bible Reading Plan: Isaiah 25:1-28:13
Galatians 3:10-22; Psalm 61:1-8; Proverbs 23:17-18

How precious to me is the blessed assurance
that You, Jesus, are the Lord God who does not change!

September 18

You Can Change a Culture

Preach the word, be ready in season and out of season, reprove, rebuke, and exhort, with all patience and teaching.

— *2 Timothy 4:2*

Using the Greeks' altar dedicated to the Unknown God as a backdrop, Paul was able to capture and hold the attention of the men of the city of Athens. He found a way to effectively communicate the gospel.

The Apostle Paul gave the crowd at Mars' Hill an opportunity to consider their deep-rooted beliefs. With eloquent and well-chosen words, he proclaimed Jesus Christ, the man God ordained as Savior of the world, and His resurrection to the Gentiles.

The Holy Spirit will give you the right words at the right moment to speak into the life of a person that will affect change, repentance within them. Paul saw immediate effects of his preaching through some who believed, namely Dionysius the Areopagite, a woman named Damaris, and others with them (Acts 17:34).

You may not see an immediate harvest as a result of obediently sharing the love of Jesus, but you will have begun the process of planting the Word in someone's heart, and God will bring the increase of eternal life.

Today's Bible Reading Plan: Isaiah 28:14-30:11
Galatians 3:23-4:31; Psalm 62:1-12; Proverbs 23:19-21

*I will obediently share the message
of Jesus today and every day.*

September 19

God's Plan

I'll give you a new heart, put a new spirit in you.
I'll remove the stone heart from your body and replace it with a
heart that's God-willed, not self-willed. I'll put my Spirit in you
and make it possible for you to do what I tell you
and live by my commands.

— Ezekiel 36:26 (MSG)

God had a plan that would produce such radical change that its inward workings would generate miraculous outward results. In Christ, we have been made into a new creation (2 Corinthians 5:17). The old life and its desires are gone. He cleanses us and replaces our hearts of stone with hearts of flesh. Then the Lord puts His Spirit – His breath, His life – within us, and His Spirit enables us to walk in His statutes.

We are no longer dead in our trespasses and sins. We are born again by the Spirit of the living God, enabled to obey His Word, and empowered to fulfill His calling upon our lives. You can experience the power of a new life in your everyday walk with God. Obey the leading of His Spirit and your heart will remain responsive to Him.

Today's Bible Reading Plan: Isaiah 30:12-33:9
Galatians 5:1-12; Psalm 63:1-11; Proverbs 23:22

Lord, thank You for giving me a heart of flesh
so that I may obey your commands.

September 20 ~ A Day with Joni

Stepping Out in Faith

The heavens declare the glory of God,
and the firmament shows His handiwork.
— Matthew 4:22

Have you come to a standstill in your spiritual walk? A plateau? You're not alone. I've been there. We've all been there. Let me share a lesson I've learned (and have to remind myself from time to time): You can't discover new lands unless you're willing to step off the familiar shore.

It is often our comfort that makes us complacent; our aversion to risk that stalls us. When Jesus called the disciples, He did not offer them a guarantee of more of the same or the comforts of the status quo. No, to follow Christ was to leave those familiar shores for a very long time.

Peter left his nets. Matthew left his tax business. Zaccheus left his tree. At a standstill? Ask yourself, What am I clinging to? What am I hiding behind? What am I afraid of? It could be that the excitement you've lost in your spiritual walk lies just beyond the boundaries of your comfort.

Today's Bible Reading Plan: Isaiah 33:10-36:22
Galatians 5:13-26; Psalm 64:1-10; Proverbs 23:23

Father, forgive me when I've dug in my heels, held on to what's known, familiar and secure. Loosen my grip on these things. Challenge me to reach for Your hand, and to step out in faith! I want life in You beyond this plateau. Be glorified in me, I pray.

September 21

Feast of Trumpets, Rosh Hashanah Begins Ten Days of Awe – Day 1

Blow the trumpet at the New Moon,
at the full moon on our feast day.

— *Psalm 81:3*

Today, as the sun sets, God's celestial calendar marks a new beginning, Rosh Hashanah (Head of the Year), or the Feast of Trumpets.

The Feast of Trumpets marks the beginning of the Ten Days of Awe, ten days when the people of God consecrate themselves and repent before Him. The blowing of the trumpets on this first day of the Ten Days of Awe herald a solemn time of preparation for the Day of Atonement (Yom Kippur).

During the Ten Days of Awe, God slips away from man and withdraws a bit. He purposely does this to create a desire, a hunger in our hearts, so that we will abandon everything else in pursuit of Him. This is a time when God wants every one of us to clear the clutter from our lives, turn away from our idols, seek Him with our whole heart and press into His presence.

Today's Bible Reading Plan: Isaiah 37:1-38:22 Galatians 6:1-18; Psalm 65:1-13; Proverbs 23:24

Jehovah Joshua Messiah,
thank You for this time of repentance.

September 22

Rosh Hashanah Ends, Sundown Ten Days of Awe – Day 2

He said to them, "Thus it is written, and accordingly it was necessary for the Christ to suffer and to rise from the dead the third day, and that repentance and remission of sins should be preached in His name to all nations, beginning at Jerusalem.

— Luke 24:46-47

Yesterday marked the beginning of the season of Atonement, not quietly, but with trumpets and shouts. In Hebrew, it is called the day of noise. Rosh Hashanah is when we celebrate the coronation of the King of all creation, royalty that will rule forever.

During the Ten Days of Awe, it is a time to come before our King, to examine our lives before Him. The dirt of this clay beneath our feet, the soil of our own sin, needs to be swept away. As you are examined by the Holy Spirit, the King will show you where you have not made Him King at all. Under the glare of His beautiful holiness, our shortcomings are very apparent.

Take time today, in day two of the Ten Days of Awe, to press into God's presence and re-examine your life and truly make Him Sovereign King.

Today's Bible Reading Plan: Isaiah 39:1-1-41:16 Ephesians 1:1-23; Psalm 66:1-20; Proverbs 23:25-28

Holy Spirit, show me my sin, that I may repent, turn to God.

September 23

Ten Days of Awe – Day 3

Therefore, bear fruit worthy of repentance…

— *Matthew 3:8*

On this, day three of the Ten Days of Awe, we are one short week away from God's holiest day of the year, the great Day of Atonement (Yom Kippur). This Feast season is different from the others.

During this season, we are not celebrating something that God did in the past, but what He is doing now, and what He is going to do. What occurs in the next seven days will mark God's plan for you and for your family for the entirety of the next year. It is that crucial and that vital.

God desires to seal His plan for you, to bless you and not to harm you, to create in you a future. But first, you have to honor God and declare Him as your Sovereign, remember His blessings and glorify His name.

We must repent, turn away from all sin and turn toward God. Press in toward Him, not away from Him. Jehovah Joshua Messiah, the Lord Jesus Christ could come at any moment, and He wants you to be ready.

Today's Bible Reading Plan: Isaiah 41:17-43:13 Ephesians 2:1-22; Psalm 67:1-7; Proverbs 23:29-35

Today I press in to You, Lord God, and I run from sin.

276

September 24

Ten Days of Awe – Day 4

For thus says the Lord GOD, the Holy One of Israel: In
returning and rest you shall be saved;
in quietness and in confidence shall be your strength...

— *Isaiah 30:15*

On this fourth day of the Ten Days of Awe, when God withdraws a bit to create a hunger and desire within our hearts, so that we will draw closer to Him, you should be getting pretty hungry for the sweet presence of the Lord.

In ancient Israel, God's people would seek Him in prayer three times a day. During the Ten Days of Awe, an extra time of prayer, the Mussaf, was added.

It is also called the crowning, when they would declare God's sovereignty. "He is King!" they would shout. "He is King over all the earth and King over our lives!"

It is incredible that the God of all creation not only rules and reigns over the Earth, but He wants to be involved and rule and reign in your life, today. What a blessing!

Today's Bible Reading Plan: Isaiah 43:14-45:10
Ephesians 3:1-21; Psalm 68:1-18; Proverbs 24:1-2

Lord God, I give you complete
rule and reign in my life today!

September 25

Ten Days of Awe – Day 5

God exalted this Man to His right hand to be a Ruler and a
Savior, to give repentance to Israel and forgiveness of sins.

— Acts 5:31

This is a very holy, awesome period on God's celestial calendar, leading up to the holiest day of the year, the great Day of Atonement.

We are right now in the middle of the Ten Days of Awe.

Today, in day five, we honor God's remembrance of His covenant with man, meaning we recognize that although God remembers what we have done in the past year and what we have not done, it is a time of reckoning when the blood must be applied, as God remembers that covenant.

John 17:20-21 says Jesus prayed on our behalf to the Father, "May they be one, as you, Father, are in me and as I am in you, that the world may believe that you sent me."

Jesus Christ, the Son of God, on Calvary's mean, angry, cruel, rugged beam became our atonement.

Today's Bible Reading Plan: Isaiah 45:11-48:11
Ephesians 4:1-16; Psalm 68:19-35; Proverbs 24:3-4

Thank You, Jesus, for atoning for my sin.
Thank You for making me whole and complete.

September 26

Ten Days of Awe – Day 6

*...testifying to both Jews and Greeks of repentance
toward God and of faith in our Lord Jesus Christ.*

— Acts 20:21

Today is day six of the Ten Days of Awe, a time when God, in His grace and mercy, strives to call our hearts back to Himself.

It is a time of repentance, a time to turn from things and turn to God, when we need to get things in order to live a holy life before the Lord, to obey His commands, to honor Him with our offerings.

It is vital right now, because this is the season when God the Father orders the trumpet to sound and when the Son of God Himself will one of these years return to earth in glory.

We do not know the day nor the hour of the return of Jesus, but we do know the season. Jesus came to Earth at an appointed time as a baby. He will return again at an appointed time, this time as King of kings and Lord of lords to reign forever.

Today's Bible Reading Plan: Isaiah 48:12-50:11
Ephesians 4:17-32; Psalm 69:1-18; Proverbs 24:5-6

Lord Jesus, I patiently await Your glorious return.

September 27

Ten Days of Awe – Day 7

Now I rejoice, not that you were made sorrowful, but that your sorrow led to repentance. For you were made sorrowful in a godly way, that you might not suffer loss in any way through us.

— *2 Corinthians 7:9*

This is day seven of God's appointed Ten Days of Awe, a time to reflect, to repent, to renew, to re-establish Jesus Christ as Sovereign Lord of our lives.

God the Father in the annals of creation set the sun, moon and stars in place to mark forever His Feast seasons, His holiest days of the entire year. In the United States, we celebrate holidays, but God's Feasts are truly holy days when He calls His people to draw near to Him, focus on Him and feast with Him.

This year began with Passover. The Feast of Passover was fulfilled by Jesus on the cruel cross of Calvary. Then 50 days later, the Feast of Pentecost was fulfilled with the birth of the New Testament church and the infilling of the Holy Spirit.

This is the only season that remains to be historically fulfilled. The Father will soon make the decision to send His Son to the Earth to claim His Bride.

Today's Bible Reading Plan: Isaiah 51:1-53:12 Ephesians 5:1-33; Psalm 69:19-36; Proverbs 24:7

Holy Spirit, fill me today.
Renew my mind, refresh my soul.

September 28

Ten Days of Awe – Day 8

When they heard these things, they were silent. And they glorified God, saying, "Then God has granted to the Gentiles also repentance unto life."

— Acts 11:18

The Ten Days of Awe on the Hebrew calendar began eight days ago on Rosh Hashanah. During this time of renewal, God wants to release a double portion of His blessings into your life of His presence, revelation knowledge, restoration, miracles, financial breakthrough and deliverance.

Embrace the Lord's blessings today. Celebrate the goodness of God that has led you to repentance (Romans 2:4). Seek the Lord with humility and contrite hearts. Gather with family and friends to eat the bread and drink the cup of the New Covenant.

Now crown Jesus as King and enjoy His embrace in a truly divine encounter.

Today's Bible Reading Plan: Isaiah 54:1-57:14
Ephesians 6:1-24; Psalm 70:1-5; Proverbs 24:8

Lord God, each day is filled with more anticipation and more excitement as we draw near to Your holiest day, Yom Kippur.

September 29

Ten Days of Awe – Day 9

Surely after I turned back, I repented...

— Jeremiah 31:19a

The Day of Atonement (Yom Kippur) is almost here, when we will celebrate and honor God for His everlasting plan of atonement through the blood of His Son, Jesus Christ.

We can never, ever earn Christ's atonement. Jesus paid the sacrificial price to redeem every single one of us, but we can and we must honor the atonement He made for our sin.

Jesus Christ, the perfect Lamb of God, made sure we would have a relationship with God through His sacrifice. This perfect Lamb then became our High Priest, offering Himself as perfect payment for our sin forever. *But this Man, after He had offered one sacrifice for sins forever, sat down at the right hand of God. Since that time He has been waiting for His enemies to be made His footstool. For by one offering He has forever perfected those who are sanctified* (Hebrews 10:12-14).

Let us honor the Lamb of God's atonement and celebrate our High Priest!

Today's Bible Reading Plan: Isaiah 57:15-59:21
Philippians 1:1-26; Psalm 71:1-24; Proverbs 24:9-10

There is no one like You, Lord, my High Priest and King!

September 30

Ten Days of Awe – Day 10
Yom Kippur
Day of Atonement

Also on the tenth day of this seventh month there shall be the
Day of Atonement. It shall be a holy convocation to you, and
you shall humble yourselves, and offer a food offering made by
fire to the LORD.
— Leviticus 23:27

This is God's holiest day on His calendar. During the Ten Days of Awe, we have repented and sought God in prayer. Our posture should mirror the shape of a shofar, the "trumpet" used to usher in this period of reflection. The shofar is bent, its head pointed to the ground. Bowing before the King of the universe is our repentant posture, inviting Jesus to be King over even the mundane details – the intricacies of our lives – as we invoke the coronation of His Kingship afresh.

Repentance is our calling every day of the year and we should be quick to seek God for forgiveness of our sins. On this day, Yom Kippur, we stand before God made righteous because of the sacrifice of His Son, Jesus Christ. We must celebrate and thank Him for His incredible atonement!

Today's Bible Reading Plan: Isaiah 60:1-62:5
Philippians 1:27-2:18; Psalm 72:1-20; Proverbs 24:11-12

Thank You, Jesus, for cleansing me
and making me righteous!

OCTOBER

Seasons Change

To everything there is a season,

a time for every purpose under heaven...

— Ecclesiastes 3:1

October 1 ~ A Day with Joni

For Such a Time as This

"And who knows if you may have attained royal position
for such a time as this?"
— *Esther 4:14*

I am constantly amazed at how God works. He delights in putting the most unlikely people in the most unique positions to affect the most amazing results. He confounds the wisdom of men.

The story of Esther and Mordecai is a great example. Were you to try and handpick the perfect people to thwart a genocidal plan to wipe out the people of God – let's just say, Esther and Mordecai aren't swimming to the top of your pool of applicants.

And that's to say nothing of the process. Twists, turns, oddities. Who does this? God – that's who! When God planned to prevent the annihilation of the Jews, He started with a beauty contest!

God is in the business of positioning ordinary people in extraordinary places, fit perfectly for peculiar moments and situations in history.

Look around. Do you think your circumstances somewhat strange? Perhaps you have been divinely placed there … for just such a time as this.

Today's Bible Reading Plan: Isaiah 62:6-65:25
Philippians 2:19-3:3; Psalm 73:1-28; Proverbs 24:13-14

O God, as I look around I have to wonder: Have You chosen me and placed me here in these unique settings and circumstances in my life today for Your ends? Open my eyes to see. Give me courage to follow Your lead. In Jesus' name I pray.

October 2

God Changes the Times and Seasons

It is He who changes the times and the seasons;
He removes kings and sets up kings;
He gives wisdom to the wise
and knowledge to those who know understanding.

— Daniel 2:21

God changes the times and seasons so that we learn to adapt to change and thereby grow and mature spiritually. Although our God never changes, we must be able to adapt to the changes in people's hearts, changes in the climate of the different seasons or changes of our circumstances.

No matter what physical, emotional or spiritual season we are in, our changeless God is faithful to see us through every one of them. Whether we face a sudden financial crisis, health issues, relationship trials, or any amount of earthly stresses, the Holy Spirit is always there to aid us and get us through the trials and tribulations of this life, and we will come forth as pure gold (Job 23:10).

Today's Bible Reading Plan: Isaiah 66:1-24
Philippians 3:4-21; Psalm 74:1-23; Proverbs 24:15-16

Holy Spirit, refine me so that I come forth as gold.

October 3

God's Celestial Timepiece

While the earth remains, seedtime and harvest, cold and heat, summer and winter, and day and night will not cease.

— *Genesis 8:22*

In God's creation, we witness His faithfulness. The sun, moon, stars and planets of our solar system do not veer off their courses. They are, in fact, a testament of God's Feast days and mark His celestial calendar. We know when to meet with God during the seasons of Passover, Pentecost and Tabernacles, because He set the sun, moon and stars in place as a sign and as His great cosmic timepiece.

Three times each year, the people of God were commanded to travel to Jerusalem for the Feasts of the Lord. Each Feast or festival marks a time to come and feast with God, according to the time of the harvest of Israel's crops. At Passover, the barley crops are harvested; at Pentecost, wheat crops are harvested; at Tabernacles, the crops of grapes, figs, pomegranates and olives are harvested.

There will be one great spiritual end-time harvest of souls when Jesus calls us home in the rapture. Are you rapture ready?

Today's Bible Reading Plan: Jeremiah 1:1-2:30 Philippians 4:1-23; Psalm 75:1-10; Proverbs 24:17-20

Holy Spirit, make me rapture ready!

287

October 4

First Day of Tabernacles (Sukkot Begins at Sundown)

The LORD spoke to Moses, saying: Speak to the children of Israel, saying: The fifteenth day of this seventh month shall be the Feast of Tabernacles for seven days to the LORD.

— Leviticus 23:33-34

As we begin our celebration of this week of Sukkot, the Feast of Tabernacles, the season of our joy, it is the concluding celebration of God's third and final Feast season of the entire year on His celestial calendar.

The Feast of Tabernacles celebrates and commemorates when God led the Israelites through the wilderness for 40 years, providing for them in every need of their daily life: water, food, clothing and shelter.

This Feast season was also a yearly reminder that God has always intended to live, to dwell gloriously in the midst of His people. God's fervent desire is to dwell, to tabernacle with you.

Today's Bible Reading Plan: Jeremiah 2:31-4:18 Colossians 1:1-17; Psalm 76:1-12; Proverbs 24:21-22

Holy Spirit, thank You for dwelling within me every moment.

288

October 5

Tabernacles – Day 2

You shall observe the Feast of Tabernacles seven days after you have gathered in your threshing floor and your winepress…

— *Deuteronomy 16:13*

God has longed to dwell with His people since He placed Adam and Eve in the Garden of Eden. The Creator longs to abide in and with His creation.

To abide means to live with, to come alive or to take up residence. When God, by the power of His Holy Spirit, takes up residence within you, He fills every part of your being: your mind, thoughts and emotions. His indwelling presence influences your way of life.

We exist to bring glory and honor to God. We are to always bear fruit, always preach the Gospel and always lead the lost to salvation in Jesus Christ. When you abide in Jesus, you have a continual revelation of Him. When you remain in Jesus, the True Vine, and His words remain in you, *you will ask whatever you desire, and it shall be done for you* (John 15:7). By this, God will be glorified (John 15:8).

Today's Bible Reading Plan: Jeremiah 4:19-6:15 Colossians 1:18-2:7; Psalm 77:1-20; Proverbs 24:23-25

Abide in me, Holy Spirit, and affect my daily life, that Almighty God will be glorified each day.

October 6

Tabernacles – Day 3

And He said, "My Presence will go with you,
and I will give you rest."

— Exodus 33:14

Today is day three of God's Feast of Tabernacles. This is a time, more than any other time of the year, when God chooses to draw closer to you and me. God is in all places at all times, but our lives are so full of the necessary day-to-day activities that it sometimes crowds out our consciousness of His presence.

The Feast of Tabernacles is our opportunity to come away for a while from a fast-paced busy lifestyle to just pause and consider the overwhelming presence of God, to think about, meditate on – the psalmist said selah – His purposes and promises to every one of us.

The children of Israel had a visible, tangible representation of God's dwelling presence on their daily journey through the wilderness. It came in the form of a cloud by day and fire by night. Even though God's presence isn't with us in such an obviously external form, today, He does remind us during the wonderful Feast of Tabernacles that He truly is an ever present help in time of need.

Today's Bible Reading Plan: Jeremiah 6:16-8:7
Colossians 2:8-23; Psalm 78:1-31; Proverbs 24:26

Thank You, Lord, for your glorious abiding presence.

October 7

Tabernacles – Day 4

And we have come to know and to believe the love
that God has for us. God is love.
Whoever lives in love lives in God, and God in him.

— 1 John 4:16

We are in day four of the Feast of Tabernacles, or as I like to call it, "The Days of God's Divine Embrace." We are at the midpoint of His appointed time for a divine encounter.

Even though man walked away from the source of his life, his substance, his sustenance, God never, ever stopped seeking reconciliation with us. He did not leave us alone.

This imagery is perhaps best conveyed in the language of love found in the Song of Solomon, the Song of Songs. It is a beautiful symbol of God's love for us portrayed during the Feast of Tabernacles.

Song of Songs 2:6 says, *His left hand is under my head, and his right hand embraces me.* Seek the Lord. Make time for Him, today, and the Feast of Tabernacles can become a life-changing encounter for you.

Today's Bible Reading Plan: Jeremiah 8:8-9:26 Colossians 3:1-17; Psalm 78:32-55; Proverbs 24:27

Jehovah Joshua Messiah, I make time for you, today.
I long to feel Your divine embrace.

October 8

Tabernacles – Day 5

"Remember, I am with you, and I will protect you wherever you go, and I will bring you back to this land. For I will not leave you until I have done what I promised you."

— *Genesis 28:15*

The days of the Feast of Tabernacles (Sukkot) are going by so very, very quickly. We are already at day five of the season of God's divine embrace.

Today, I want to encourage you to find a place where you can be alone with God. During the first part of the Feast of Tabernacles, God is placing His left hand under your head (Song of Songs 2:6).

His desire is to bring you face-to-face with Him. The face, of course, is where our inner self is revealed. The eye is the window of the soul.

We become adept at hiding our true feelings. We do it all day from one another, from friends, family and coworkers. But God knows it all, and He wants you to take the mask off and reveal yourself to Him fully. Think how much God must love us. He already knows everything about us; yet, He puts His left hand under our head and draws us close to look deeply within His eyes.

Today's Bible Reading Plan: Jeremiah 10:1-11:23 Colossians 3:18-4:18; Psalm 78:56-72; Proverbs 24:28-29

Draw me close, Lord Jesus; I long to see Your face.

October 9

Tabernacles – Day 6

You will make known to me the path of life;
in Your presence is fullness of joy;
at Your right hand there are pleasures for evermore.

— Psalm 16:11

It is day six of the season of our joy, of God's divine embrace, the Feast of Tabernacles. I pray you are experiencing God's presence in your life, today, at a much deeper level than you ever have before. During the time when God places His left hand under your head, He wants you to return His love and devotion face-to-face with praise and adoration.

After that divine encounter, after you have given Him the very depths of your being, Almighty God reaches out with His right arm. He no longer looks for reciprocation or expression. While He was holding your head in His left hand, you could respond with your eyes, your voice, your expressions, your devotion, your countenance and your words. But now God holds you close with His right hand; and by doing so, He says to you that He doesn't expect anything in return. He just wants to be with you.

Today's Bible Reading Plan: Jeremiah 12:1-14:10
1 Thessalonians 1:1-2:8; Psalm 79:1-13;
Proverbs 24:30-34

I long to be with You, Lord God, to express how deeply
I adore you and how much I praise You and thank You.

October 10

Tabernacles – Day 7

Those who trust in the LORD shall be as Mount Zion,
which cannot be removed, but abides forever.
As the mountains are around Jerusalem,
so the LORD surrounds His people,
from now and forever.

— Psalm 125:1-2

Sukkot means dwelling place, a secret place, a hiding place where God overshadows us with His presence, covers us with His wings, and fills us with His glory.

At Sukkot we dwell as one with the living God. Psalm 91:1-2 decrees this eternal truth: *He who dwells in the shelter of the Most High shall abide under the shadow of the Almighty. I will say of the LORD, "He is my refuge and my fortress, my God in whom I trust."*

When you and I dwell in the presence of our Father, He covers us and protects us from every attack of the adversary; and in our very, very troubled world, we need God's presence and protection more than ever. Tabernacles is a witness of His abiding presence, protection, provision and peace, not just for one season, but for every day of the entire year.

Today's Bible Reading Plan: Jeremiah 14:11-16:15
1 Thessalonians 2:9-3:13; Psalm 80:1-19; Proverbs 25:1-5

Jehovah Joshua Messiah, thank You for hiding me in the secret place. Thank you for being my refuge and fortress.

October 11

Tabernacles – Day 8

"As the Father loved me, I also loved you. Remain in my love...I have spoken these things to you, that My joy may remain in you, and that your joy may be full.

— John 15:9, 11

It is the final day of Sukkot, the season when God's plan and purpose is for you to feel the embrace of His loving arms around you more than ever before, when He holds you close to Himself and says to you, "I want all of you: the inside, the outside, the part of you that can respond by praising and worshiping and the part that cannot do anything. I want the best parts. I want all of you. I will never leave you. I want you to abide with me forever."

God's purpose in drawing you near to Him during the Feast of Tabernacles is not to blame you for something, but to draw you closer to His indwelling Holy Spirit, as you journey through your everyday life.

Your body is the temple, the tabernacle, the meeting place of God. Follow His still, small voice every day, as He walks with you, and as you walk with Him.

Today's Bible Reading Plan: Jeremiah 16:16-18:23
1 Thessalonians 4:1-5:3; Psalm 81:1-16; Proverbs 25:6-8

*I praise You, dear Lord, for Your divine embrace.
Thank You for drawing me close to You,
by the power of Your Spirit.*

October 12

Shemini Atzeret

And I heard a loud voice from heaven, saying, "Look! The tabernacle of God is with men, and He will dwell with them. They shall be His people, and God Himself will be with them and be their God.

— *Revelation 21:3*

Shemini Atzeret means to abide, tarry or hold back. The wise rabbis through the centuries have concluded that it is as though God is asking those who have observed Sukkot to stay another day and tarry with Him, to remain, to stay with Him a while longer.

Our God calls us to His dwelling place, stirs us to worship Him in the intimacy of His blessing and presence, and then says, in essence, "Stay a little while longer. I love you. I want you close another day."

No wonder teachers and mystics through the years have viewed this festival as a sign of eternity. We will dwell with our God. He, in turn, will dwell with us and even bid us to tarry with Him forever in an eternity of celebration and fellowship when we will tabernacle with Him and He with us forever.

Today's Bible Reading Plan: Jeremiah 19:1-21:14
1 Thessalonians 5:4-28; Psalm 82:1-8; Proverbs 25:9-10

Hallelujah! We will dwell with our God forever!

October 13

Simchat Torah

Many people shall go and say, "Come, and let us go up to the mountain of the LORD, to the house of the God of Jacob, and He will teach us of His ways, and we will walk in His paths." For out of Zion shall go forth the law, and the word of the LORD from Jerusalem.

— Isaiah 2:3

In Israel there is another celebration after Sukkot. It is called Simchat Torah the day after Shemini Atzeret. Both immediately follow the last day of Sukkot, but are not part of that Feast.

Simchat Torah is defined as "rejoicing in the Torah" and marks the completion of the annual cycle of Torah reading, which begins again immediately. This is symbolic that the Word of God is never-ending and inexhaustible. Jesus says to us in Matthew 24:35, *"Heaven and earth will pass away, but My words will never pass away."* Solomon reminds us wisely, *"My son, attend to my words; incline your ear to my sayings. Do not let them depart from your eyes; keep them in the midst of your heart; for they are life to those who find them, and health to all their body."* (Proverbs 4:20-22).

Today's Bible Reading Plan: Jeremiah 22:1-23:20 2 Thessalonians 1:1-12; Psalm 83:1-18; Proverbs 25:11-14

I will celebrate the commandments of my God!

297

October 14 ~ A Day with Joni

Rest

"Come to Me, all you who labor and are heavily burdened, and I will give you rest."
— *Matthew 11:28*

We live in a chaotic world. We keep chaotic schedules. Our days are a blur. You know what I mean – a whole year passes and we're like, "Where did it go?" Our senses are under assault. Our minds are working overtime. And if we're not careful, it's our spiritual lives that can pay the price. "Pray and study the word? Where can I find the time?"

Read the words of Jesus, above. It's an invitation that we are wise to heed! "Come," He says. And bring your burdens, concerns, worries and fears with you when you come – He's offering rest! He's offering to take those burdens; to lighten their load upon your heart and soul. Doesn't it sound wonderful? Doesn't it sound like just the respite and remedy you need?

Remember, against the backdrop of a raging storm, Jesus is a safe and quiet place.

Don't make this another of those, "As soon as I have a moment, I'll do it!" intentions. Pull out of the fast lane. Park the car. Go on in and sit a while. Breathe.

Today's Bible Reading Plan: Jeremiah 23:21-25:38
2 Thessalonians 2:1-17; Psalm 84:1-12; Proverbs 25:15

Lord, I come to You needy. I need You, Your peace, Your solace. I confess I'm often running, burning the candle at both ends. Help me to prioritize a time – today and every day – to bring my burdens into Your presence, and to embrace Your offer – rest!

October 15

Recognize Your Season

And God said, "Let there be lights in the expanse of the heavens to separate the day from the night, and let them be signs to indicate seasons, and days, and years."

— Genesis 1:14

Over the course of time, rivers often change course. Where a mighty river once coursed, only stagnating pools of water remain.

What would have happened to the children of Israel if they had refused to move when God was ready? They would have noticed the cloud was gone and would have said, "Wait a minute. The cloud was right here yesterday. Maybe it will come back. We should wait right here." The cloud would be miles ahead while Israel stagnated, apart from the presence of God.

Jesus boldly declared, *"He who believes in Me, as the Scripture has said, out of his heart shall flow rivers of living water"* (John 7:38). He was speaking about believers carried along in the power of the Holy Spirit.

Be instant in season and out of season. Many times I approach the pulpit with a message ready to deliver; then the Holy Spirit prompts me in an entirely different direction. Always listen for God's voice.

Today's Bible Reading Plan: Jeremiah 26:1-27:22
2 Thessalonians 3:1-18; Psalm 85:1-13; Proverbs 25:16

Lord, speak to me today; I long to hear Your voice.

299

October 16

The Message Does Not Change

I will send My messenger, and he will prepare the way before Me. And the Lord, whom you seek, will suddenly come to His temple, even the messenger of the covenant, in whom you delight. He is coming, says the LORD of Hosts.

— *Malachi 3:1*

The Messenger of the covenant has a delivering word. It is a message that brings comfort to the depleted soul and peace to the troubled mind. It is the good news that every person longs to hear, and it does not change. Even though the style of delivery may change, the message does not.

Your *suddenly* or *now* season begins the moment your faith apprehends the message of the Messenger. How does it happen? Faith *comes* by hearing and hearing by the word of God (Romans 10:17). When the Lord arrives, it will be with awe-inspiring speed! He may not appear when you want Him to, but He is always right on time. When Jesus comes, He will come suddenly. He is the answer to every prayer you will ever pray. Your miracle is about to manifest by the power of His perfect presence!

Today's Bible Reading Plan: Jeremiah 28:1-29:32 1 Timothy 1:1-20; Psalm 86:1-17; Proverbs 25:17

Jesus, I stand expecting You to come suddenly, to manifest Your power in my life!

October 17 ~ A Day with Joni

Strength

...that He would give you, according to the riches of His glory,
power to be strengthened by His Spirit in the inner man...
— *Ephesians 3:16*

"Lord, give me strength." That's a mother's prayer, for sure. We all need it.

How can we stand up under the weight of the world? How can we bear up when circumstances turn sour? What remedy can be found to alleviate the pressures that mounts when life goes crazy?

What we need, the Bible calls the strengthening of the inner man. If the inner man is compromised, the soul will be crushed under the weight of the world.

Consider this truth: *He who is in you is greater than he who is in the world (1 John 4:4).* The stress in our culture must be met by the ever-increasing strength of God in us. We'll be able to say, like the apostle Paul, *"We are troubled on every side, yet not distressed; we are perplexed, but not in despair" (2 Corinthians 4:8).*

Before this day is over, you will run up against it – you'll encounter some kind of pressure to compromise. Turn to Him! Christ in you, overcomes the world.

Today's Bible Reading Plan: Jeremiah 30:1-31:26
1 Timothy 2:1-15; Psalm 87:1-7; Proverbs 25:18-19

God of strength! Will You meet me today, strengthening the inner-me, for whatever lies ahead? I am glad You know how this day will unfold. Nothing in it will surprise You or overwhelm You. I cannot say the same about me. Help me, Jesus! Give me strength, I pray.

October 18

The Seasons of God

He set the moon to mark the appointed seasons;
the sun knows its time for going down.

— Psalm 104:19

Our God is a God of timing, a God of seasons and a God of cycles; and just as there are physical seasons, there are spiritual seasons.

There are more than 800 verses in the Bible where God declares He is concerned with times, seasons and cycles. That is almost one verse for every page of Scripture. This is one of the most important truths you can know about God. Yet it is more than a truth; it is an invitation. It is like the insight a husband gets into his wife's soul that helps him love her more deeply and fill her days with greater joy. It is knowledge that invites relationship, knowledge that issues a call.

From the very beginning, God set in motion His times, cycles and seasons. As you journey through life, you will encounter different seasons, some good and some bad. Always trust God and have faith to know that every season you experience is ordered by God to help you grow in your relationship with Him.

Today's Bible Reading Plan: Jeremiah 31:27-32:44
1 Timothy 3:1-16; Psalm 88:1-18; Proverbs 25:20-22

Lord God, thank You for
Your seasons that help me grow.

October 19

The Shortest Season

He who gathers in summer is a wise son,
but he who sleeps in harvest is a son who causes shame.

— Proverbs 10:5

Harvest time is the shortest season. The planting and growing season take months, but the reaping season is very short. The Bible warns that if someone sleeps through the harvest, they cause shame.

It brings shame to expend all the time and energy to plant crops, but then miss the harvest. This has a spiritual implication as well. There are those who spend time carrying out the religious rudiments of outreach and ministry, but it is little more than a business to them. What a shame it would be if they were to miss the final harvest, the rapture of the church, because their heart was not right with God.

You can go through all the religious gestures and still not have a meaningful relationship with Jesus Christ. Take time today to bow your heart to Him and let His Spirit minister to you. Cry out for the Holy Spirit to bring you into a deeper relationship with Almighty God.

Today's Bible Reading Plan: Jeremiah 33:1-34:22
1 Timothy 4:1-16; Psalm 89:1-13; Proverbs 25:23-24

Holy Spirit, draw me deeper today into the heart of God.

October 20

God Will Visit You

Fear came on everyone. And they glorified God, saying,
"A great prophet has risen up among us!"
and "God has visited His people!"

— Luke 7:16

Jesus had a habit of breaking up funeral services. It happened first in the streets of Nain, when a widow woman's son was raised from the dead (Luke 7:11-16).

Jesus visited the city of Nain, and because of that visitation, the widow's only son, whose life had been cut short, came to life again. Now *that* is a visitation – not a crowd, not a small group gathering, not a women's get together over tea, not men bonding over hunting or golf.

A visitation is to impart life! It is to rescue and redeem! It was similar to when God visited Israel in Egypt. During this visitation, God took note of their suffering and declared, "I have come to redeem you" (Exodus 3).

A visitation produces redemption. To redeem means *to buy back by paying the price.*

Today's Bible Reading Plan: Jeremiah 35:1-36:32
1 Timothy 5:1-25; Psalm 89:14-37; Proverbs 25:25-27

Visit me, Lord, in Your great power and unending love!

October 21 ~ A Day with Joni

When the Past Comes Calling

Therefore if the Son sets you free, you shall be free indeed.
— John 8:36

An elephant in the room – that moment when you come face to face with someone who knows your past mistakes. Memories rush back, as do the feelings of guilt, shame and embarrassment. Who speaks first? What do you say? Do you gloss over the obvious? The elephant? Here's how I feel about the past in a nutshell. We can benefit from it in two ways: (1) Learning from it, and (2) Not repeating it.

We can grow forward from our past. We don't need to dwell there. Remember, the Bible tells us Satan is the accuser. Our God is the God of forgiveness and restoration. He brings beauty from ashes! His love set you free!

Freedom has no limit or expiration date. Freedom belongs to us forever – and forever is a long, long time! This freedom flies on the wings of God's incomparable love and takes us, in the profound words of Buzz Lightyear, from the movie Toy Story: "To infinity and beyond!"

Today's Bible Reading Plan: Jeremiah 37:1-38:28
1 Timothy 6:1-21; Psalm 89:38-52; Proverbs 25:28

Dear God – it hurts! Those things I cannot go back and undo, words I cannot unsay, Father when thoughts or recollections of them resurface, I am ashamed. May I learn from them, grow on them, and be set free from them! Will You bring beauty from these ashes? In Jesus' name.

October 22

Know the Time of Your Visitation

"They will dash you, and your children within you, to the ground. They will not leave one stone upon another within you, because you did not know the time of your visitation."

— Luke 19:44

The Lord is searching the landscape of humanity to reveal Himself strong on behalf of those whose hearts are perfect toward Him. This does not mean He is looking for those who never mess up. The word *perfect* means devoted, consecrated, faithful or loyal.

This is a remnant deeply devoted to God. They are men and women who are eagerly moving toward their divine appointment with His wondrous plan to stand in the gap for humanity. He responds to these devoted saints who long for Him with vast exploits so they may reap the end time harvest of souls.

Our Master will return with an eternal reward and righteous commendation for every good and faithful servant. Check your devotion to the Lord. He stands ready to reveal His power to the fully consecrated.

Today's Bible Reading Plan: Jeremiah 39:1-41:18
2 Timothy 1:1-18; Psalm 90:1-91:16; Proverbs 26:1-2

*Lord, show Yourself strong through me
as I commit to be fully devoted to You.*

October 23

The Circle of Life

*For they themselves declare how we were received by you, and
how you turned to God from idols, to serve the living and true
God, and to wait for His Son from heaven, whom He raised
from the dead—Jesus, who delivered us from the wrath to come.*

— *1 Thessalonians 1:9-10*

There is a circle of life. We are born. We live. Then
we will eventually die should Jesus tarry in His return.

While on this earth we are to, in the words of Paul,
serve the living and true God (1 Thessalonians 1:9b). No
matter our station in life, we will all one day step
through the door from this life into eternity.

*As it is appointed for men to die once, but after this comes the
judgment…* (Hebrews 9:27). Every Sunday, all across
the world, you can hear beautiful messages about Jesus
coming out of the grave, but His resurrection is past
and yours is yet to come. If you are part of the first
resurrection, then the second one will have no power
over you. If you are waiting for the Son from heaven,
then you will be delivered from the wrath that is to
come upon the earth.

Today's Bible Reading Plan: Jeremiah 42:1-44:23
2 Timothy 2:1-21; Psalm 92:1-93:5; Proverbs 26:3-5

> *I bow my knee to the Son of heaven and I choose
> to serve You, Lord, the only true and living God.*

307

October 24

The Greatest Transition

He is the head of the body, the church. He is the beginning,
the firstborn from the dead, so that in all things
He may have the preeminence.

— Colossians 1:18

God was dead. The earth convulsed. Women began to weep. Graves began to burst open. The sun cloaked itself in darkness in the middle of the day and became as black as midnight.

How does God die? He became a man.

As it is appointed for men to die once (Hebrews 9:27).

Jesus breathed His last breath. He gave up the ghost.

Jesus was the Firstborn from the dead. "How?" you may wonder. After all, others had been raised from the dead. The widow of Nain's son preceded Him. Jairus' daughter preceded Him. Lazarus preceded Him.

The Apostle Paul declared that Jesus was appointed by God the Father to be "the first fruits of those who are asleep."

Today's Bible Reading Plan: Jeremiah 44:24-47:7
2 Timothy 2:22-3:17; Psalm 94:1-23; Proverbs 26:6-8

Jesus, You have made me free from the fear of death!

October 25

There Was None Like Jesus

*But now is Christ risen from the dead and become
the first fruits of those who have fallen asleep.*

— 1 Corinthians 15:20

There was none like Jesus. How was He different?

He that ascended is also He that first descended (Ephesians 4:9). For three days following, Jesus was on a mission in the dark reaches of the underworld. He stopped by Abraham's bosom and preached the message of His life, death and impending resurrection. He revealed His purpose for coming to the earth: to destroy the works of the devil.

Jesus then waded through the ashes of by-gone millennia of time. He plundered the corridors of the doomed and the damned. He grabbed the devil by the nape of the neck and took away the keys of death, hell and the grave. Finally, He tore death's dark veil asunder!

Jesus delivered you from this body of death (Romans 7:24). Now the law of life in Christ Jesus has made you free from the law of sin of sin and death (Romans 8:2)!

Today's Bible Reading Plan: Jeremiah 48:1-49:22
2 Timothy 4:1-22; Psalm 95:1-96:13; Proverbs 26:9-12

Jesus, You are the Firstborn from the dead!

October 26

There's a Change Coming

Your word is a lamp to my feet and a light to my path.

— *Psalm 119:105*

Man is hopelessly, eternally lost. Left to his own devices, he will not only destroy himself, but everything and everyone around him. But on a cross hung a bleeding, dying Savior who said, "I am doing this for you."

If you are saved, it is because of the shed blood of Jesus. If you are saved, you will not have to ask the deacon or the preacher if you are saved nor will you have to get a confirmation letter from denominational headquarters to give validity to your decision. You will know that you know, that you know, that you know.

When you are saved, everything looks different. The birds sing louder and the sun shines brighter, because you have been touched by God, and you have been changed.

Today's Bible Reading Plan: Jeremiah 49:23-50:46 Titus 1:1-16; Psalm 97:1-98:9; Proverbs 26:13-16

Jesus, thank You for the change You have made in me!

October 27

The Unchangeable Covenant

*I will establish My covenant between Me and you
and your descendants after you throughout their generations
for an everlasting covenant, to be God to you and your
descendants after you.*

— *Genesis 17:7*

We live in a time when a person's word means nothing. Marriages are dissolved daily with no regard to the vows of "until death we do part." Our courts are flooded with lawsuits.

It has not always been this way. In ancient times a covenant, sealed in blood, was a promise of enduring responsibility, never entered into lightly and never disregarded.

This is the kind of relationship we have with God. The entire Bible is a legal contract signed in Jesus' blood! When God said, "I will never leave you nor forsake you (Hebrews 13:5), He did not add, "maybe" or "if."

This is the unchangeable fact of His absolute faithfulness! Study the promises of God in the light of His blood covenant and learn how sure and secure is the Rock on which you stand.

Today's Bible Reading Plan: Jeremiah 51:1-53
Titus 2:1-15; Psalm 99:1-9; Proverbs 26:17

*Jesus, Your unchangeable covenant
frees me forever from death!*

311

October 28 ~ A Day with Joni

Embody the Gospel Message

You are our letter written in our hearts,
known and read by all men.
— 2 Corinthians 3:2

How do you share the gospel with others? First, be the gospel, alive and in living color before them.

The apostle Paul told the believers in Corinth, "Your very lives are a letter that anyone can read by just looking at you." It's so true.

People are watching us and actions speak louder than words. Exemplary behavior says it all.

"Love your neighbor," Jesus commanded. How are you doing with that?

You have probably heard the expression, "The best sermons are the ones that are seen." I'd go even a step further: The best sermons are the ones that are seen *and experienced.*

When we share the gospel tangibly – the watching world sees it in our behavior and experiences it in the manner of our love – then we're really communicating God's good news!

Today's Bible Reading Plan: Jeremiah 51:54-52:34
Titus 3:1-15; Psalm 100:1-5; Proverbs 26:18-19

My gracious Heavenly Father, "Love the Lord your God with all your heart ... and love your neighbor as yourself" – may it be so in my life! I pray for opportunities to share the gospel tangibly, in words and deeds, so others can hear, see and feel the love of Christ through me.

October 29

The Great Exchange

Know therefore that the LORD *your God, He is God, the faithful God, who keeps covenant and mercy with them who love Him and keep His commandments to a thousand generations,*

— Deuteronomy 7:9

God promised Moses that any of his enemies who came against him must inevitably face the Lord, not just Moses. God will fight your battles for you when you walk in covenant with Him.

When you walk in covenant, you can be confident of possessing the promises of God in your life. He has promised in His Word that when we are weak, He will give us His strength and when we have no ability, He will give us His ability (2 Corinthians 12:9-10; Philippians 4:13; Isaiah 40:29-31).

You have nothing but debits and He has nothing but credits. You have poverty; He is Jehovah Jireh, who has all wealth. You have sickness; He is Jehovah Rapha, your healing and your Healer. You have sin; He Jehovah Joshua Messiah, the Lord Jesus Christ who is absolutely holy. What a glorious exchange!

Today's Bible Reading Plan: Lamentations 1:1-2:22 Philemon 1:1-25; Psalm 101:1-8; Proverbs 26:20

Thank You, Jehovah Joshua Messiah, for who You are!

October 30

The Struggle Can Bring Dynamic Change

*Jacob was left alone, and a man
wrestled with him there until daybreak.*

— Genesis 32:24

Throughout the Bible, the name of a thing is its very nature. Jacob means "Deceiver," supplanter, liar, thief. All his life, Jacob was called a deceiver. When conflict arose from his deceitful actions against his brother, he didn't see any way out. In fear and desperation, he returned to Bethel. He climbed the mountain where he first made an altar to the Lord, and it was there that the angel of the Lord wrestled with him.

Jacob said to the angel, "It took too long to find you; I'm not letting you go!" In that struggle, Jacob was forever changed. God gave Jacob a new nature. He carried God's mark, and he carried a new name: Israel. In Christ, old things pass away and all things become new. He did it for Jacob, and He will do it for you. Seek God with all your heart. Refuse to let go until you have been forever changed!

Today's Bible Reading Plan: Lamentations 3:1-66
Hebrews 1:1-14; Psalm 102:1-28; Proverbs 26:21-22

*In You, Lord Jesus, I know that I am a new creation,
a new species of being that has never existed before.*

314

October 31

Make An Exchange

And it must be, when you come into the land which the LORD your God is giving you for an inheritance, and you possess it, and dwell in it, that you shall take from the first of all the produce of the ground which you shall bring from your land that the LORD your God is giving you, and put it in a basket and go to the place where the LORD your God chooses to make His name abide.

— Deuteronomy 26:1-2

Life is a process of exchange. We enter to leave, get in to get out, go up to come down. God wants to make exchanges in your life and lead you out of bondage and into a land of promises.

The "status quo" is the greatest enemy of the cause of Christ. The Israelites were comfortable in Egypt and begged to go back to the tyranny they had known for so long. Your abundance is tied to the process of exchange. God wants you to exchange your bondage for freedom. He wants to bring you out of the kingdom of the world and into His glorious kingdom.

Determine to break through the boundaries the devil has raised up around you. Exchange your way of doing things and go forward with God.

Today's Bible Reading Plan: Lamentations 4:1-5:22 Hebrews 2:1-18; Psalm 103:1-22; Proverbs 26:23

Holy Spirit, give me a dynamic breakthrough today!

315

NOVEMBER

Only Believe

"Do not be afraid, only believe."

— *Mark 5:36b*

November 1

The Word of God

For you are prominently declared to be the letter of Christ,
prepared by us, written not with ink but with
the Spirit of the living God, not on tablets of stone
but on human tablets of the heart.

— 2 Corinthians 3:3

The Word of God enters your life through the eye gate, through the ear gate, and goes past your mind into the hard, calloused surface of mental reasoning, from there to be deposited into the fertile soil of your human spirit.

You are primarily and foremost a spirit man or woman. Don't check with your mind first; always check with your spirit first. When the Word of God is in your heart, the Holy Spirit will bring the Word to your remembrance when you're in a situation where you need His divine guidance.

Under the anointing and inspiration of the Holy Spirit, declare and decree the Word of God over your life today. Don't take this day for granted. Frame your world with the Word of God!

Today's Bible Reading Plan: Ezekiel 1:1-3:15
Hebrews 3:1-19; Psalm 104:1-23; Proverbs 26:24-26

Almighty God, thank You for reminding me that
my spirit is forever gloriously connected to Your Spirit.

November 2

The Way, the Truth, the Life

Jesus said to him, "I am the way, the truth, and the life.
No one comes to the Father except through Me."

— John 14:6

There is one way to live eternally with the Father, and that is through Jesus Christ the Son of God. If you know Jesus, you know the way to the Father. Without Jesus, you cannot know the way.

Jesus provides an abundant life now and for eternity. Don't let your lifestyle rob you of eternal life. Once you get a hold of truth, let nothing turn your plow.

Do not let the stresses of everyday life deprive you of daily victories. Press on! God is not so far from us that He cannot have compassion for us. Even though God is holy, high and lifted up, and seated on the throne, you now have access to God through Jesus Christ.

Pray to the Father, in Jesus' name, and God will answer you. Jesus stepped in the place of judgment and took the punishment meant for you, what you rightly deserve, and He is now the way for you to receive everlasting life!

Today's Bible Reading Plan: Ezekiel 3:16-6:14
Hebrews 4:1-16; Psalm 104:24-35; Proverbs 26:27

Thank You, Jesus, for paying a debt you did not owe
in order to cancel a debt I could never repay.

November 3

Have Faith

Jesus answered them, "Have faith in God. For truly I say to you, whoever says to this mountain, 'Be removed and be thrown into the sea,' and does not doubt in his heart, but believes that what he says will come to pass, he will have whatever he says. Therefore I say to you, whatever things you ask when you pray, believe that you will receive them, and you will have them."

— Mark 11:22-24

It may sound strange, but I number my mountains, and as I remove them and cast them into the sea, I tell them to stay there! I tell those mountains to go back to their overlord, Satan, and tell him that his mission against me failed.

Whether you recognize it or not, we live on a cursed planet, and we dwell among men of unclean lips. This is not a recreation room; it is a battlefield. Just above your head, a battle is raging. There are forces of light, forces of darkness, forces of good and forces of evil.

Don't become at ease in Zion. (Amos 6:1). In faith, speak to your mountains and watch God move!

Today's Bible Reading Plan: Ezekiel 7:1-9:11
Hebrews 5:1-14; Psalm 105:1-5; Proverbs 26:28

In the mighty, matchless name of Jesus and by the power of the Holy Spirit, mountains of bondage, lack and disease, be removed and cast into the sea and never return!

November 4 ~ A Day with Joni

Always

And remember, I am with you always…
— Matthew 28:20b

Have you ever experienced a huge shift in your life that leaves you feeling out of sync?

It's a strange feeling, as though life slipped off track and you're out of place. It's disorienting.

I'll bet you have experienced it. Maybe you or someone you love is feeling that way today. Your job description was rewritten and you're feeling like a stranger at your own desk. Your last child left for college and the house has lost that "homey" feeling. A loved one has departed for heaven and suddenly you don't feel so at home here on earth.

What do you do when life slips out of gear? Get closer to the One who never changes. Turn to Him. Read a Psalm. Whisper a prayer. Sing a song of praise.

Jesus told us to remember – and it is so important that we do – He is with us always!

Surely, it must be one of the great treasures of the Bible … the word always.

Today's Bible Reading Plan: Ezekiel 10:1-11:25
Hebrews 6:1-20; Psalm 105:16-36; Proverbs 27:1-2

Thank You, Lord, for the word always – and that You are always God, always present, always with me! I confess there are times when I take my eyes off You, forget this precious promise. Overwhelm me with this truth: today, tomorrow, always … I am never without You.

November 5

Faith, Hope & Love

So now abide faith, hope, and love, these three.
But the greatest of these is love.

— *1 Corinthians 13:13*

We are instructed in Ephesians 4:15 to speak the truth in love. How do we do that? The great Apostle Paul, in 1 Corinthians 13, explains the God kind of love.

Love is patient and kind. It is not jealous or boastful. The God kind of love is not proud, arrogant or rude. Love is not selfish, is not easily provoked, and it keeps no record of wrongs. Love doesn't rejoice in evil, but rejoices in the truth. Love always protects, trusts, hopes, and perseveres.

God's love is perfect and seeks to build up, not tear down. Love never fails. Because we long to advance God's kingdom, we must exhibit His character and demonstrate how He wants His kingdom to operate.

In Matthew 6:9-13, Jesus instructs us to pray for God's kingdom to come and His will to be done. Since God's kingdom lives within us (Luke 17:21), we must be sure His character is evident in our actions.

Today's Bible Reading Plan: Ezekiel 12:1-14:11
Hebrews 7:1-17; Psalm 105:37-45; Proverbs 27:3

Holy Spirit, help me to demonstrate the love of God.

November 6

A New Covenant for a New Culture

Surely, the days are coming, says the LORD, when I will make a new covenant with the house of Israel and with the house of Judah ... this shall be the covenant that I will make with the house of Israel after those days, says the LORD: I will put My law within them and write it in their hearts; and I will be their God, and they shall be My people ... for I will forgive their iniquity, and I will remember their sin no more.

— Jeremiah 31:31, 33, 34b

God has given us a do-over. He hit the refresh button, and we have been given another chance. It is not too late to begin again with the Lord Jesus Christ.

Jeremiah so eloquently prophesied what God knew from the beginning: we were going to mess up. But let's not wallow in the ditch and be satisfied with our plight. As a culture, we don't have to stay in the ditch. I believe we, as a nation, can turn and start over.

With God, we can become a compassionate culture, a culture of life, a culture set apart by God to accomplish His purpose and His plan.

Today's Bible Reading Plan: Ezekiel 14:12-16:41 Hebrews 7:18-28; Psalm 106:1-12; Proverbs 27:4-6

Lord Jesus Christ, thank You for another chance.

322

November 7

Clap Your Hands!

For you shall go out with joy, and be led out with peace; the mountains and the hills shall break forth into singing before you, and all the trees of the field shall clap their hands.

— *Isaiah 55:12*

What a marvelous scene described in Isaiah 55:12. There is such a time of rejoicing that even the mountains and hills break out in praise and the trees start clapping their hands!

As followers of Christ, when we clap our hands in praise, clapping skin on skin, we're exercising our authority in the earth, telling Satan he has no authority over us. We are making the choice to offer the Lord Jesus Christ, Jehovah Joshua Messiah praise!

Offering praise to our King frustrates the enemy. Matthew 21:15 says, *But when the chief priests and scribes saw the wonderful things that He did, and the children crying out in the temple, "Hosanna to the Son of David," they were extremely displeased.*

The religious leaders were <u>extremely</u> displeased at the exuberant worship the children exhibited for Jesus. It disturbed the religious that the children were crying out to Jesus for salvation and not them.

Today's Bible Reading Plan: Ezekiel 16:42-17:24 Hebrews 8:1-13; Psalm 106:13-31; Proverbs 27:7-9

Hosanna! Lord, save us!

November 8

Glory to God

My mouth will be filled with Your praise
and with Your glory all the day.

— Psalm 71:8

To give God glory means to give Him honor, praise and worship as described in Romans 4:20.

He did not waver at the promise of God through unbelief, but was strong in faith, giving glory to God.

Followers of Christ have been called into the kingdom priesthood and anointed with the power of the Holy Spirit to minister the saving Gospel of Jesus Christ. Just as the priests of the Old Testament gladly bore the ark on their shoulders, we are to bear an unwavering faith-filled testimony of the Lord Jesus Christ and give Him glory in the malls, the streets, the workplace, the park, the grocery store, wherever we go.

God is now fulfilling His original plan through you and me, His church! He expects us to mature and become strong in our faith. The stronger we become, the more glory we give Him.

Today's Bible Reading Plan: Ezekiel 18:1-19:14
Hebrews 9:1-10; Psalm 106:32-48; Proverbs 27:10

Be glorified in me today, Lord,
that I may give you glory everywhere I go.

324

November 9

Prayer & Praise Are Weapons

What is it then? I will pray with the spirit, and I will pray with the understanding. I will sing with the spirit, and I will sing with the understanding.

— 1 Corinthians 14:15

Someone once told me, "I guess the only thing left to do is pray." My reply, "The first thing we should ever do is pray." As the battle of the ages rages on, we must get on a war footing.

Even though the war has already been won in the spirit at Calvary, we must now take practical steps today to fight through our specific battles in this war. There are battles in our families, on our jobs and in our neighborhoods.

Thoroughly study the Scriptures and find verses that deal specifically with spiritual warfare, then apply them to your battles. Study the Word as if your life depended on it, because it does.

God gave us powerful weapons to fight in this war: prayer and praise. When we speak God's Word back to Him, it shakes the foundations of the alien armies of the antichrist that have been arrayed against you. Pray and praise your way through to victory!

Today's Bible Reading Plan: Ezekiel 20:1-49
Hebrews 9:11-28; Psalm 107:1-43; Proverbs 27:11

I am safely sheltered in the loving arms of my God.

November 10

Resurrection Power

Jesus said to her, "I am the resurrection and the life. He who believes in Me, though he may die, yet shall he live. And whoever lives and believes in Me shall never die. Do you believe this?"

— John 11:25-26

God is looking for a church flowing both in the message of the cross and in the miracle of the resurrection. The Gospel of Jesus Christ is powerful, but we have to believe it to experience its power.

Sadly, many who say they believe in Jesus do not believe His healing power can heal them today or that they can trust Him to be their provider.

The precious blood of Jesus became our cure against the ravages of sin, death and disease, and it became our prescription for complete victory and total triumph in every area of our lives. Just one drop of the crimson red blood of Christ can renew your joy, mend your marriage, fix your broken finances and heal you.

One drop of the precious blood of the Lamb of God is sufficient in power to forgive the sins of humanity. That same power is available today to heal your body, break the chains of every stronghold and swing wide the gates to your miracle!

Today's Bible Reading Plan: Ezekiel 21:1-22:31
Hebrews 10:1-17; Psalm 108:1-13; Proverbs 27:12

*I believe the message of the cross
and the miracle of the resurrection.*

November 11 ~ A Day with Joni

Sowing and Reaping Alert

For they sow the wind, and they will reap the whirlwind.

— Hosea 8:7a

You know the principle of sowing and reaping. There is a great positive side to it. There is also a sobering reality to recognize.

Whatsoever a man sows, accelerates.

You and I have heard many sad tales of unintended consequence. It started with a couple of beers and ended in vehicular manslaughter. It started with flirtation and ended with broken homes and shattered children. It started with a little gossip and ended a treasured friendship.

Sparks turn to flames. When we allow ourselves to flirt with moral and ethical boundaries we are standing on a slippery slope, falling away to a pool of great regret.

The seed you sow today can generate a windfall of blessing or a whirlwind of sorrow. Be careful. Be wise.

Today's Bible Reading Plan: Ezekiel 23:1-49
Hebrews 10:18-39; Psalm 109:1-31; Proverbs 27:13

Gracious Lord, I don't want to become one of those stories, a testimony of unintended consequences. Will You give me guidance as I sow, to avoid folly and always sow in wisdom and faith. I commit the harvest to You! It is rightfully in Your hands!

November 12

The Ends of the Earth

All the ends of the earth have seen the deliverance of our God.

— Psalm 98:3b

Have you ever reached the ends of the earth, where it seems there's nothing to reach out to? Well, in Christ, you've got more to reach out for than to hold on to. You can curse yourself by trying to hold on to what God told you to let go of. Let go and lay hold!

Isaiah 54:16 reveals it is God who created the blacksmith that blows the coals in the fire and who brings forth the weapon to kill, and it is God who has created the destroyer to cause ruin and wreak havoc.

God is releasing His mighty army against the alien armies of the antichrist that have been arrayed against you. All the Lord wants you to do is stand there and rejoice and give Him praise, just as Israel did on the battlefield in 2 Chronicles 20:22.

You are under an everlasting covenant, and you do not need a physical weapon. You are fighting a spiritual battle, and the enemy cannot cross the blood line. You are fighting by the power of the Holy Spirit, and the fruit of your battle is absolute victory!

Today's Bible Reading Plan: Ezekiel 24:1-26:21 Hebrews 11:1-16; Psalm 110:1-7; Proverbs 27:14

Lord, my praise is a weapon, and I praise You always!

November 13

Dunamis Power

Now to Him who is able to do exceedingly abundantly beyond all that we ask or imagine, according to the power that works in us, to Him be the glory in the church and in Christ Jesus throughout all generations, forever and ever. Amen.

— Ephesians 3:20

God's power is working and being generated right now in you. When you lay down at night, the Spirit of God is ministering to you, the holy angels are ministering to you, and you have overwhelming peace.

Dunamis is a Greek word that means power. It supplies its own power. Its exhaust creates energy that it then burns. That means it can never be depleted.

I found out something else about this power. Dunamis means the working out of power. The most accurate translation is it is the weapon of power. The cross is the weapon of God's power.

What is that weapon? What is so mighty about that mean, ugly, angry, biting beam that would make it God's power? The cross is the instrument, the weapon of His power: power to save, power to heal, power to deliver.

Today's Bible Reading Plan: Ezekiel 27:1-28:26
Hebrews 11:17-31; Psalm 111:1-10; Proverbs 27:15-16

Thank You for Your cross, Lord,
for it is the power of my salvation.

329

November 14

The Seed Is in the Ground

Now in the place where He was crucified there was a garden, and in the garden was a new tomb in which no one had ever been buried.

— John 19:41

The perfect Lamb of God was offered. Jesus went from a virgin womb to a virgin tomb, where no one had ever been buried.

The flawless, incorruptible Seed that would change everything forever was planted in the ground. Would there be a harvest on the Seed God had planted?

Now everyone waited. Heaven waited, earth waited, hell waited. Would there be a resurrection, or would God forever be branded a liar? Would the spotless Lamb of God fulfill God's purpose, or would the precious Son of God be forever known as a murdered sacrifice?

Some of the disciples seemed to forget the words Jesus spoke to them regarding His resurrection: *And if I be lifted up from the earth, I will draw all men to Myself* (John 12:32).

Never finish writing your story on Friday, because Resurrection Day is on the way!

Today's Bible Reading Plan: Ezekiel 29:1-30:26 Hebrews 11:32-12:13; Psalm 112:1-10; Proverbs 27:17

> *Holy Spirit, help me to never, ever forget the words of Jesus.*

November 15

Your Maker Is Your Husband

For your Maker is your husband, the LORD of Hosts
is His name; and your Redeemer is the Holy One of Israel;
He shall be called the God of the whole earth.

— Isaiah 54:5

Not only is God your Maker, He is the Head of your house and your Redeemer. Jesus, the Holy One of Israel, is God of the whole earth!

God's love is beyond anything we could possibly understand as human beings. His love is unconditional and is exceedingly, abundantly above what we could ever ask or imagine.

You do not have to earn God's love. It was poured out at Calvary in the most amazing demonstration of love and compassion ever displayed on earth. Some might die for a friend. But how many would die for their enemies while their enemies spat on them and pummeled them with thousands of blows to the head and body, while their enemies whipped them until their flesh hung like ribbons from their bones and while their enemies utterly humiliated them?

One died for us under those conditions: Jesus our Savior and Deliverer!

Today's Bible Reading Plan: Ezekiel 31:1-32:32
Hebrews 12:14-29; Psalm 113:1-114:8; Proverbs 27:18-20

There is none, no not one, who loves me like You do.

November 16

Call on God

Call to Me, and I will answer you, and show you great and mighty things which you do not know.

— Jeremiah 33:3

When we call on God, according to Jeremiah 33:3, we can expect an answer. God does not say that if we pray just the right way He might answer. He does not say that He will only answer on certain days if we are at a specific location. He simply says call, and He will answer.

Sometimes we get so busy with the activities of our daily lives that we forget to call on God. There is no part of your life that is too mundane or too difficult for God to handle. He cares about the seemingly small things concerning your life, as much as He cares about the big things in your life.

He loves it when you have a conversation with Him, as though He were your best friend, because He is. God loves when you have an open communication with Him throughout your day. You don't have to wait until morning devotions or evening prayers to talk to God. He wants to hear from you throughout your day.

Today's Bible Reading Plan: Ezekiel 33:1-34:31 Hebrews 13:1-25; Psalm 115:1-18; Proverbs 27:21-22

I will to talk to You and praise You all day long!

November 17

The Counselor

"But when the Counselor comes, whom I shall send to you from the Father, the Spirit of truth who proceeds from the Father, He will bear witness of Me."

— John 15:26

Jesus warned us that we would be hated by the world (John 15:18). He further tells us that a servant is not greater than his Master; if the world persecuted Him, they will persecute His followers (John 15:20).

The world hated Jesus because He exposed their sin. Their hatred was so intense they could not receive the miracles that He performed on their behalf. As Jesus pointed out in John 15:25, *"They hated Me without a cause."*

Jesus called the Holy Spirit the Spirit of truth and explained that the Holy Spirit would come to bear witness of Him. That is why it is so important to operate in the gifts of the Spirit for the purpose of expressing the love and power of Jesus and showing people who He is.

Satan's purpose is always to steal, kill and destroy, but Jesus came so that we could have abundant life (John 10:10).

Today's Bible Reading Plan: Ezekiel 35:1-36:38 James 1:1-18; Psalm 116:1-19; Proverbs 27:23-27

Thank You, Lord, for the One
You've called alongside to help.

November 18 ~ A Day with Joni

Where Are You?

"...he was lost and is found."

— Luke 15:32b

God's first question for man after the fall was, "Where are you?" We're still struggling with the question, "Where are we?" Apart from Christ we don't know who we are, why we are, or where we are going. Our search for significance has us trying to fill a God-shaped void with things of our own making, our own vices and devices.

Possessions rust. Pleasures fail. Power corrupts. Philosophies disappoint. The Bible warns us of it all – folly, chasing after the wind.

Where are you? Just like Adam, are you scared to reply? Are you crouching in the bushes, trying to fashion leaves for loin-covers? Come home, beloved.

It's really not complicated. When you don't know where you are, you're lost. The Bible speaks of that, too. In Christ, the lost are found.

Today's Bible Reading Plan: Ezekiel 37:1-38:23 James 1:19-2:17; Psalm 117:1-2; Proverbs 28:1

Here I am, Lord, in need of You! I confess that often times I run after lesser affections trying to fill a void only You can truly satisfy. Forgive me. Welcome me into Your arms – found and free.

November 19

The Gift of Faith

But the manifestation of the Spirit is given to everyone for the common good...to another faith by the same Spirit...

— 1 Corinthians 12:7, 9

The gift of faith is different from the measure of faith that God gives to everyone (Romans 12:3) The gift of faith is wonder-working faith that believes for incredible miracles from God.

The gift of faith can see your child instantly healed of a fever. This gift can produce a miracle of financial blessing that would be impossible in the natural. The gift of faith is a supernatural ability to trust God in the darkest of circumstances and then witness a miracle.

The gift of faith is an expression of God's love that is manifested so that people can see God's power on display and know that He alone is God. The gift of faith cannot be earned. It is God's gift to equip the body of Christ to do exploits in the name of Jesus.

Faith in God can move your mighty mountain.

Today's Bible Reading Plan: Ezekiel 39:1-40:27 James 2:18-3:18; Psalm 118:1-18; Proverbs 28:2

Holy Spirit, increase my faith to believe for the miraculous.

November 20

The Gift of Serving Others

*We have diverse gifts according to the grace
that is given to us…if service, in serving…*

— *Romans 12:6-7*

The gift of serving others is needed in the body of Christ. Jesus Himself was and is a servant. *"…the Son of Man did not come to be served, but to serve and to give His life as a ransom for many."*

The Holy Spirit manifests abundant grace in those who serve. If it were not for this gift, there would be no practical daily ministry to the body of Christ.

In Acts 6:3 the qualifications of a servant are that they be full of the Holy Spirit and full of wisdom. So, these were not just people who waited tables. These were true servants of the Most High God who ministered to the body of Christ daily.

In the parable of the talents (Matthew 25:14-30), Jesus explains that of the three men entrusted with the talents, only two received approval. Their master's commendation to both was, "Well done, good and faithful servant." It's not position, fame or fortune that receives God's approval; it is the act of serving. My wife, Joni, always says, "We are at our best when we are serving."

Today's Bible Reading Plan: Ezekiel 40:28-41:26
James 4:1-17; Psalm 118:19-29; Proverbs 28:3-5

*Holy Spirit, grant me the gift of serving;
I want to be like Jesus.*

November 21

Build Up the Body of Christ

He gave some to be apostles, prophets, evangelists, pastors, and teachers, for the equipping of the saints, for the work of service, and for the building up of the body of Christ, until we all come into the unity of the faith and of the knowledge of the Son of God, into a complete man, to the measure of the stature of the fullness of Christ...

— Ephesians 4:11-13

The fivefold ministry office gifts were given to equip the saints of God to do the ministry and to build up the body of Christ. Through these gifts, we are being trained by the Holy Spirit to work within the body of Christ to move, as the Message Bible says in Ephesians 4:13, *rhythmically and easily with each other, efficient and graceful in response to God's Son, fully mature adults, fully developed within and without, fully alive in Christ.*

These gifts are such a blessing to the body of Christ, as they devote their lives to serving the people of God. Whether it be establishing and building churches, preaching the Gospel across the country and around the world, caring for a congregation or teaching a Bible study, these men and women of God are anointed by the Holy Spirit to help the church grow.

Today's Bible Reading Plan: Ezekiel 42:1-43:27 James 5:1-20; Psalm 119:1-16; Proverbs 28:6-7

Lord, thank You for those You have anointed to serve.

November 22

An Everlasting Covenant

Now may the God of peace, who through the blood of the eternal covenant brought again from the dead our Lord Jesus, the Great Shepherd of the sheep...

— Hebrews 13:20

Jesus paid the price and became the perfect sacrifice. God came into covenant with Himself. With His own blood He entered into the Most Holy Place and secured our redemption forever (Hebrews 9:12). Our Savior became the eternal link between God and man. His purpose was so that He may be in us and we may be in Him. Through this covenant relationship, we can know God intimately and receive His love and His blessings.

If you are a born-again believer, then you are the recipient of an everlasting covenant of perfection! As a child of God, you are an heir and joint heir with Jesus Christ. Through Jesus' better covenant you are now adopted into the family of God. You are no longer under the curse of sin. As an heir in God's house, the covenant benefits of this new spiritual bloodline belong to you!

Today's Bible Reading Plan: Ezekiel 44:1-45:12
1 Peter 1:1-12; Psalm 119:17-32; Proverbs 28:8-10

I receive your healing power by faith
because I am under a better covenant!

November 23

Be Made Whole

*When Jesus saw him lying there, and knew that he had been in
that condition now a long time, He said to him,
"Do you want to be healed?"*

— John 5:6

The Lord's work did not end on the cross. Like a surgical instrument, He wants to remove the pain and heartache that have invaded your life. Jesus, the Great Physician, longs to step into the arena of your affliction to make you whole.

Jesus asks you, today, "Do you want to be healed?" The man in John 5:6 had been in that condition for 38 long years. Could it be that after a few years with this illness, he had grown too weak to fight and too weary to believe for his healing any longer? He tells Jesus he had no one to help him into the pool. All had abandoned him, leaving him to fend for himself.

Take a step of faith toward your miracle. It is easy to hear about Jesus' healing blood, but the real test comes when you are faced with a situation in your own life or family that only the Great Physician can mend. When you determine to stand upon His Word with faith, your trial can become your testimony.

Today's Bible Reading Plan: Ezekiel 45:13-46:24
1 Peter 1:13-2:10; Psalm 119:33-48; Proverbs 28:11

Thank You, Jesus, for turning my test into a testimony.

November 24

Turn Your Gaze to Jesus

The LORD *said to Moses, "Make a poisonous serpent, and put*
it on a pole, and it will be, that everyone who is bitten,
when he looks at it, will live."

— *Numbers 21:8*

"Why did you drag us out of Egypt to die? Why did you bring us to this worthless country? The food is bland, tasteless!" The Israelites were once again complaining to Moses. Due to their ingratitude, God sent serpents to bite them and many died.

Moses interceded for God's people, and at His command he fashioned a snake. Anyone in the camp of Israel who looked at the bronze serpent in faith and obedience received deliverance from the effects of the snakes that plagued the camp.

The bronze serpent was a type of Jesus' sacrifice. Jesus said, *"Just as Moses lifted up the serpent in the wilderness, even so must the Son of Man be lifted up, that whoever believes in Him should not perish, but may have eternal life"* (John 3:14-15). Healing is your rightful possession Jesus purchased for you when He gave His life on the cross. Look to Him and receive your miracle today.

Today's Bible Reading Plan: Ezekiel 47:1-48:35
1 Peter 2:11-3:7; Psalm 119:49-64; Proverbs 28:12-13

I turn my gaze upon You, Lamb of God,
who bore all of my sicknesses and diseases
so that I may walk in divine health.

November 25 ~ A Day with Joni

Dry Bones

He said to me, "Son of man, can these bones live?"

— Ezekiel 37:3a

The question would have never crossed my mind.

I'm a mother. I think practically. Dry, sun-bleached bones, a dismembered skeleton – they don't reassemble and reanimate. Ezekiel even said, "The bones were very dry." That's enough for me. I'd have concluded, all hope is gone. You would have too.

Have you a valley of dry bones in your life? Somewhere, something – maybe even someone-- where the promises of God seem impossible?

The Bible is a great encourager to me because it's full of impossible settings where God showed up, and the miraculous happened. Drop in on Noah. Moses. Joshua. David. Daniel.

Then look back at your situation. Can these bones live? Oh, you betcha!

Today's Bible Reading Plan: Daniel 1:1-2:23
1 Peter 3:8-4:6; Psalm 119:65-80; Proverbs 28:14

Lord, this is another of those times when I believe, but I need You to help my unbelief. Dry bones, difficult seasons in life, challenges I cannot imagine my way through – You've got this! Lord, hear my prayer. Allow me to lift these weighty matters before You, I pray. Amen.

November 26

More Will Be Given

For to him who has, will more be given,
and he will have abundance.
But from him who has not,
even what he has will be taken away.

— Matthew 13:12

Although this parable is about a sower sowing seed, the explanation Jesus gives for the parable has a spiritual meaning, as well. Jesus is stressing that the parable was given to the disciples to unlock the mysteries of the kingdom of heaven.

When we study the Word and gain wisdom from God, more wisdom will be given; because we are diligent to study and show ourselves approved by God (2 Timothy 2:15), and God is a rewarder of those who diligently seek Him (Hebrews 11:6).

So, though in the natural, it appears unfair to give more to the one who already has and take away from the one who does not have, this is a spiritual lesson to encourage those who have the Word to pursue the kingdom of God even more.

Receive the Word of God on good ground today and bear abundant fruit for His kingdom.

Today's Bible Reading Plan: Daniel 2:24-3:30
1 Peter 4:7-5:14; Psalm 119:81-96; Proverbs 28:15-16

Holy Spirit, give me understanding
as I read the Word today.

November 27

The Power to Get Wealth

But you must remember the LORD your God, for it is He who gives you the ability to get wealth, so that He may establish His covenant which He swore to your fathers, as it is today.

— Deuteronomy 8:18

Very few enjoy overwhelming wealth that gives us the ability to give on <u>every</u> occasion, exceedingly and abundantly, to help the poor, feed the hungry, help the homeless or extend help in a disaster. The problem is the wealth is in the wrong hands. Unfortunately, much of the wealth in the world is hoarded and used for selfish and ungodly purposes. The wealth God provides is for building His kingdom spiritually and physically. We cannot hoard wealth and then allow the poor to suffer and God's kingdom to be neglected.

For instance, you come upon an old friend dressed in rags and half-starved and say, "Good morning, friend! Be clothed in Christ! Be filled with the Holy Spirit!" and walk off without providing so much as a coat or a cup of soup—where does that get you? Isn't it obvious that God-talk without God-acts is outrageous nonsense? (James 2:15-17 MSG)

God gives us the power to get wealth so that we can establish His covenant of love.

Today's Bible Reading Plan: Daniel 4:1-37
2 Peter 1:1-21; Psalm 119:97-112; Proverbs 28:17-18

Holy Spirit, convict me and help me put my faith in action.

343

November 28

Invest in God's Kingdom

Be generous: Invest in acts of charity.
Charity yields high returns.
Don't hoard your goods; spread them around.
Be a blessing to others. This could be your last night.

— *Ecclesiastes 11:1-2 (MSG)*

One important step to take with regard to finances is to tithe ten percent of your gross income and give offerings to help the poor and others who are in need. God repays those who invest in His kingdom. *Mercy to the needy is a loan to GOD, and GOD pays back those loans in full* (Proverbs 19:17 MSG).

Another important aspect with regard to finances is to keep a budget. Keeping a budget is scriptural. Forty percent of the parables Jesus taught were about money and investment. Jesus gave His approval to the budgeting process in Luke 14:28. *"For who among you, intending to build a tower, does not sit down first and count the cost to see whether he has resources to complete it?"*

Budgeting is God's will. Failing to plan will create failure. You must set goals for your life. Do not let life happen to you. Attack it. Set financial goals.

Today's Bible Reading Plan: Daniel 5:1-31
2 Peter 2:1-22; Psalm 119:113-128; Proverbs 28:19-20

Holy Spirit, teach me how to budget
so that I can be a blessing to the kingdom of God.

November 29

Stuff Means Nothing to God

"Why take thought about clothing? Consider the lilies of the field, how they grow: They neither work, nor do they spin. Yet I say to you that even Solomon in all his glory was not dressed like one of these. Therefore, if God so clothes the grass of the field, which today is here and tomorrow is thrown into the oven, will He not much more clothe you, O you of little faith? Therefore, take no thought, saying, 'What shall we eat?' or 'What shall we drink?' or 'What shall we wear?' (For the Gentiles seek after all these things.) For your heavenly Father knows that you have need of all these things. But seek first the kingdom of God and His righteousness, and all these things shall be given to you.

— Matthew 6:28-33

Material things don't mean anything to God. You don't have to wear hand-me-downs. You can put your faith in God.

If you believe you can lose everything in a day by an attack of the adversary, why not believe you can gain it all in a day through a blessing from God? As a man thinks in his heart, so is he (Proverbs 23:7).

Change your thinking to believe for outrageous miracles from God.

Today's Bible Reading Plan: Daniel 6:1-28
2 Peter 3:1-18; Psalm 119:129-152; Proverbs 28:21-22

Holy Spirit, increase my faith
to believe for outrageous miracles.

November 30

Out of Sight, Out of Mind

*Let your lives be without love of money, and be
content with the things you have. For He has said:
"I will never leave you, nor forsake you."*
— *Hebrews 13:5*

Here is an exercise you can do at home to keep out of debt. Let's, as an example, say you're paid $500 this week. Instead of putting the $500 in a bank where you won't see it, put it in envelopes where you can see where it goes. Pay for all of your expenses out of these envelopes.

From your $500 income, as an example, in separate envelopes each week you put $50 for your tithe, $10 for offerings, $50 for savings, $100 to set aside this week for housing (mortgage or rent), $50 for food, $20 for the electric bill, $10 for the water bill, $10 for the phone, $20 for clothing and $20 for entertainment. You've set aside $340 for your basic monthly expenses; $160 is set aside for emergencies.

When you run out of money in the envelope, you don't go in debt to pay for something. If it is not a life or death situation that you have to have the money, you go without. Make adjustments to your lifestyle to stay within your budget. You have to be disciplined.

Today's Bible Reading Plan: Daniel 7:1-28
1 John 1:1-10; Psalm 119:153-176; Proverbs 28:23-24

*Holy Spirit, teach me to adjust my lifestyle
so that I can live within the resources God gives me.*

DECEMBER

God's Design

Again, Jesus spoke to them, saying,
"I am the light of the world.
Whoever follows Me shall not walk in the darkness,
but shall have the light of life."

— John 8:12

December 1

Jehovah Jireh My Provider

Abraham called the name of that place
The LORD Will Provide, as it is said to this day,
"In the mount of the LORD it will be provided."

— *Genesis 22:14*

At the top of the mountain, Abraham obediently bound his compliant son hand and foot to the altar. As the blade was just about to strike Isaac's chest, God spoke to him and told him not to harm his son. God took note of Abraham's faith. For Abraham knew that if he slew his son, the Lord was able to raise him up. He did not question or waiver. He only believed, and it was counted to him for righteousness. In the distance, he heard the faint bleating of a ram caught in the thicket. God had provided the sacrifice.

Like the ram, the Messiah was caught in the thicket of human need. Jesus said, *Your father Abraham rejoiced to see My day. He saw it and was glad."* (John 8:56). Abraham was willing to offer Isaac as a sacrifice. By faith He saw another sacrifice: God Almighty would willingly give His Son as a ransom for many. Before you ever cried out, God already provided a way of deliverance. He is Jehovah Jireh. He is your Provider.

Today's Bible Reading Plan: Daniel 8:1-27
1 John 2:1-17; Psalm 120:1-7; Proverbs 28:25-26

Jehovah Jireh, You have already met my need.

December 2 ~ A Day with Joni

Our God of Second Chances

For He knows how we are formed;
He remembers that we are dust.
— Psalm 103:14

Pick up your Bible and see for yourself. Cover to cover, they're there – people who needed, and got, second chances. Adam and Eve. Jonah. David. Elijah. Peter. John-Mark. Onesimus. Oh, and that's just the beginning of the list.

Think of the stories in the Bible. Redemption through and through. Mary Magdalene lived a troubled life. She got a second chance. Zacchaeus was a notorious cheat, and he was given a second chance.

The truth is, we need a second chance because we are all sinners. We all fall short of glory of God. Yet God loves, forgives, restores, and renews. The patience of our God stretches as far as the east is from the west.

You may be thinking, "Oh, but I've really blown it!" The key to God's patience is this: He never forgets that we are children and He loves us. He is the perfect parent, exercising restraint born of love. Let me say that more clearly, beloved – He loves you!

Today's Bible Reading Plan: Daniel 9:1-11:1
1 John 2:18-3:6; Psalm 121:1-8; Proverbs 28:27-28

Father, I am so grateful for Your love and patience with me. You know who I am, all of my needs, even my shortcomings, and yet You are still my Father; I am still Your child. I'm amazed and in awe of You. Thank You! In Jesus' name.

349

December 3

Jehovah Tsidkenu
My Righteousness

In his days Judah will be saved, and Israel will dwell safely.
And this is the name by which he will be called:
THE LORD OUR RIGHTEOUSNESS.

— *Jeremiah 23:6*

Jehovah Tsidkenu is the Lord our Righteousness. Jesus, who knew no sin, became sin for us so that we could become the righteousness of God in Christ Jesus (2 Corinthians 5:21).

Faith in Christ brings righteousness in God, to live in right standing with God. This only comes through the blood of the Savior. It has nothing to do with what we can offer Him. *For by grace you have been saved through faith, and this is not of yourselves. It is the gift of God, not of works, so that no one should boast.* (Ephesians 2:8-9).

When you are born again, God declares you righteous. You literally put on Christ. You take on His character; therefore, you do not have to commit sin because in you dwells the resurrected power and presence of Christ!

Today's Bible Reading Plan: Daniel 11:2-35
1 John 3:7-24; Psalm 122:1-9; Proverbs 29:1

Father, I am so grateful that I can be in right standing with You because of the obedience of Jesus at the Cross.

350

December 4

Jehovah Elyon Most High

Then Melchizedek king of Salem brought out bread and wine.
He was the priest of God Most High.

— Genesis 14:18

We are children of the Most High God. As children of the Most High, we are blessed with all that God has. He fills us with His character: love, joy, peace, kindness, goodness, gentleness, faithfulness and discipline. He equips us with gifts flowing from His Spirit: healing, miracles, wisdom, knowledge, wonder-working faith, discernment, tongues, interpretation and prophecy.

As our High Priest, Jesus provided free, unhindered access to the highest place of authority, the throne of the Most High. When we are full of faith, we will boldly go into the presence of God even in the face of weakness, adversity and temptation. When we approach this Holy Place, we will confidently make our petition known and receive the divine help that we so desperately need. What a glorious entry has been made through our Great High Priest.

Jehovah Elyon withholds nothing from us. We serve the Most High God. There is none above Him!

Today's Bible Reading Plan: Daniel 11:36-12:13
1 John 4:1-21; Psalm 123:1-4; Proverbs 29:2-4

Jehovah Elyon, You are above all!

December 5

Jehovah Mephalti My Deliverer

But I am poor and needy; yet the LORD thinks about me. You are my help and my deliverer; do not delay, O my God.

— Psalm 40:17

Jesus has the power to deliver you! Deliverance does not just mean that you get set free from whatever has bound you. It also means that you are propelled all the way to where God wants you to go.

A letter is never considered delivered when it leaves your hand; it is only delivered when it arrives at its destination. Too many have settled for just being released from whatever has held them back. They are satisfied with the status quo, unwilling or unable to go on in God. Our purpose is not only salvation; it is to walk in the fullness of all the blessings that Jesus, our Deliverer, offered up His life to provide for us.

The Lord wants to deliver you. He desires not only to bring you out of the land of bondage, but also into the land overflowing with His goodness and provision. Whatever you need, He will release you into a greater anointing as you receive His delivering power in your life today.

Today's Bible Reading Plan: Hosea 1:1-3:5
1 John 5:1-21; Psalm 124:1-8; Proverbs 29:5-8

Jesus, I acknowledge You as My Deliverer. Thank You for setting me free. I yield in total commitment to You.

December 6

Thy Kingdom Come

From that time Jesus began to preach, saying,
"Repent! For the kingdom of heaven is at hand."

— Matthew 4:17

Every time God comes into the presence of humanity in any form to speak, the first thing He says is "Repent."

"Repent" is not a negative message, but a positive one. Romans 2:4 says it is the goodness of God that leads us to repentance. We need to understand God's will in order for repentance to be accomplished. It is not merely sorrow, although sorrow may accompany repentance. Repentance is changing your mind.

We must change our minds. When we change our minds about God and toward God, then we will have true repentance. When we have truly repented, the kingdom of heaven is laid out before us.

Today's Bible Reading Plan: Hosea 4:1-5:15
2 John 1:1-13; Psalm 125:1-5; Proverbs 29:9-11

Help me, Holy Spirit, as I go through this day,
that I will recognize the areas in which I need to repent.

December 7

Change Your Mind

I urge you therefore, brothers, by the mercies of God, that you present your bodies as a living sacrifice, holy, and acceptable to God, which is your reasonable service of worship. Do not be conformed to this world, but be transformed by the renewing of your mind, that you may prove what is the good and acceptable and perfect will of God.

— Romans 12:1, 2

What must happen for the kingdom of heaven to come? You have only to change your mind. Christians sometimes sing, "When we all get to heaven, what a day of rejoicing that will be!" Why not rejoice now? You are in the kingdom now.

Begin to think like a child of the King. When trouble comes, speak words of faith: "I am not having the worst day of my life. I am in the middle of the will of God! I am in the kingdom of heaven. The kingdom has come because the King has come! He has raised me up and given me joint seating together with Christ in heavenly places!"

Change your mind, because the kingdom of heaven is at hand. It is here right now. You can enter into it right now!

Today's Bible Reading Plan: Hosea 6:1-9:17
3 John 1:1-15; Psalm 126:1-6; Proverbs 29:12-14

Holy Spirit, help me change my stinkin' thinkin'.

354

December 8

God Is Changeless

For I am the LORD, *I do not change…*

— Malachi 3:6a

God is changeless. He has been the same since the beginning of time.

The Lord's covenants never change. The covenant ratified between God and His Son still stands today. There is still only one way to heaven and it is through the blood of Jesus Christ. He *is the same yesterday, and today, and forever* (Hebrews 13:8).

The Bible is still true today. It is timeless. Sin is still sin. Jesus is still our Healer. Jesus is still our Deliverer. No matter what men, philosophy or contemporary religion say, His truth never changes. Your spiritual target is always the same, and you will never miss it if your focus is on His Word.

You can base your life on who God is, what He does and what He says. We must turn, change the way we think and act to reflect who He is. He is the only sure thing in this world.

Today's Bible Reading Plan: Hosea 10:1-14:9 Jude 1:1-25; Psalm 127:1-5; Proverbs 29:15-17

In a world that is constantly changing, Lord, my security is in You, because You never change.

December 9 ~ A Day with Joni

Leaning on the Everlasting Arms

What then shall we say to these things?
If God is for us, who can be against us?
— *Romans 8:31*

Not just who, but what can be against the children of God? If we concentrate on our troubles, we become afraid. Fear strangles faith, but trust will be our companion on the path of safety when we go knowing that God goes before us.

Though it may seem like one to us, nothing is an emergency to God! We never walk alone. I admit, sometimes the path seems like an uphill climb. Though I may wobble, I know to lean on the One who is with me. I'm reminded of the powerful words of the classic hymn, Leaning on the Everlasting Arms:

What have I to dread, what have I to fear, Leaning on the everlasting arms? I have blessed peace with my Lord so near, Leaning on the everlasting arms.

This I know – God greets our bad news with His good news. I'll take that exchange any day! How about you?

Today's Bible Reading Plan: Joel 1:1-3:21
Revelation 1:1-20; Psalm 128:1-6; Proverbs 29:18

O Lord, help me to lean into You! I confess, I often lose sight of the forest through the trees; my perspective shrinks; I fret and worry. You are for me! Who or what could ever stand against me? Lord, will You help me to embrace and embody this marvelous truth today? Amen.

356

December 10

God Makes Everything Beautiful

He has made everything beautiful in its appropriate time.

— Ecclesiastes 3:11a

Seasons change, but God does not. He is the same yesterday, today and forever (Hebrews 13:8). The moniker, "Altogether Lovely," ascribed to the Messiah (Song of Solomon 5:16 KJV) first appears a contradiction of terms, compared to the prophet Isaiah's description: *He has no form or majesty that we should look upon him nor appearance that we should desire him* (Isaiah 53:2).

Consider first the Suffering Savior. Jesus was flogged and bloodied beyond recognition. He was paraded through the streets of Jerusalem, repulsed and reviled by the growing mob. His appearance was so marred by our sin and iniquity that His own Father turned His back on Him. Yet it pleased the Lord to bruise His Son (Isaiah 53:10). Why? Everything is made beautiful in its time (Ecclesiastes 3:11).

Jesus was lovely at the conception of creation, at the bedside of Jairus' dead daughter returned to life, lovely in the eyes of the Heavenly Father, lovely at the end of a vacant tomb. The Redeemer is still altogether lovely.

Today's Bible Reading Plan: Amos 1:1-3:15
Revelation 2:1-17; Psalm 129:1-8; Proverbs 29:19-20

Holy Spirit, reveal to me the loveliness of Christ.

December 11

Seasons of Transition

I will instruct you and teach you in the way you should go;
I will counsel you with my eye on you.

— Psalm 32:8

Times of transition and change can be stressful on individuals, companies, churches and even nations.

Joseph had an excruciating transition from the pit to the palace. (Genesis 37, 39-41). Israel transitioned from slavery to freedom and wandered in the wilderness before going into the Promised Land. It was prophesied that David would be King of Israel, but his time of transition saw many battles and threats on his life before he took the throne and even while he reigned. The Lord Jesus Christ was not exempt from a season of transition; He had a horrendous season of transition from the time He was arrested in the Garden of Gethsemane until He was crucified on the angry, mean, cruel, rugged beam of Calvary.

No matter what transition you face, God is with you and has already gone before you. You never walk alone. Walk through each day under the anointing of the Holy Spirit, and your transition will be smoother. Give it all to God. He is the Master of Transition.

Today's Bible Reading Plan: Amos 4:1-6:14
Revelation 2:18-3:6; Psalm 130:1-8; Proverbs 29:21-22

Chaos always comes at the curvature of change.

December 12

Possess Your Land

Therefore all who devour you will be devoured; and all your adversaries, every one of them, will go into captivity. And those who plunder you will become plunder, and all who prey upon you I will give for prey.

— Jeremiah 30:16

Under Moses' leadership, Israel experienced mighty manifestations of God. They were *all* delivered from the pursuing Egyptian army through the parting of the Red Sea. They *all* enjoyed the spiritual food from heaven and the spiritual drink from the rock in the desert (Exodus 17:6).

The Spiritual Rock that followed them and supernaturally sustained them was none other than Jesus Himself. He was their provision in the wilderness. Yet in spite of this, they displeased God by their lack of self-control. In the end, between one and three million Jews who drank from the Spiritual Rock of Christ, died in the wilderness. Only two from that generation, namely Joshua and Caleb, made it into the Promised Land. We all need to drink daily and deeply from the river of God's provision. Do not fall prey to the lusts of the flesh today. Break through into your land of promises.

Today's Bible Reading Plan: Amos 7:-9:15
Revelation 3:7-22; Psalm 131:1-3; Proverbs 29:23

Father, with Your help, I will inherit the land of promises.

December 13

Your Appointed Time

Indeed, the stork in the sky knows her appointed times.
And the turtledove and the crane and the swallow
observe the time of their coming.
But My people do not know the judgment of the LORD.

— Jeremiah 8:7

When Jesus spoke, even death had to listen. The grave itself had to loose its hold. In the city streets, the grieving widow, her family, all who were part of the funeral procession, and the gathering crowd recognized that a Great Prophet was among them.

Humanity began to see that there might be hope beyond the scope of human limitation. They began to get a glimpse of light beyond the veil of their darkness. The greatest, most powerful, most far-reaching, love-inspired visitation of all time in the entire history of mankind had come in the person of Jesus Christ, the Great Prophet, the Messiah, the King.

Jesus is still visiting His people with resurrection power and new life. He will impart hope, peace and life in you. Call His name and He will hear and answer.

Today's Bible Reading Plan: Obadiah 1:1-21
Revelation 4:1-11; Psalm 132:1-18; Proverbs 29:24-25

Visit me today, Lord Jesus, in the everydayness of my life.

December 14

A New Name

"There is no salvation in any other, for there is no other name under heaven given among men by which we must be saved."

— Acts 4:12

When partners entered into a covenant they also took each other's names. God, whose name was YHWH took the "H" from His own name and gave it to His covenant partner. The "H" representing the breath of God, breathed life into two childless old people with no hope for their future.

He changed the name of Abram to Abraham, "the father of many nations." He changed Sarai's name to Sarah, "a princess." As God confirmed His covenant with Abraham and His successors, He took on their names and became "The God of Abraham, Isaac and Jacob," and later, "The God of Israel."

We are given a glimpse of those who have entered into His covenant: *and his name shall be on their foreheads* (Revelation 22:4). We will be called by His wonderful name as we live in the joy of His presence forever!

Today's Bible Reading Plan: Jonah 1:1-4:11
Revelation 5:1-14; Psalm 133:1-3; Proverbs 29:26-27

Thank You, Abba YHWH for the amazing change and breath of life Your name brings!

361

December 15

Righteous Seed

Look, children are a gift of the LORD,
and the fruit of the womb is a reward.

— *Psalm 127:3*

When our children were teenagers, someone came up to my wife, Joni, and said, "Your family seems like the Brady Bunch," to which Joni replied, "No, we're the Adams family; it's just that nobody knows it."

Being the parents of teenagers is quite the experience. There's lots of eye-rolling, emotional outbursts, and thoughts of running away – and that's just the parents.

All jokes aside, children, at any age, can cause upheaval in a home. Whether you are a parent, caregiver, teacher, or part of an extended family and friends, give children clear direction and boundaries, so that they know what is expected of them.

As you submit to God, children will sense His presence surrounding them. Creating an atmosphere of godliness and love gives the next generation a fighting chance to make a difference in the culture around them.

Today's Bible Reading Plan: Micah 1:1-4:13
Revelation 6:1-17; Psalm 134:1-3; Proverbs 30:1-4

Holy Spirit, make me a godly example
to children I encounter.

December 16 ~ A Day with Joni

Forgetting the Past

...but this one thing I do, forgetting those things which are behind and reaching forward to those things which are ahead...
— Philippians 3:13

The apostle Paul encouraged, "forgetting those things which are behind us." It's like cleaning out the basement – or for my friends down south, the garage or an attic. How do you decide what to keep and what to throw away? We should forget anything that God has forgotten. His promise to "remember our sins no more" is one of the crown jewels of grace. Holding ourselves captive to forgiven sin is sheer folly.

We should forget anything that centers on self. Paul summed up his former life of personal ambition and achievement with a pungent word: dung. Read Philippians 3. I'm not kidding.

We should forget the sins of others against us. We are to forgive. This one, I know, is the hardest.

When we settle in among clutter from the past, we rob ourselves of a new frontier. When we forget these things, we make room for something better – we reach forward. Beloved, look around. Is it time to sweep out things of the dusty past?

Today's Bible Reading Plan: Micah 5:1-7:20
Revelation 7:1-17; Psalm 135:1-21; Proverbs 30:5-6

Lord, just like cleaning out the basement or the garage – these things feel so meaningful. They're hurts I've held on to; treasures I've stored. Will You give me wisdom and insight? Which things in my past are a hindrance to my future joy in You? Help me pack them up and send them away – forever. Amen.

December 17

The Power of the Holy Spirit

And he said to me: "This is the word of the LORD to
Zerubbabel, saying: Not by might nor by power,
but by My Spirit, says the LORD of Hosts.

— Zechariah 4:6

Battles come and battles go. Seasons change. When you are a child of God, you do not have to be stuck in a battle nor trapped in a season. After all, it is neither our might nor power that defeats the enemy. It is the Spirit of God who breaks us free and mightily propels us forward.

When you belong to God, at any time you can get a sudden breakthrough that propels you through every line of Satan's defense. God can turn your desperate situation around in the blink of an eye. One touch from the Spirit of God will instantly change your life.

John was baptizing in the Jordan River, and suddenly Jesus appeared, the Lamb of God. Jesus was God's perfect seed planted in the earth that radically changed everything forever! The Holy Spirit fills those who believe in Jesus, and mighty miracles of salvation, healing, deliverance and provision are being poured out in abundance by the Spirit of God!

Today's Bible Reading Plan: Nahum 1:1-3:19
Revelation 8:1-13; Psalm 136:1-26; Proverbs 30:7-9

Holy Spirit, move my life forward
today in a very dramatic way.

December 18

Seek the Healer

Do not yield your members to sin as instruments of
unrighteousness, but yield yourselves to God,
as those who are alive from the dead, and your bodies to God
as instruments of righteousness.

— Romans 6:13

Do not seek a healing as much as you seek the Healer. Always remember God is the one who blesses. God is your deliverer. God is the baptizer in the Holy Spirit. Give yourself wholly and completely to God. The seven most precious syllables that can be spoken in one breath are, "Abba, I belong to You."

Because the Lord wants a deeper relationship with His people, He wants us to move into a greater depth of relationship with the Holy Spirit. The Holy Spirit is our Helper. He is exactly like Jesus in every essential detail and quality. He is not different from God. He is God dwelling inside you. Whatever may be trying to drag you down today – whether depression, sickness, bondage, poverty, a broken relationship – remember that the greater One lives on the inside of you. God has taken up personal residence inside your mortal body and quickens you and makes you alive!

Today's Bible Reading Plan: Habakkuk 1:1-3:19
Revelation 9:1-21; Psalm 137:1-9; Proverbs 30:10

Holy Spirit, regardless of my current circumstances,
quicken me today and make me come alive!

December 19

You Can Change a World

"Get up, go to Nineveh, the great city,
and proclaim to it the message that I tell you."

— *Jonah 3:2*

Jonah was an unwilling missionary. He received a divine mandate to preach repentance to what he perceived was a group of unworthy Ninevites. Jonah at first chose to run from God, but then he repented and did God's will after being swallowed and regurgitated by a whale.

Jesus was a greater missionary. He left the splendor of heaven and went willingly to sinful mankind despite the cost (Matthew 12:41). He endured the shame and stigma of the cross for the joy that was set before him: lost humanity, you and me (Hebrews 12:2).

The world is our mission field, and we are its laborers. There is something within you that God wants to use to change the world. You have power to change your generation. Ask the Holy Spirit to give you passion for the lost. With that passion will come a renewed power to see supernatural signs and wonders and an unprecedented harvest of souls, unlike the world has ever seen.

Today's Bible Reading Plan: Zephaniah 1:1-3:20 Revelation 10:1-11; Psalm 138:1-8; Proverbs 30:11-14

Holy Spirit, fill me with a
burning passion to reach the lost.

December 20

Pray in the Spirit

Pray in the Spirit always with all kinds of prayer
and supplication. To that end be alert with all perseverance
and supplication for all the saints.

— Ephesians 6:18

This is a powerful spiritual weapon. You must stay alert and persevere in prayer for the saints. You never know what a brother or sister in Christ, or a family member, friend, neighbor, or coworker may be going through. Pray in the spirit as you walk through the grocery store. Pray in the spirit as you're driving to work. Pray for your coworkers throughout the day.

Instead of complaining about a situation, take up your spiritual weapons and do warfare by praying in the spirit. Many complain about the toxic political climate in our nation. Instead of complaining, pray in the spirit.

The government we follow is on Christ's shoulders. Jesus and His body are not separated. He is the Head, and we are His body. God has seated you in heavenly places in Christ, and all powers that would oppose you have been placed under your feet.

Today's Bible Reading Plan: Haggai 1:1-2:23
Revelation 11:1-19; Psalm 139:1-24; Proverbs 30:15-16

I am part of the body of Christ
and Jesus is the Head of this body;
I am seated together with Him in heavenly places.

December 21

The True Tabernacle

A minister in the sanctuary and the true tabernacle,
which the Lord, not man, set up.
— *Hebrews 8:2*

A close examination of the building specifications of the Old Testament tabernacle reveals a type and shadow of our Lord and Savior, Jesus Christ. Virtually every piece of that structure shouts of a coming redeemer. Outside the tent is the altar of brass, where a bleeding sacrifice is offered before any attempt to approach God can be made. Jesus is our sacrifice for sin (Hebrews 10:12). Then there is the laver, where cleansing must take place before access is admitted. The blood of the Lamb of God washes us from all impurity (John 1:29)

Located inside the tent is the lampstand, giving light to all within. Jesus said He is the Light of the world (John 8:12). There also is the table of showbread, representing fellowship and sustenance. Jesus is the Bread of Life (John 6:35). There is hidden meaning in every piece and particle of the tabernacle. Even the Ark of the Covenant speaks of Jesus Christ, since it was made of wood, representing humanity, overlaid with gold, representing deity. Just as the ark was wood and gold in one piece of furniture, Jesus was all God and all man inhabiting one vessel. God's children have the True Tabernacle living inside of them. We can dwell in His presence each and every day!

Today's Bible Reading Plan: Zechariah 1:1-21
Revelation 12:1-17; Psalm 140:1-13; Proverbs 30:17

I celebrate the True Tabernacle, Jesus Christ!

December 22

A Life of Change

Therefore we were buried with Him by baptism into death, that just as Christ was raised up from the dead by the glory of the Father, even so we also should walk in newness of life.

— *Romans 6:4*

Jesus died to pay for your sins and to make you a new creation. You come into your new life for one purpose: to become more like Jesus.

What should this new life look like? *These signs will accompany those who believe: In My name they will cast out demons; they will speak with new tongues; [18] they will take up serpents; if they drink any deadly thing, it will not hurt them; they will lay hands on the sick, and they will recover."*

You have a new language with which to commune with God. You have power from another realm that is over all the works of the enemy. Heal the sick. Walk in love. Step into the newness God has for you.

Continue to grow from glory to glory and from one manifested presence of the Lord to another. As you begin the New Year, meditate on God's Word so you might live abundantly in Him and become all you are meant to be for Him.

Today's Bible Reading Plan: Zechariah 2:1-3:10 Revelation 13:1-18; Psalm 141:1-10; Proverbs 30:18-20

> *Holy Spirit, ready me for this new year, change my life so that Almighty God is glorified and people are drawn to Jesus.*

December 23 ~ A Day with Joni

Burdens to Blessings

Cast your burden on the LORD,
and He will sustain you;
— Psalm 55:22a

Burdens. They can be hard to even put into words. Sometimes when I find myself unable to explain what I'm feeling, I'll just stare off in silence, trying to process it.

What happened? What am I feeling? Why am I feeing this way? What will I do with it? Here's what I've learned: God is our safety net when we walk the tightrope of uncertainty. We weren't built to bear our own burdens. We're told to bring our burdens to Him – to cast them upon Him because He loves us. He doesn't promise an easy way out. He doesn't promise a shortcut to happiness. But He does promise His presence. He does promise He will sustain you.

Where are you at today? Uncertain? Having difficulty sorting out what happened, what you're feeling, and what to do with it? Your Father stands with open arms, ready to take it all. Will you let Him?

Today's Bible Reading Plan: Zechariah 4:1-5:11 Revelation 14:1-20; Psalm 142:1-7; Proverbs 30:21-23

Lord, I need You! You invite me to cast my burdens upon You. Will You give me courage to do that, to let go, and to look to You? When I can't see it, when I can't make sense of it, help me to rest in You. In Jesus' name.

December 24

The Light of the Morning

The God of Israel said, the Rock of Israel spoke to me: He who rules over man justly, who rules in the fear of God, is like the light of the morning when the sun rises, a morning with no clouds, gleaming after the rain like grass from the land.
— *2 Samuel 23:3-4*

There is nothing like the dawning of the sun into the clear, blue morning sky radiating brilliant colors off the tender grass and blooming flowers after a steady evening rain shower. This is the picture David portrays of the coming Messiah. This is the One of whom he prophesied one last time. A just Ruler would arise to exercise dominion over mankind. The Rock of Israel would execute righteousness and judgment.

Like the light of the morning Jesus Christ dawned upon the horizon of humanity. His salvation illuminated a world fearfully wandering in the darkness of sin, sickness, and despair. His radiance brought safety, security, hope, and help.

In the Bible rain generally represents the blessing. Like the rain upon the grass the Messiah also made available all the blessings of salvation—provision, health, peace, joy, deliverance, and restoration. Jesus has arisen. He has provided everything you will need. He is the Light of the Morning, the Rock of Israel!

Today's Bible Reading Plan: Zechariah 6:1-7:14
Revelation 15:1-8; Psalm 143:1-12; Proverbs 30:24-28

Lord, I thank You that the Light of Jesus shines upon my life, and Your blessings rain down upon me!

371

December 25

Glory to God!

Suddenly there was with the angel a company of the heavenly host praising God and saying, "Glory to God in the highest, and on earth peace, and good will toward men."
— Luke 2:13-14

Did you know that when God sent Jesus to earth it was the greatest act of benevolence ever? It was an act of unprecedented generosity. God gave us the person that He loved most…and Jesus laid down everything for us: His position, wealth and eventually His life.

Why? Because of love! God loved us so much that He did not consider the cost. God gave His best in spite of the number who would accept His gift.

God showed us favor in our fallen condition. Jeremiah 29:11 says, *For I know the plans that I have for you, says the LORD, plans for peace and not for evil, to give you a future and a hope.* He showed us love though we were separated from Him and gave us a gift that cost Him what He treasured most.

Luke 19:38 says, *"Blessed is the King who comes in the name of the Lord! Peace in heaven and glory in the highest!"* As you celebrate the birth of Christ Jesus, rejoice in the benevolence of God.

Today's Bible Reading Plan: Zechariah 8:1-23
Revelation 16:1-21; Psalm 144:1-15; Proverbs 30:29-31

Glory to our Savior, our King and our God!

December 26

Sweet Perfume

Therefore be imitators of God as beloved children. Walk in love, as Christ loved us and gave Himself for us as a fragrant offering and a sacrifice to God.
— Ephesians 5:1-2

As children of God, we are to follow His example in everything we do. We are to love one another because God so loved us that He gave His only Son for us. We are to follow the example of Jesus because He willingly sacrificed His life so that we could live and have forgiveness of sin.

We are called to live lives full of love for others, following the life of Christ. We are to live lives that are pleasing to God, lives that are sweet perfume to Him, lives of sacrifice, putting others before ourselves.

Romans 12:1 says, *I urge you therefore, brothers, by the mercies of God, that you present your bodies as a living sacrifice, holy, and acceptable to God, which is your reasonable service of worship.* God gave us His best on that first Christmas day 2,000 years ago. Jesus gave us His all, and we are called to do the same. Let us lift up our lives before God as sweet aromas, spread the perfume of Christ throughout the world, demonstrate we are His and show the world His love by the lives we choose to live.

Today's Bible Reading Plan: Zechariah 9:1-17
Revelation 17:1-18; Psalm 145:1-21; Proverbs 30:32

Holy Spirit, guide me through this day and help me to demonstrate the love and power of God.

December 27

Looking at the Unseen

While we do not look at the things which are seen, but at the things which are not seen. For the things which are seen are temporal, but the things which are not seen are eternal.
— 2 Corinthians 4:18

There is hope for you beyond the scope of human limitation, but you are not going to get it by looking at the natural and being dictated by your feelings.

Get ready: things are going to be shaken up. You may have to walk through a lonesome valley. Satan has a plan. It doesn't matter if it's a fever, a bad report or some kind of destruction, his plan is to take you out. But when the devil has a plan to take you out, God has a plan to keep you in. Fix your eyes on the unseen.

Have you read of the perseverance of Job? God rewarded Job with double for all the pain he face (Job 42:10-17). Fix your eyes on Jesus in this new year, because He went into the grave and came out the other side victorious.

You're going through; do not quit in the middle of the storm. Grab the reins of life, hold on and steer the wild wings of the wind toward hope. Pursue the things of eternity. God will reward you for your faithfulness to His everlasting Word.

Today's Bible Reading Plan: Zechariah 10:1-11:17
Revelation 18:1-24; Psalm 146:1-10; Proverbs 30:33

Jesus, thank You for Your perfect sacrifice.
Because of You, I have an intimate relationship with God.

December 28

What Is Left

And this statement, "Yet once more," signifies the removal of those things that can be shaken, things that are created, so that only those things that cannot be shaken will remain.
— Hebrews 12:27

What can we count on in perilous times? What rock are we to build our lives on? When everything else has faded, three things will remain: faith, hope and love (1 Corinthians 13).

We have inherited a kingdom that cannot be moved, cannot be shaken and cannot fall apart. It is going to endure. Quit looking at what you can see and focus on what you cannot see – angels walking around you, the fiery hosts of heaven surrounding you in all you do.

Look! See that blood covering you? That is the blood of Jesus! You are in a kingdom that cannot be moved. The only reason you have to fear is that you have stepped outside that kingdom. The devil is a thief; he does not have to be strong. He just has to walk until you are not paying attention, not holding steadfast to God's Word. Do not be entangled again with a yoke of bondage. Walk in the Spirit! Build your life on the sure foundation of the Word of God; and when everything else around you is being shaken, you will remain standing.

Today's Bible Reading Plan: Zechariah 12:1-13:9
Revelation 19:1-21; Psalm 147:1-20; Proverbs 31:1-7

Holy Spirit, help me stand
on the sure foundation of Christ.

375

December 29

Be Ready

He showers down rains for you,
the early rain and the latter rain, as before.

— Joel 2:23b

We are in the latter rain. Stay firm in the Lord, study the Word and pray always. Jesus is coming back, and we want to be ready.

Do not be like the five foolish virgins who took no oil with them and were not prepared to meet the bridegroom (Matthew 25:1-13).

Just because you are saved does not mean you will hear the sound of the trumpet when the Lord returns to gather His church. You must be vigilant, in His will and seeking the things of the kingdom.

If Jesus returns on Sunday or Wednesday evening, will He find you in church? Where will He find you on Tuesday or Thursday? Will you miss His call? Seek the Lord always, every day, every hour. Be ready, for the coming of the Lord draweth nigh.

Today's Bible Reading Plan: Zechariah 14:1-21 Revelation 20:1-15; Psalm 148:1-14; Proverbs 31:8-9

Lord Jesus, I eagerly anticipate Your return;
I will be ready!

December 30 ~ A Day with Joni

Joy in Today's Journey

In Your presence if fullness of joy...
— Psalm 16:11b

You ever had one of those mornings?

It was starting out to be a bad day! I got up early to walk the dogs. They weren't listening. Next thing I knew, I was chasing them in my pajamas! Breakfast? I burned the French toast and spilled the syrup. I got Austin to school on time and decided to swing into a drive-thru carwash. I rolled down my window to pay, pulled in – *and forgot to roll it up.*

If I was one of the seven dwarfs, I'd have been Grumpy.

It was certainly nothing major, but isn't it just like the enemy to steal our joy over, "the little foxes that spoil the vines" (Song of Songs 2:15)? I prayed, "Lord, I really don't want to have a bad day." I heard the Holy Spirit say, "Worship your way through it."

The interesting thing about worship is that we have to take our eyes off of everything and everyone else, including ourselves, and focus on God. It takes discipline to throw off everything that hinders us, but when we do, peace comes and joy returns.

Today's Bible Reading Plan: Malachi 1:1-2:17
Revelation 21:1-27; Psalm 149:1-9; Proverbs 31:10-24

Father, I want to worship my way through this and every day. As obstacles arise, as frustrations grow, will You help me refocus my attention and reorient my affections to You? Joy is in Your presence! I long for You.

December 31

New Year's Eve

I am...the beginning and the end...
— Revelation 22:13

Most of the time when we think of the beginning and the ending of something, we think in terms of something beginning, moving through time to its conclusion, and then ending. But God is not limited by time nor space, nor is He limited by our perception of things. If we think of beginning and ending as a circle rather than a straight line, it helps us understand the truth Jesus is trying to convey.

If our endeavors always move in a straight line, we will think of our lives as a series of disjointed tasks that seem to have no relationship to one another. But if we think of our efforts as moving in a circle, we see that when one thing ends, another is ready to begin. It is not that we just go back to the starting point of where we were before, but we are ready for a new beginning, going somewhere we have never been. Jesus knows the end from the beginning. He is both at once!

God is the only One who truly knows the end from the beginning. That is why it is so important to view those things in light of Him who is Alpha and Omega. He sees what seems hopeless and lifeless full of potential, full of life and full of blessing.

Today's Bible Reading Plan: Malachi 3:1-4:6
Revelation 22:1-21; Psalm 150:1-6; Proverbs 31:25-31

Jesus, You see my ending from my beginning
and it is even greater than I could imagine!

About the Author

Rod Parsley began his ministry as an energetic 19-year-old in the backyard of his parents' Ohio home. The fresh, "old-time gospel" approach of Parsley's delivery immediately attracted a hungry, God-seeking audience. From the 17 people who attended Parsley's first 1977 backyard meeting, the crowds rapidly grew.

Today, as the pastor of Columbus, Ohio's 5,200-seat World Harvest Church, Parsley oversees Harvest Preparatory School; Valor Christian College; Bridge of Hope missions and outreach; a second campus in Elkhart; Ind.; the Center for Moral Clarity, a non-partisan Christian grassroots advocacy organization; World Harvest Ministerial Alliance; and four television programs:

- *Breakthrough*, a daily and weekly television broadcast airing six days a week on multiple networks and cable outlets;
- *120 Live With Rod Parsley*, a monthly interview and ministry program on Word Network;
- *World Harvest Alive,* a weekly program featuring the congregation of World Harvest Church; and
- *Seriously?! With Ashton Parsley*, a weekly program airing on Word Network and featuring Pastor Rod and Mrs. Joni Parsley's daughter.

Pastor Parsley's message to "Raise the Standard" of spiritual intensity, moral integrity and physical purity not only extends across North America, but also spans the globe to nearly every nation via television and shortwave radio.

Thousands in arenas across the country and around the world experience the saving, healing and delivering message of Jesus Christ as Pastor Parsley calls people back to Bible basics.

Rod Parsley currently resides in Pickerington, Ohio, with his wife, Joni, and their two young adult children, Ashton and Austin.

CONNECT
WITH **ROD PARSLEY**

For more information about *Breakthrough*, World Harvest Church, Valor Christian College, Harvest Preparatory School, the Center for Moral Clarity, or to receive a product list of the many books, CDs, and DVDs by Rod Parsley, contact:

BREAKTHROUGH/WORLD HARVEST CHURCH
P.O. Box 100
Columbus, OH 43216-0100
(800) 637-2288
www.RodParsley.com

VALOR CHRISTIAN COLLEGE
P.O. Box 800
Columbus, OH 43216-0800
(614) 837-4088
www.ValorCollege.com

HARVEST PREPARATORY SCHOOL
P.O. Box 400
Canal Winchester, OH 43110-0400
(614) 382-1111
www.HarvestPrep.org

THE CENTER FOR MORAL CLARITY
P.O. Box 100
Columbus, OH 43216-0100
(614) 837-1990
http://CMC.RodParsley.com

If you need prayer, Breakthrough Prayer Warriors are ready to pray with you 24 hours a day, 7 days a week at (866) 241-4292 Visit Rod Parsley at his website address:
www.RodParsley.com

Deut 32:2